War Dept.  United States

**Manual for army cooks**

War Dept.  United States

**Manual for army cooks**

ISBN/EAN: 9783744789646

Printed in Europe, USA, Canada, Australia, Japan

Cover: Foto ©Andreas Hilbeck / pixelio.de

More available books at **www.hansebooks.com**

FOR

# ARMY COOKS

PREPARED UNDER THE DIRECTION

OF THE

COMMISSARY GENERAL OF SUBSISTENCE.

PUBLISHED BY AUTHORITY OF THE SECRETARY OF WAR

FOR USE IN THE

ARMY OF THE UNITED STATES.

WASHINGTON:
GOVERNMENT PRINTING OFFICE.
1896.

# WAR DEPARTMENT.

## Document No. 18.

### OFFICE COMMISSARY GENERAL OF SUBSISTENCE.

# CONTENTS OF PART I.

## RECIPES.

CONTENTS.

# 8

# 10 CONTENTS.

# MANUAL.

## PART I.

# THE ARMY RATION IN GARRISON.

(15)

# MANUAL FOR ARMY COOKS.

## METHODS OF COOKING.

The ordinary methods of cooking are as follows: Roasting, Baking, Boiling, Simmering, Stewing, Broiling, Frying, and Sautéing.

**Roasting** is that process by which a substance is cooked by the direct heat of a fire, without interposition of utensils, and generally in the open air. This method is seldom used at present, baking being substituted for it.

### HINTS ON ROASTING MEAT.

In roasting beef allow to fifty pounds, four hours, if pieces are cut in chunks of about seven to ten pounds each; remove bones from large roasts; dredge both sides with flour, salt, and pepper; on each piece place a piece of fat suet, bacon, or pork. Pour over hot meat broth or water (boiling is best) to moisten and set the juices, and basting is not required. Turn the meat and when about half done add onions and broth to make enough gravy, and an hour before it is done put in the pared potatoes with the meat and gravy to bake brown. Keep oven *closed* until ready to serve.

To roast mutton it requires to the fifty pounds, three hours.

To roast veal it requires to the fifty pounds, four and one-half to five hours.

To roast pork it requires to the fifty pounds, four and one-half to five hours.

Allow meat broth sufficient to make gravy for the command. Season to taste, remembering that to season correctly is one-half of good cooking.

**Baking** is that process by which a substance is cooked by heat in an oven. The temperature for baking most articles is about 400° F.

This, of all cooking, requires great care and constant attention to detail. The action of the weather, exposure, locality, and fuel are hardly ever the same; thus it will be seen that allowance must be made for these changes. Nothing is gained by the slightest haste. Full time must be allowed and, with attention, you may be sure of the most excellent results at all times.

*An easy method to test the heat of an oven.*—If the hand and naked arm can be held in the oven for fifteen seconds the temperature is about right. If this can not be done without distress the oven is too hot. If the exposed part can be held comfortably in the oven for a greater length of time, it is too cold. This method allows the cook to determine approximately the proper degree of heat. Experience will enable him to arrive at it precisely.

**Boiling** is the most abused method of cooking. Rapid boiling should be avoided. Additional heat is not generated by furious boiling, and much of the aroma of a substance escapes when steam is rapidly generated. To boil properly, the fire should be clear, and after the boiling has commenced the vessel so separated from the heat by the interposition of stove covers, or so far removed from the fire that the liquid shall have only a regular and very gentle movement, with slow steam generation and consequent slow evaporation. In boiling at least two articles of the Army ration— beans and peas—it is desirable to use soft water.

Hard water, if hardness depends upon the presence of carbonate of lime, can be rendered soft by boiling it an hour and then allowing it to cool, when most of the lime will be precipitated.

For cooking beans and peas the water thus treated can be used at once, after carefully decanting it. But if it is to be used for drinking or for making coffee or tea, it should, after decanting, be agitated in the air in order to aerate it.

The boiling point of water is raised three or four degrees by the ordinary proportion of salt recommended for cooking vegetables.

### HINTS ON BOILING MEATS AND VEGETABLES.

Boiled fresh meats and vegetables should be put on in boiling water, which sets and retains the juices, and boiled slowly; they should be salted and seasoned while cooking.

Cold water should be used when putting on salt meats and meats for soups, stews, corned meats, etc.

Ham, bacon, and pork should be boiled from fifteen to twenty minutes per pound, mutton about fifteen minutes per pound, and beef until the bones are free or a fork will pierce easily.

Meat, except hams, before boiling, should be cut into chunks of about five pounds each, all soup bones cracked (the more the better), and all scum arising while boiling carefully removed and burned.

The broth, except from salt meats, should be kept for stews, gravies, soups, etc.

Onions should be slowly boiled in two or three · waters from one to two hours, seasoned to taste, and thickened before serving, being barely covered with liquid.

Cabbage should be boiled (with pork or bacon) from one-half to one hour.

### LOSS IN COOKING.

During the operations of boiling, roasting, and baking, fresh beef and mutton, when moderately fat, lose, on the average, about as follows:

|  | In Boiling. | In Baking. | In Roasting. |
|---|---|---|---|
| Four pounds of beef lose _____ | 1 pound. | 1 lb. 3 oz. | 1 lb. 5 oz. |
| Four pounds of mutton lose _____ | 14 ounces. | 1 lb. 4 oz. | 1 lb. 6 oz. |

## TIME REQUIRED IN COOKING.

Many of the recipes indicate the time of cooking. The following is a fair average, when specific directions are not given in the recipe:

*Roasting.*—Ten pounds of beef about two and one-half hours.

Ten pounds of mutton about two and one-half hours.

*Boiling.*—Ten pounds of beef about two and one-half hours, after the water boils.

Ten pounds of mutton about two and one-half hours, after the water boils.

Ten pounds of ham about four hours, after the water boils.

*Baking.*—About twenty minutes to the pound.

**Simmering** is to boil slowly, *i. e.*, to have the liquid so far removed from .the direct heat of the fire as to keep it up to the slow-boiling point. *To simmer is in most cases to boil properly.*

**Stewing** is that process by which the substance is placed in a small portion of fluid and cooked by simmering.

**Broiling** is that process by which the substance is acted upon by the direct heat of the fire, with only the interposition of a gridiron or some similar apparatus. In broiling, the fire should be clear, bright, and free from smoke.

It is better to broil before a fire than over it. By the former process the juices of the meat can be caught in a dripping pan, and used, while in the latter manner they are lost in the fire, and tend to give a smoky flavor by their ignition.

In broiling, the article should be turned frequently, so as to have it cooked evenly.

**Frying** is practically boiling in fat, and is considered the least wholesome of all kinds of cooking. Fat (lard, etc.) raised to 400° Fahr. is sufficiently hot for frying purposes. A substance fried at this temperature can not absorb fat, since the moment it is dropped into the fat the great heat closes its pores. If, however, the fat is not hot enough, or if it is chilled by dropping too much in it at a time, the substance will absorb it, and be injured in lightness and flavor. When cooked, food should be taken from the lard or fat and allowed to drain a few moments in a sieve or colander.

*To test hot fat.*—If little jets of smoke issue from the top of it, the fat is hot enough for frying.

### FRYING MEATS, VEGETABLES, ETC.

There are two methods of frying: One with very little fat in the pan, the other with enough to boil. Chops or fat meats are best prepared by putting them in the pan when it is very hot, with just enough fat to prevent them from sticking when first put in. They should be cooked quickly and turned frequently by use of a turnover. Forks should never be used in turning or trying meats, as each stab means a loss of the juices. They should not be salted when cooking, as salt releases the juices. They should be seasoned before serving and served hot and quickly. Meats prepared in the foregoing manner are equal to broiled.

If the other method is followed, a deeper vessel and plenty of fat should be used; the fat heated until it bubbles and boils, and then the meats, chips (potatoes), doughnuts, or whatever the article is, dropped in and cooked until brown and well done. Meats should first be rolled in dry crumbs, cracker dust, corn meal, or flour.

Articles cooked this way should be turned over once and when done set in a strainer to drip or dry; if doughnuts, dipped in powdered sugar; if potatoes or meats, seasoned and served very hot.

Steak for frying, if tough, can be made tender by pounding to mash the fiber and rolling in flour before frying. When frying, meats should be covered.

**Sautéing** is that process by which a substance is cooked in a frying pan or skillet with just sufficient fat to cover the bottom of the pan. The fat must be frying hot before the substance is put in it.

**Seasoning.**—As salt and pepper are always at hand for use on the table, they should be used sparingly in the kitchen. It is much easier to add these articles to the prepared food than to eliminate them from it. The seasonings given in the recipes are suggestive and not arbitrary. They can be varied to suit individual taste or convenience.

**Mixing.**—Preciseness in the preparation of ingredients is an important element of success in cooking. Accurate measuring is the habit of the careful and industrious cook; guessing at proportions is the practice of the indifferent and lazy cook.

After the ingredients have been carefully determined, they should be incorporated as laid down in the recipe. Failure to make a good dish when ingredients have been carefully prepared is often due to the fact that they have not been mixed properly.

In many cases recipes for cooking are printed upon the packages containing food, such as cornstarch, chocolate, gelatin, condensed milk, hominy, macaroni, yeast powders, etc. In such cases these printed recipes should be followed instead of those printed in the books or handed down by old housekeepers, since manufacturers know the strength and quality of their special productions, and are better capable of giving instructions than those who have experimented only with the general products. It often happens that failures in cooking occur from lack of attention to these printed recipes, and by misapprehension as to the strength and character of the substances used.

## TO CLEAN UTENSILS.

New utensils should be cleaned before they are used.

A new iron pot should have a handful of sweet hay or grass boiled in it, then be scrubbed with sand and soap; afterwards clean water should be boiled in it for about half an hour.

A new tin should be filled with boiling water in which has been dissolved a spoonful of soda, and placed over the fire to simmer. Afterwards it should be scoured with soap and rinsed with hot water. The soda renders soluble the resin used in soldering. Tins can be kept clean by rubbing them gently with sifted wood ashes.

After being thoroughly washed in very hot soap-suds and wiped dry, tin vessels should be set on the top of the stove for a few moments and then vigorously scoured for a few minutes, with dry flour rubbed on with a wad of newspaper crumpled and softened.

In this way tinware may be kept free from rust and almost as bright and glistening as silver, care being taken that it is never put away damp and that it is kept in a dry place.

A coffee or spice mill can be cleansed by grinding a handful of raw rice in it. The particles of spice, pepper, or coffee will not adhere after the rice is ground through the mill.

A copper stew pan or vessel can be cleaned with fine sand and salt, half the quantity of salt to that of sand; rub it thoroughly with the hand or a brush. If there are many stains, an old lemon (or vinegar) may be used to remove them.

N. B.—In washing any greasy utensil, it is best, if possible, to use the hand instead of flannel or rags, as they retain the grease, and so keep putting it on again, instead of scrubbing it off.

All utensils after being used should be at once filled with hot water and set over the fire to scald thoroughly, and before being set away should be cleaned and dried. Grease remaining in a vessel will make it rancid, and moisture will rust it.

Before being used for cooking purposes, *all* utensils should be thoroughly clean.

All utensils should, if possible, be exposed to the sun daily. The practice of keeping them in cupboards until absolutely needed for use should be discouraged.

Knives and forks (unless plated) should be cleaned with brick and flannel; if rusty, rub with a fresh-cut potato dipped in ashes.

Plate or plated articles can usually be kept clean and bright by washing them with soap and boiling water and rubbing dry while hot with soft cloths.

In case of bone, ivory, or wooden handles, care must be taken that they shall never be placed in hot water, which will crack the bone or dissolve the cement which joins them.

### TABLES OF APPROXIMATE WEIGHTS AND MEASURES.

| | |
|---|---|
| Three teaspoonfuls | = One tablespoonful. |
| Four tablespoonfuls | = One wineglass. |
| Two wineglasses | = One gill. |
| Two gills | = One tumbler or cup. |
| Two cupfuls | = One pint. |
| One quart sifted flour | = One pound. |
| One quart powdered sugar | = One pound seven ounces. |
| One quart granulated sugar | = One pound nine ounces. |
| One pint closely packed butter | = One pound. |
| Three cupfuls sugar | = One pound. |
| Five cupfuls sifted flour | = One pound. |

One tablespoonful salt _____ = One ounce.
Seven tablespoonfuls granulated
   sugar _____ _____ _____ = One-half pint.
Twelve tablespoonfuls flour ___ = One pint.
Three coffee-cupfuls ____ _____ = One quart.
Ten eggs _____ _____ ___ _____ = One pound.

A tablespoonful is frequently mentioned in a recipe, and it is generally understood as a measure or bulk equal to that which would be produced by *half an ounce* of water.

## CHOICE AND DESCRIPTION OF MEATS.

### BEEF.

Contracts for the Army require that fresh beef shall be good in quality and condition, fit for immediate use, and from fore and hind quarter meats proportionally, including all the best cuts thereof. Beef from bulls, stags, or diseased cattle shall not be delivered. The necks of the cattle slaughtered for beef shall be cut off at the fourth vertebral joint, and the breasts trimmed down; the shanks of fore quarters shall be cut off four inches above the knee joint, and of hind quarters eight inches above the hock joint. Necks, shanks, and kidney tallow shall be excluded from delivery.*

Beef cattle may be placed in the following order, as to the character of eating beef:

1. Spayed heifer from four to seven years old.
2. Steer or bullock (never worked) from four to six years old.
3. Free-martin (or barren heifer) not over eight years old.

---

* It was found by weighing a steer and dressing it according to contract that the—
   Fore quarters weighed 310 pounds 15 ounces.
   Hind quarters weighed 268 pounds 13 ounces.
   Excess of fore quarters, 42 pounds 2 ounces.
This proportion has been found to be general; consequently, in receiving fresh beef under contract it should be expected that the proportion of fore-quarters meat to hind-quarters meat would be about as 8 is to 7.

4. Ox from five to eight years old.

5. Heifer from three to four years old.

6. Cow from three to eight years old.

Besides having a knowledge of cooking and preparing food, the cook should be also conversant with the nature and quality of meat, and the way in which oxen and sheep, when killed, are divided into joints.

*Method of cutting.*

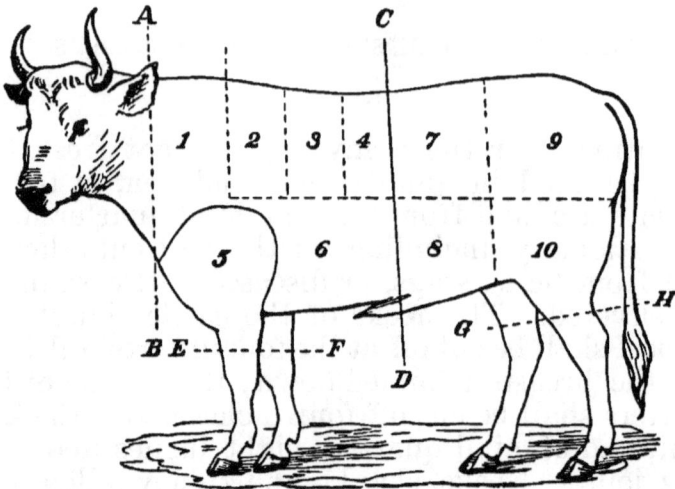

A B.—Cut at the neck.

C D.—Cut to divide fore and hind quarters.

E F.—Cut at fore leg.

G H.—Cut at hind leg.

### FORE QUARTERS.

No. 1.—Chuck. Stews and stock.

No. 2.—Chuck roast, 5 ribs. Roast.

No. 3.—Second cut, 3 ribs. Roast.

No. 4.—First cut, 3 ribs. Roast.

No. 5.—Shoulders. Boiling.

No. 6.—Plates and brisket. Stews.

### HIND QUARTERS.

No. 7.—Sirloin. Roast.

No. 8.—Flank. Stews.

No. 9.—Rump. Steaks.

No. 10.—Round. Boiling.

A *baron* of beef is two sirloins cut in one joint.

Nos. 1, 6, and 8 do not keep as well as other parts and should be consumed first.

The following table exhibits about the average proportion of meat to bone in the most ordinary joints of meat; the joints, when raw, being first weighed, and afterwards the bone, when dressed, and the meat removed with a knife:

| | Gross weight. | | Weight of bone. | |
|---|---|---|---|---|
| | Pounds. | Ounces. | Pounds. | Ounces. |
| Sirloin | 13 | 6 | 1 | 9 |
| Rump | 18 | 7 | 4 | 0 |
| H bone | 10 | 6 | 1 | 6 |
| Round | 18 | 4 | 1 | 12 |
| Mouse buttock | 3 | ½ | 0 | 0 |
| Veiny piece | 7 | ½ | 0 | 0 |
| Thick flank | 11 | 4 | 1 | 7 |
| Thin flank | 8 | 12 | 0 | 0 |
| Leg | 12 | 6 | 3 | 5 |
| Ribs (best end) | 14 | 8 | 1 | 15 |
| Ribs (middle) | 12 | 2 | 2 | 3 |
| Ribs (chuck) | 8 | 6 | 1 | 12 |
| Shoulder | 10 | 6 | 2 | 0 |
| Sticking piece | 8 | 4 | 0 | 11 |
| Shin | 9 | 6 | 2 | 6 |
| **Total** | 165 | 14 | 24 | 6 |

Or, about 15 per cent of bone to that of meat.

The hind quarter and ribs are considered far preferable; the remainder of the fore quarter and neck are coarse and of inferior worth.

The ration is twenty ounces of beef, as delivered from the block; an allowance of twenty per cent for bone will leave sixteen ounces of meat.

## MUTTON.

The contracts for fresh mutton require that the carcasses shall be trimmed as follows: The heads shall be cut off at first vertebral joint, the shanks of fore quarters at the knee joint, and of hind quarters at the hock joint.

*Method of cutting.*

No. 1.—The leg or haunch.
No. 2.—The loin.
No. 3.—The fore quarter.
No. 4.—The neck.

No. 5.—The breast and fore leg.
A *chine* is two necks.
A *saddle* is two loins.

## PORK.

Hogs make the best bacon when they weigh about 150 pounds. They should be fed on *corn* six weeks before killing time.

*Method of cutting.*

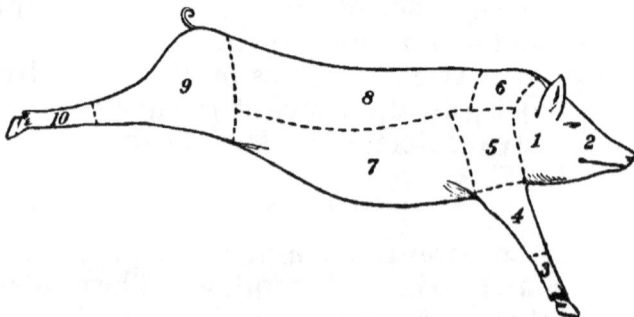

Nos. 1 and 2.—Head and snout.
No. 3.—Hock, for boiling.
No. 4.—Fore leg, for boiling.
No. 5.—Shoulder, for steaks.
No. 6.—Top of neck, for sausage.

No. 7.—Side meat or bacon.
No. 8.—Loins, for chops or roast.
No. 9.—Ham, to fry, boil, or bake.
No. 10.—Feet, for jelly or pickle.
A *chine* is two loins undivided.

## METHOD OF CUTTING VEAL.

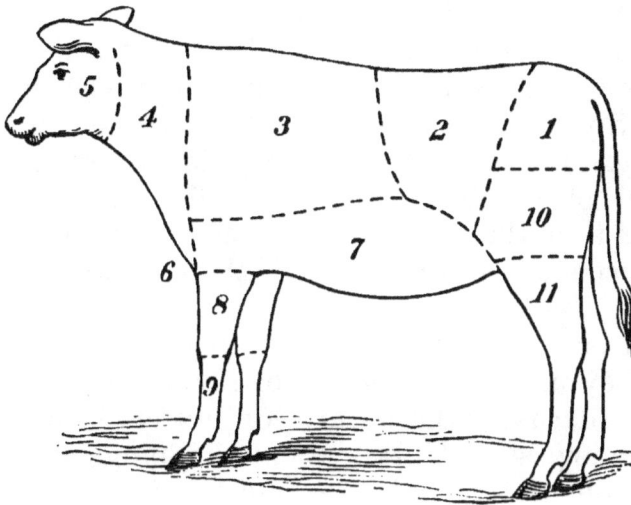

No. 1.—End of loin, for roasts.
No. 2.—Loin, for roasts or cutlets.
No. 3.—Rib, for roasts or chops.
No. 4.—Neck, for stew or soup.
No. 5.—Head, for soup or jelly.
No. 6.—Sweetbreads, located between the neck and stomach, on each side of the windpipe, between the fore legs.

No. 7.—Breast, for stew.
No. 8.—Shank, for stew or soup.
No. 9.—Feet, for jelly.
No. 10.—Fillet, for roasting.
No. 11.—Knuckle, for stewing.

The fore quarter is divided into two pieces called the brisket or breast, and rack.

## HOW TO SAVE DRIPPINGS.

A nutritious and palatable soup can be made from the drippings of roasted meats. Mutton fat is not suitable for drippings, being too strongly flavored.

When meat has been roasted there is always a mixture of juice and fat at the bottom of the pan.

Carefully pour the grease which is on the top into a sauce pan, keeping the juice underneath to serve with the meat. Place the grease on the fire and let it cook until it stops sizzling. The sizzling indicates that there is still liquid in the fat which must be thoroughly evaporated or it will prevent its preservation. Pour through a fine strainer into·an earthen jar, and it will keep indefinitely, if in a cool place. The grease of different meats can be kept in the same jar just as they may happen to be cooked; in fact their mixture is an improvement.

Not only can soup be made from these drippings, but they may also be used for frying or cooking in most all cases where lard or butter is used for those purposes. Three jars of drippings should be kept constantly on hand—one for frying fish, one for vegetables, and one for soup and meats. This number is necessary, so the grease left from frying can always be strained back into the jar from which it was taken without injuring the other fat. About once a month, unless entirely used, all the grease should be removed, melted, and strained anew back into the jars, after they have been thoroughly cleansed and scalded.

### BUTTER.

When butter has become rancid it may be rendered again eatable by melting it and shaking it repeatedly with boiling water for the purpose of removing the free fatty acids.

Slightly rancid butter may be made fresh for immediate use on the table by rechurning it in fresh milk, and then washing and salting as in the original process for making butter.

## TO GET A VERY GOOD QUALITY OF COOKING BUTTER FROM SUET.

Place suet in a kettle, over hot fire, with just enough water to prevent it burning or frying. After boiling a minute, turn entire contents of kettle into ice water (or very cold water) in a large flat tub. The white fat will rise to the surface, and is to be skimmed off and placed back in kettle and allowed to boil. Change the water in the tub, and again turn the fat into cold water and skim and again put back in the kettle and allow to boil. Again change the water in the tub, turn the fat in, and skim it off at once so that before it is quite cold you can place it in a churn and work it with milk. This is afterwards placed in a wooden or earthen bowl, a little salt added, and when worked over will yield a very acceptable quality of butter, good for cooking vegetables, pastry, sauces, etc., where butter is ordinarily used. *If milk can not be obtained* the suet may be turned into a wooden or earthen bowl and worked out with water and salt. It then produces a very good quality of fat, suitable for all cooking purposes and with the strong taste of the suet removed.

In the first instance, if the fat is too cold on placing in churn or bowl to work easily, heat it very slightly. The butter produced from working this in milk has been used to great advantage on hot breads, in vegetables, etc., and will prove a good substitute for the original article.

In the latter case (where worked out with only salt and water) it is to be used solely for cooking. This may be packed away in jars, rolled in cloth well salted, and will keep for a long time.

It is recommended to use only beef suet, as that from mutton hardens too speedily.

### DRIPPING PAN.

The *dripping pan* provides the fatty element especially necessary for good pies and puddings, and which is also required for frying purposes. *It should be thoroughly understood that the presence of fat and fatty matters in soups or stews is not only unpalatable, but it is deleterious to health.*

Dripping is provided as follows: (1) By removing the fatty substance rising to the surface of stock, soup, or stews, which must be frequently *skimmed off* and placed in the pan. By removing the white substance which adheres to the iron dishes or rises on the surface of the meat, etc., when baking; this should be carefully placed in the pan as above. (2) Before cooking, the excessive portions of fat (for instance, the suet around the kidneys) should be removed from the meat ration, cut up into small pieces, placed in a *second* pan, and kept distinct from the other.

The fatty substances, alluded to in (1), having been placed in a pan or baking dish, should be melted down and allowed to come to a simmer. A small quantity of water is then added and the fat allowed to cool; the water is then removed and the residuum, forming a solid block, is turned out and the bottom scraped. The fatty substances in (1) are retained exclusively for cooking. The contents of (2) is fat, and may be reduced as shown above. It may be sold or otherwise disposed of.

### AN INEXPENSIVE ICE BOX.

The arrangement consists of two boxes, the larger one about three feet square and the other one just enough smaller to allow a space of about three inches between the two around the four sides and also at the bottom. This space should be filled closely with sawdust or with fine charcoal. Let the cover be attached to the smaller box by straps or hinges and the cover to the larger box be placed in position.

Line the inside of the inner box with zinc, and through the bottom bore a hole that will admit a half-inch lead pipe. A hole should also be bored in the bottom of the larger box right under that in the smaller one, and the lead pipe must be long enough to go through both holes and carry off the water that will come from the ice. The latter may lie upon the bottom of the box without support of any kind. The pipe may be soldered to the inside to prevent the water from percolating through.

This box will be found a good preserver of ice, and it should not exceed $1 in cost. If shelves are desired, strips of tin can be hung over the edge of the inner box, with cleats attached on which the shelves may rest.

## RANGES AND UTENSILS.

The Quartermaster's Department is charged with the duty of providing the kitchens, the ranges, and the usual fixtures that accompany them. Utensils needed for the preparation of food, that are not furnished by that Department, can be provided by purchases made from the company or mess fund.

## ARMY RANGE, No. 4.

The following is a diagram of Army Range No. 4. These cuts represent the latest pattern and the plates used in its construction are numbered and named, so that in ordering repair plates it will be impossible to make any mistakes:

## Numbers and names of parts.

No. 400  Back top.
"   401  Right and left end rails.
"   402  Front top rail.
"   403  Front and back protector.
"   404  Flue cover in back top.
"   405  Inside fire-door lining.
"   406  U water back.
"   407  Right and left side linings.
"   408  Large grate frame.
"   409  Grate rest.
"   409½ Crossbar bolts to grate rest.
"   410  Right half of duplex grate.
"   410½ Wheel for duplex grate.
"   411  Left half of duplex grate.
"   411½ Duplex-grate shaker.
"   412  Draft door.
"   412½ Draft-door latch.
"   413  Draft-door register.
"   413½ Draft-door catch.
"   414  Casing plate.
"   415  U-shaped lining.
"   415½ Left guide for feed door.
"   416  Monogram for feed door.
"   416½ Right feed-door guide.
"   417  Feed door.
"   417½ Feed-door frame.
"   418  Front grate.
"   419  Rest for top panel in oven protector.
"   420  Rest for top-panel bolts to oven.
"   421  Oven protecting plate.
"   422  Protecting strip above water back.
"   423  Top panel (with flange).
"   424  Key panel (no flange).
"   425  Range cover.

No. 426  Flue door.
"   427  Hinge for flue door.
"   427½ T knob with catch for flue door.
"   428  Oven door.
"   428½ Army range name plate on oven doors.
"   429  Oven-door latch.
"   430  Left movable pivot for oven-door latch.
"   430½ Right movable pivot for oven-door latch.
"   431  Hollow bars for oven-door latch.
"   431½ Socket for hollow bars on oven door.
"   432  Guide for latch of oven door.
"   432½ Oven-door catch.
"   433  Right and left oven-door support.
"   434  Right and left outside oven bracket.
"   435  Right-hand bracket for oven and draft door.
"   435½ Left-hand bracket for oven and draft door.
"   436  Ash pan.
"   436½ Ash-pan handle.
"   437  Smoke box.
"   437½ Smoke-box collar.
"   438  Right and left damper blade for smoke box.
"   439  Smoke-box partition.
"   440  Oven rack.
"   441  Right and left bar brackets.
"   442  Bar in front of range.
"   443  Knob for bar.
"   444  Knob for draft-door register.
"   445  Shelf.

To repair the grates in this range, remove plate No. 418 (front grate) by taking out the bolt that holds it in place. Then draw out the entire grate through the draft door, repair, and replace as before.

## LIST OF ONE SET OF TINWARE FOR ARMY RANGE, NO. 4.

One square boiler 31 by 24 by $16\frac{1}{2}$ inches, capacity 20 gallons.

One steamer to fit 20-gallon boiler, size 13 by 24 by 9 inches.

One square boiler 24 by 12 by 13 inches, capacity 15 gallons.

One square boiler 24 by 12 by 13 inches, same as above, with addition of a $\frac{3}{8}$-inch patent lever bib cock and sliding strainer.

One square boiler $12\frac{1}{2}$ by $12\frac{1}{2}$ by 18 inches, capacity 12 gallons.

One square boiler $12\frac{1}{2}$ by $12\frac{1}{2}$ by 18 inches, same as above, with addition of a $\frac{3}{8}$-inch patent lever bib cock and sliding strainer.

Two square boilers $12\frac{1}{2}$ by $12\frac{1}{2}$ by $12\frac{1}{2}$ inches, capacity 8 gallons.

Two steamers to fit 8-gallon boilers, size $12\frac{1}{2}$ by $12\frac{1}{4}$ by 7 inches.

Two bake pans 21 by 21 by 4 inches, top measure 1-inch flare.

Four bake pans 21 by 10 by 4 inches.

Three joints of 9-inch stovepipe.

One 9-inch elbow.

## LIST OF TABLEWARE AND COOKING UTENSILS.

The equipment of tableware and kitchen utensils under paragraph 285 of the Regulations is as follows, in addition to the tinware that comes with the range, viz:

| Articles. | | Allowance for troop of cavalry, battery of artillery, or company of infantry. | Allowance for light battery of artillery. | Allowance for regimental headquarters, including band. |
|---|---|---|---|---|
| Dinner plates | | 60 | 65 | 24 |
| Soup plates | | 60 | 65 | 24 |
| Meat plates | | 6 | 6 | 3 |
| Cups and saucers | | 60 | 65 | 24 |
| Water pitchers | | 6 | 6 | 3 |
| Vegetable dishes | | 30 | 33 | 12 |
| Saltcellars | [Articles of china and glassware upon which an allowance of 20 per cent per annum of total value is made.] | 12 | 12 | 6 |
| Pepper boxes | | 12 | 12 | 6 |
| Sirup pitchers | | 12 | 12 | 6 |
| Bowls | | 60 | 65 | 24 |
| Pickle dishes | | 8 | 8 | 4 |
| Sugar bowls | | 12 | 12 | 6 |
| Gravy boats | | 12 | 12 | 6 |
| Mustard pots | | 12 | 12 | 6 |
| Tumblers | | 60 | 65 | 24 |
| Dippers | | 6 | 6 | 3 |
| Soup ladles | | 6 | 6 | 3 |
| Skimmers | | 2 | 2 | 1 |
| Dish pans | | 4 | 4 | 2 |
| Basting spoons | | 6 | 6 | 3 |
| Teaspoons | | 60 | 65 | 24 |
| Tablespoons | | 60 | 65 | 24 |
| Table forks | | 60 | 65 | 24 |
| Table knives | | 60 | 65 | 24 |
| Bread knives | | 4 | 4 | 2 |
| Butcher knives | | 4 | 4 | 2 |
| Chopping bowls | | 4 | 4 | 2 |
| Coffee mills | | 1 | 1 | 1 |
| Meat saws | | 2 | 2 | 1 |
| Scales and weights | | 1 | 1 | 1 |
| Frying pans | | 4 | 4 | 2 |
| Meat forks | | 6 | 6 | 3 |
| Meat choppers or meat cutters | | 2 | 2 | 1 |
| Carving sets | | 2 | 2 | 1 |
| Cleavers | | 1 | 1 | 1 |
| Mustard spoons | | 12 | 12 | 6 |
| Flour sieves | | 1 | 1 | 1 |
| Can openers | | 6 | 6 | 3 |
| Graters | | 2 | 2 | 1 |

The dishes are of vitrified china.

The following additional articles would probably embrace all essential utensils, viz:

One teakettle.

Two griddles.

Two gridirons.

Two stew pans.

One butchers' steel.

One nutmeg grater.

Two strainers.

One colander.

Six pudding pans.

Two cake turners.

Two bread pans for mixing pastry.

A monthly allowance of unbleached muslin is necessary for use as cooks' aprons, dishcloths, etc. Soap and concentrated lye for scrubbing tables, and some suitable material with which to clean metal utensils are also needed.

### SUGGESTIONS IN RELATION TO CARE OF TABLE-WARE.

Articles of tableware and kitchen utensils lost, damaged, broken, or destroyed, through the carelessness of enlisted men, should be charged on the muster rolls to the men at fault, and a "statement of charges," on the prescribed form, should be filed as a voucher with the return from which any article so charged is dropped.

Breakage of china and glassware not due to carelessness is usually replaced on requisition, at the public expense, provided it does not exceed 5 per cent per quarter of the total value of the outfit of china and glassware to which a mess is entitled. The value may be determined by prices stated in the price list of clothing and equipage published annually to the Army, and articles so replaced should be destroyed and dropped from returns, on proper certificates or affidavits, under paragraph 697 of the Regulations.

Breakage in excess of 5 per cent per quarter of the value of china and glass outfits should be replaced on requisition only under extraordinary circumstances, or when the value of the articles has been charged against enlisted men. Requisitions therefor should clearly set forth the extraordinary circumstances, or that the value of the articles to be replaced has been charged against enlisted men, stating to whom charged and upon what roll.

Estimates and requisitions calling for articles other than china and glassware necessary to maintain a mess equipment, should show clearly the necessity and propriety of such renewal, and if to replace articles lost or stolen, should be accompanied by the proceedings of a board of survey, except in cases where the value has been charged against enlisted men.

Estimates for tableware and kitchen utensils should be made quarterly, commencing with the one for the fourth quarter of the present fiscal year, and should cover such articles only as, with those on hand, will complete the mess outfit as established by this order. To meet emergencies, special requisitions may be made, wherein shall be set forth the circumstances causing such emergencies.

#### MESSING.

In camp or barracks, where companies are not joined in a general mess, a company commander should supervise the cooking and messing of his men. He should see that his company is provided with at least two copies of the Manual for Army Cooks, and that suitable men in sufficient numbers are fully instructed in managing and cooking the ration in the field; also that necessary utensils in serviceable condition are always on hand, together with the field mess furniture for each man. At a

post where all the companies are joined in a general
mess, the post commander should see that the instruction above mentioned is given.  At such a post
a company commander confines his supervision of
the mess of his company to observation and to noti-
fying the officer in charge, in writing, of anything
requiring remedy.  Should this officer fail to apply
proper remedy, report may then be made to the post
commander.  A department commander should see
that each company of his command has the necessary
field practice each year.

Kitchens will be better conducted if they are
placed under the immediate charge of non-commissioned officers, who should be held responsible for
their condition and for the proper use of rations.
No one should be allowed to visit or remain in the
kitchen except those who go there on duty or are
employed therein.  The greatest care should be
observed in cleaning and scouring cooking utensils.

Special regulations for soldiers' fare cannot be
made to suit each locality and circumstance.  Personal care and judgment on the part of company
officers are relied on to prevent waste or misuse.

By due economy, some part of the ration can be
saved and sold, and the proceeds applied to provide
additional articles of diet.

The food of prisoners is usually sent to their places
of confinement, but post commanders may arrange
to send prisoners, under proper guard, to their
messes.

Such proportions of company allowances of fuel,
illuminating supplies, brooms, and scrubbing brushes
as may be necessary for the service of a general mess
should be allotted by the post commander.

In the field the mess furniture of soldiers is limited
to the smallest possible quantity, usually to one tin
cup, knife, fork, and spoon, and such device for
individual cooking as may be furnished by the
Ordnance Department.

## DETAILS FOR SERVICE IN POST MESS.

The following details for service in a "Post Mess" have been found to be very satisfactory.

One officer.

One non-commissioned officer—steward.

One private as chief cook.

Two privates as assistant cooks.

Two privates, as kitchen police, from each organization; detailed for seven days, and to be excused from all company duties.

One private, as a waiter, to be detailed by first sergeants daily for each table occupied by their respective companies.

### Duties, etc.

#### OFFICER IN CHARGE.

Under the immediate supervision of the post commander, the officer who is specially selected for this duty takes charge of the entire messing establishment, and gives all directions for carrying out the system of messing and cooking. He has charge of all persons on duty in connection with the establishment and gives his constant personal attention and oversight to all matters connected with the receipt, examination, and disposition of the ration, the care and disposal of the savings, the procuring, preparing, and cooking of food, and the serving of meals. He hears all complaints and corrects or reports any that seem to be well founded. In case of his failure to remedy subjects of complaint, report may be made to the post commander. He also has charge of the post garden, which should be the only garden cultivated at the post (except the hospital garden).

The post mess fund may be administered by a mess council, which should consist of all the company commanders present for duty; an account of which should be forwarded, through proper military channels, every three months, to the department commander.

The post mess fund is collected and held by the officer in charge, whose account is subject to inspection by the post commander and the mess council, and he makes payments or purchases, on the warrants of the post commander, which warrants are only drawn in pursuance of specific resolves of said council.

At the end of June and December of each year he renders a detailed report of the working of the system to the post commander, with such remarks and recommendations as he may deem expedient.

He has full charge of the lighting and heating of the mess buildings, with which he should make himself thoroughly familiar; also with everything pertaining to the post mess, the buildings being under his immediate and personal control.

The officer in charge makes frequent daily visits to the buildings and carefully inspects the dishes, kettles, boilers, steamers and roasters, etc.

The following are important general matters for care by the officer in charge:

1. To maintain a regular and abundant supply of provisions.

2. To economize the funds and to justify receipts and expenditures by well-vouched accounts.

3. To decide with care upon the articles which should form the soldiers' food.

4. To see as far as practicable that every article of diet is wholesome and nutritious.

5. To acquaint himself as far as practicable with the peculiar properties of the different articles of food, or that food most conducive to the soldiers' health.

### STEWARDS, OR NON-COMMISSIONED OFFICERS.

The non-commissioned officer detailed for duty in the post mess is known as "steward."

Under the immediate supervision of the officer in charge, the steward has immediate charge of the messing and is responsible for the discipline and police of the establishment, and cases of neglect, inattention, and insubordination are reported to him.

The steward, notwithstanding his general supervision of the entire management, is immediately and directly responsible that the food of the men is properly prepared, served, and cooked, and requires the cooks to give the closest attention to their duties.

To insure uniformity, the steward sees that everything has a place and that it is kept there when not in use.

He sees that the floors are at all times scrupulously clean, the utmost care being taken and means devised to prevent soup, grease, etc., from dropping on the floor and on the clothes of the men while seated at the table. The officer in charge gives this matter his personal attention.

He sees that the white caps, jackets, and aprons are kept clean, that they are not used by the men except while at work in the mess hall, and that when not in use they are hung up in the place set apart for that purpose; that they are numbered in regular series, and sent to the laundry to be washed, etc.—the aprons three times a week and the caps and jackets once a week.

## THE COOKS, THE PREPARATION AND COOKING OF THE FOOD, AND THE CLEANSING OF UTENSILS, BOILERS, ETC.

The chief cook exercises general control over the cooking and all details immediately connected therewith.

He has immediate control of all cooking apparatus and is held responsible for its good order and cleanliness, and while exercising general control of all cooking, gives particular attention to the roasting ovens, coffee urns, coffee-roasting machine, and refrigerator.

The first assistant cook has immediate charge of the steamers and soup kettles, and renders such assistance to the chief cook in the general preparation of meals as he may require.

The second assistant cook has immediate charge of the roasting ovens, and gives such assistance to the chief cook in the general preparation of meals as he may require.

### KITCHEN POLICE.

The duties of the kitchen police are as follows: The preparation of vegetables and bread, the setting of the tables and placing the food thereon under supervision of the cooks, and the removing and cleansing of the dishes after each meal, and all work incident thereto, and such duties as the steward may prescribe.

### WAITERS.

There is no regular force of waiters. At meals each of the first sergeants of companies details a waiter for each table occupied by his company, whose duty it is to assist his comrades in obtaining food in addition to that served.

The waiters march in with their companies and leave the mess hall as soon as they have eaten their meals, and are required to do no other work about the establishment.

The non-commissioned officers in charge of the companies are held strictly accountable that the waiters perform their work with neatness and dispatch, and in order that the non-commissioned officers may give their men their strictest attention, they do not eat their meals until their companies are through, and they have seen that the food is fairly and properly divided.

## GENERAL SUGGESTIONS.

Meals should be served at hours designated by the commanding officer.

All men should march with their companies to the mess hall, except the guard and prisoners, unless otherwise directed. No man should have his meal in advance of the time, except the guard and prisoners, or as ordered.

The first sergeants should march their companies to meals and remain in the mess hall as already described until the meals are finished, and should be charged with the duty of preserving order in their respective companies.

The following men only should be allowed to sleep in the mess building:

1. The steward.
2. The chief cook and the two assistant cooks.

The steward should see that the occupied rooms are thoroughly ventilated and properly policed. They should be ready for inspection as soon as practicable after guard mount.

The mess hall may be ventilated in winter by opening the doors or windows for a short time after each meal.

The wash room should be cleansed after use in the morning, and the water-closet properly disinfected by one of the kitchen police designated.

### The Officer of the Day.

He inspects and tastes each meal during his tour and submits with his report to the post commander the bill of fare for the day, upon the form annexed, with his guard report, with such remarks and recommendations as may seem proper.

MANUAL FOR ARMY COOKS.

## POST MESS.

—

### BILL OF FARE.

—

#### Dinner.

—

#### Supper.

—

#### Breakfast.

—

Remarks:

## BILLS OF FARE.

What to provide for meals is sometimes a perplexing question, and the following tables are given as suggestions only. The number of dishes can be readily increased or diminished according to the locality and state of the funds of the company or mess.

A variety in even the same kinds of food can be obtained by consulting the recipes in the Manual. It should be remembered that no good results can be assured unless the *company commander makes it his personal duty* to supervise the table management of his company and indicate the bills of fare at least weekly. When unable to personally attend he should direct some other *commissioned* officer to visit the kitchen and mess hall, and these visits should be made irregularly at *all* meals and not solely at dinner time.

He should know what his resources are and so use them that the best results may be obtained.

The following is the legally authorized daily allowance of food to each person entitled to draw rations, viz:

## THE RATION.

| KINDS OF ARTICLES. | QUANTITIES PER RATION. | | QUANTITIES PER 100 RATIONS. | | |
|---|---|---|---|---|---|
| MEAT COMPONENTS | *Oz.* | *Gills.* | *Lbs.* | *Oz.* | *Galls.* |
| Fresh beef | 20 | ------- | 125 | ------- | ------ |
| Or fresh mutton, when the cost does not exceed that of beef | 20 | ------- | 125 | ------- | ------ |
| Or pork | 12 | ------- | 75 | ------- | ------ |
| Or bacon | 12 | ------- | 75 | ------- | ------ |
| Or salt beef | 22 | ------- | 137 | 8 | ------ |
| Or, when meat can not be furnished, dried fish | 14 | ------- | 87 | 8 | ------ |
| Or pickled fish | 18 | ------- | 112 | 8 | ------ |
| Or fresh fish | 18 | ------- | 112 | 8 | ------ |

## THE RATION—Continued.

| Kind of Articles. | Quantities Per Ration. | | Quantities Per 100 Rations. | | |
|---|---|---|---|---|---|
| | Oz. | Gills. | Lbs. | Oz. | Galls. |
| **BREAD COMPONENTS.** | | | | | |
| Flour | 18 | ------ | 112 | 8 | ------ |
| Or soft bread | 18 | ------ | 112 | 8 | ------ |
| Or hard bread | 16 | ------ | 100 | ------ | ------ |
| Or corn meal | 20 | ------ | 125 | ------ | ------ |
| Baking powder, for troops in the field, when necessary, to enable them to bake their own bread | $1\frac{8}{25}$ | ------ | 4 | ------ | ------ |
| **VEGETABLE COMPONENTS.** | | | | | |
| Beans | $2\frac{3}{8}$ | ------ | 15 | ------ | ------ |
| Or peas | $2\frac{2}{5}$ | ------ | 15 | ------ | ------ |
| Or rice | $1\frac{3}{8}$ | ------ | 10 | ------ | ------ |
| Or hominy | $1\frac{3}{8}$ | ------ | 10 | ------ | ------ |
| Potatoes | 16 | ------ | 100 | ------ | ------ |
| Or potatoes, $12\frac{4}{5}$ oz., and onions $3\frac{1}{5}$ oz. | 16 | ------ | 100 | ------ | ------ |
| Or potatoes, $11\frac{1}{5}$ oz., and canned tomatoes or other fresh vegetables not canned, $4\frac{4}{5}$ oz. | 16 | ------ | 100 | ------ | ------ |
| **COFFEE AND SUGAR COMPONENTS.** | | | | | |
| Coffee, green | $1\frac{3}{5}$ | ------ | 10 | ------ | ------ |
| Or roasted coffee | $1\frac{7}{25}$ | ------ | 8 | ------ | ------ |
| Or tea, green or black | $\frac{8}{25}$ | ------ | 2 | ------ | ------ |
| Sugar | $2\frac{2}{5}$ | ------ | 15 | ------ | ------ |
| Or molasses | | $1\frac{16}{25}$ | ------ | ------ | 2 |
| Or cane syrup | | $1\frac{16}{25}$ | ------ | ------ | 2 |
| **SEASONING COMPONENTS.** | | | | | |
| Vinegar | | $\frac{8}{25}$ | ------ | ------ | 1 |
| Salt | $\frac{16}{25}$ | ------ | 4 | ------ | ------ |
| Pepper, black | $\frac{1}{25}$ | ------ | ------ | 4 | ------ |
| **SOAP AND CANDLE COMPONENTS.** | | | | | |
| Soap | $1\frac{9}{25}$ | ------ | 4 | ------ | ------ |
| Candles (when illuminating oil is not furnished by the Quartermaster's Department) | $\frac{6}{25}$ | ------ | 1 | 8 | ------ |

## SAVINGS.

Articles of the ration (excluding fresh vegetables, bread, and baking powder) due a bakery, a company, or any organization, not needed for consumption, are retained by the commissary if required for reissue, and purchased as savings at the invoice prices. Savings and sales of fresh beef (except that issued for the sick in hospital, the detachment of the Hospital Corps, and the hospital matron serving therein) are prohibited; baking powder issued but not used will be returned to the commissary. The commissary purchases the savings of hospitals (including fresh beef) at cost prices, when the surgeon in charge so requires; but does not purchase savings of companies, bakeries, batteries, or any organization when public loss would result. When not required for reissue, savings may be sold to any person.

## COMPANY FUNDS.

The savings arising from an economical use of the ration constitute the company fund, which is kept in the hands of the company commander, and disbursed by him for the purchase of food, or articles to produce food, for the improvement of the soldiers' table fare, and for the purchase of white aprons and jackets for enlisted men employed in company kitchens and mess rooms, and for knife brick, dish towels, and other authorized articles.

A prudent commander can, by carefully watching the economy of his kitchen, manage to save a quantity from the ordinary ration as issued to him, and by the sale of these articles, purchase substitutes, in other foods, that will be more satisfactory by giving a variety.

## THE TRAVEL RATION.

When troops travel otherwise than by marching, or when for short periods they are separated from cooking facilities and do not carry cooked rations, the following articles are issued in lieu of *all* components of the ordinary ration.  They constitute the travel ration.

| ARTICLES. | PER 100 RATIONS. |
|---|---|
| Soft bread_____ pounds__ | 112½ |
| Or hard bread_____do ____ | 100 |
| Beef, canned _____do ____ | 75 |
| Baked beans, 1-lb. cans_____ number__ | 33 |
| Or baked beans, 3-lb. cans _____do ____ | 15 |
| Coffee, roasted_____ pounds__ | 8 |
| Sugar _____do ____ | 15 |

After troops have been subsisted upon the travel ration for four consecutive days, they may be allowed canned tomatoes in addition to the travel ration at the rate of one pound of tomatoes per man per day.  Unconsumed articles of the travel ration are not sold as savings but turned over to the commissary.  When supplied with cooked or travel rations, they may be allowed 21 cents per man per day for the purchase of liquid coffee, in lieu of the coffee and sugar portion of the ration.  If traveling under command of an officer, funds for the same purpose, at the same rate, are transferred to him, and at the end of the journey he transfers the unexpended balance, if any, to the nearest commissary

## BILLS OF FARE.

The following bills of fare are suggestive only; additional articles may be added as the company fund increases:

## Table No. 1.

| | BREAKFAST. | DINNER. | SUPPER. |
|---|---|---|---|
| SUNDAY | Beef stew. Coffee. Bread. | Roast beef, or pork and cabbage. Potatoes. Rice pudding, or duff. Bread. | Dried fruit, stewed. Coffee. Bread. |
| MONDAY | Codfish hash. Coffee. Bread. | Beef soup. Bread. | Beef stew. Coffee. Bread. |
| TUESDAY | Meat hash. Coffee. Bread. | Pork and beans. Bread. | Dried fruit, stewed. Coffee. Bread. |
| WEDNESDAY | Codfish hash. Coffee. Bread. | Roast beef. Potatoes. Bread. | Beef stew. Coffee. Bread. |
| THURSDAY | Meat hash. Coffee. Bread. | Pork and cabbage. Potatoes. Bread. | Dried fruit, stewed. Coffee. Bread. |
| FRIDAY | Codfish hash. Coffee. Bread. | Beef soup. Bread. | Beef stew. Coffee. Bread. |
| SATURDAY | Meat hash. Coffee. Bread. | Roast beef. Potatoes. Bread. | Dried fruit, stewed. Coffee. Bread. |

## Table No. 2.

| | BREAKFAST. | DINNER. | SUPPER. |
|---|---|---|---|
| SUNDAY | Baked meat hash. Coffee. Bread. | Roast beef and gravy. Mashed potatoes, pickles, coleslaw. Coffee. Bread. | Rice or bread pudding. Coffee. Bread. |
| MONDAY | Irish stew. Coffee. Bread. | Beef soup, with vegetables. Roast beef and gravy. Bread. | Stewed fruit. Coffee. Bread. |
| TUESDAY | Fried pork and gravy. Coffee. Bread. Corn cakes. | Beef stew. Bread. Pickles. | Boiled mush and sirup. Coffee. Bread. |
| WEDNESDAY | Roast beef and gravy. Coffee. Bread. | Boiled beef, with gravy. Beef soup, with beans. Bread. | Boiled rice and sirup. Coffee. Bread. |
| THURSDAY | Baked meat hash. Coffee. Bread. | Baked pork and beans. Bread. Coleslaw. | Stewed fruit. Coffee. Bread. |
| FRIDAY | Irish stew (or fish balls). Coffee. Bread. | Vegetable soup. Roast beef and gravy. Bread. | Bread pudding. Coffee. Bread. |
| SATURDAY | Meat hash. Coffee. Bread. | Roast beef or pork and gravy. Mashed parsnips. Pickles. Bread. | Boiled mush and sirup. Coffee. Bread. |

## Table No. 3.

| | BREAKFAST. | DINNER. | SUPPER. |
|---|---|---|---|
| SUNDAY | Sirup, butter. Hash. White bread. Coffee. | Bean soup. Corned beef and cabbage. Mashed potatoes. Bread and rice pudding. | Stewed apples. Tea. Bread. Cheese. |
| MONDAY | Boiled hominy and bacon. Coffee. Bread. Butter. | Vegetable soup. Roast beef. Mashed potatoes and vegetables. Bread and pickles. | Tea. Bread and sirup. Cheese. |
| TUESDAY | Baked hash, with onion gravy. Coffee. Bread. | Vegetable soup. Baked beans and bacon. Mashed potatoes, bread. Boiled mush, with sirup. | Stewed dried fruit. Tea. Bread. |
| WEDNESDAY | Bacon. Coffee. Bread, sirup, butter. | Roast beef, with onion gravy. Mashed potatoes and vegetables. Pickles, bread pudding. | Cheese. Tea. Bread, butter. |
| THURSDAY | Baked hash, with gravy. Coffee. Bread, butter. | Boiled beef. Mashed potatoes. Vegetables, bread. | Stewed dried fruit. Tea. Bread. |
| FRIDAY | Fish. Potatoes. White bread and cakes. Butter, sirup. | Roast beef, with gravy. Fish, with sauce. Mashed potatoes, vegetables. Bread and boiled mush, with sirup. | Cheese. Tea. Bread. Butter. |
| SATURDAY | Hominy and bacon. Coffee. Bread, sirup. | Irish stew. Baked beans. Vegetables, pickles, bread. | Stewed dried fruit. Tea. Bread, butter. |

## Table No. 4.

| | BREAKFAST. | DINNER. | SUPPER. |
|---|---|---|---|
| SUNDAY | Beef stew. Mush and sirup. Bread. Coffee. | Mutton broth. Boiled mutton. Rice. Bread pudding. Coffee. | Dried fruit. Cold meat. Tea. |
| MONDAY | Boiled mackerel. Fried mush. Bread. Coffee. | Bean soup. Roast beef. Rice. Pudding. Coffee. | Beef hash. Rice and sirup. Bread. Tea. |
| TUESDAY | Fried bacon. Corn bread. Coffee. | Vegetable soup. Roast beef. Cracker pudding. Coffee. | Cold meat. Mush. Bread. Tea. |
| WEDNESDAY | Codfish balls. Brown bread. Coffee. | Pea soup. Baked pork and beans. Bread. Coffee. | Stewed apples or peaches. Cold pork and beans. Bread. Tea. |
| THURSDAY | Stewed beef. Bread. Coffee. | Bean soup. Bacon and greens. Baked hominy, coffee. | Corn-meal batter cakes. Mutton stew. Tea. |
| FRIDAY | Broiled mackerel. Bread. Coffee. | Vegetable soup. Boiled codfish and potatoes. Baked batter pudding. Bread, coffee. | Dried fruit, stewed. Mush and sirup. Tea. |
| SATURDAY | Fried bacon. Fried mush. Bread, coffee. | Bean soup. Roast beef. Rice pudding, coffee. | Stewed beef. Bread. Tea. |

# RECIPES

## COOKING IN GARRISON.

(55)

## REMARKS ON SOUP.

Meat soup should have for its base uncooked meat and bone, and the water with which it is to be made should be soft. There may be added to the fresh meat the bones and remnants of cooked beef, veal, lamb, and mutton, but the principal nourishment of the soup comes from the raw meat, the usual quantity being one pound of clear lean meat to a quart of water. Success largely depends upon the cooking and skimming, and failure is generally owing to rapid boiling and neglecting to skim the pot. The soup pot must be perfectly clean. The meat must be cleaned. The water must heat gradually and simmer until the soup is cooked; the pot must be kept covered while the soup is cooking, removing the cover only to skim and add the necessary ingredients. From the time the soup commences to boil till it is done the fat and scum should frequently be removed. If cooked meat or bones are to be used, they may be added after the soup has cooked three-quarters of an hour. If the soup is allowed to simmer, the allowance of water given in the recipes will not require replenishing. If, however, it is allowed to boil hard, the water will evaporate fast and require replenishing with boiling water. Fast boiling drives off much of the aroma of the ingredients. Where soup requires seven hours or longer to cook, it is advisable to *make it the day previous*, especially in the winter months, when it will keep fresh and sweet for a week. If it is made in an iron pot, it must be strained as soon as cooked, or while hot, into a tin or earthen vessel, for if allowed to remain in an iron pot over night it will be discolored and have an unpleasant taste. When vegetables are used, they should be added only in time to become thoroughly done. To prepare vegetables for soup they must be picked over, washed, pared, and cut into small pieces from a quarter to a half inch thick, put into a pan of cold water, rinsed, and drained. Tomatoes should be scalded, peeled, and sliced. Onions fried give a richer color and a different flavor to soup than when used raw. Vegetables should be put into the soup one hour and a quarter or one hour and a half before it is cooked. Potatoes are an exception to this rule; they should be put in only thirty minutes before the soup is cooked. To prepare rice it must be picked over, washed, and drained. Season the soup lightly with salt and pepper when it is to be served. Good rich soup can be made from the heads, tails, and soup bones of cattle. The heads must be skinned and split into pieces. Remove the eyes and brains; wash out with cold water all impurities; skin, wash, and chop the tails into small pieces. Crack soup bones well open. The canned soups are in effect soup stock, and, when used according to the recipes printed upon the cans, furnish a good substitute in case sudden calls are made for soup. Fresh stock is, however, the most satisfactory.

## STOCK POT.

A *stock pot* should be established to provide good soup and gravies. It consists of a cooking utensil, either a boiler or large boiling pot, into which should be placed all available bones, etc., such for example as are collected when the ration meat is cut up, in preparing boned meat, meat pies, meat puddings, and stews. This boiler should be kept gently simmering for three or four hours daily immediately before its contents are required for use. If the meat is properly boned it will provide soup for the men at a nominal cost—of beans, peas, tomatoes, vegetables, etc.

In order to insure a constant change of stock, and that no bones remain longer than three days in the pot, the following system should be adhered to: The bones extracted from the meat rations should be placed in a net, with a tally attached, before being boiled; the bones of the second and third days should be similarly treated; after the third day the bones boiled upon the first day should be removed, and similarly the bones of the subsequent days, the stock being continually replenished from day to day. The bones should always be removed from the stock before the vegetables and other ingredients are added. They should be carefully drained, placed in a dish, and kept in a cool dry place until required the following morning. This process adds enormously to the strength of the soup made. The amount of water to be added to the boiler in making stock must depend on the quantity and the quality of the bones.

### STOCK SOUP (BOUILLON).

(*See remarks on soup.*)

| 4 pounds fresh lean beef. | 1 gallon cold water. |
|---|---|
| 1 soup bone. | 2 onions, sliced. |
| Pepper and salt. | |

Time, seven and one-half to eight hours.

Put the meat and bone into a pot with the cold water and a tablespoonful of salt. One hour before the stock is cooked, put in the sliced onion. Pepper, and, if necessary, salt, a few minutes before straining. When cooked, strain while hot through a colander into the vessel in which it is to be kept, preferably an earthen jar, put it away in a cool place to stand over night. In the morning the stock will be a jelly, with a layer of fat on top. Take off this fat and use it as drippings for cooking purposes. As stock will not keep longer than twenty-four hours in the summer, it is recommended that none be made in warm weather, but in the winter months it could be made twice a week. Scraps of cooked meat and bones may be economically utilized in the manufacture of stock.

Stock soup is sometimes served as soon as it is made; the name *Bouillon* is then given it. If it is cold, and it is desired to serve it, it should be slowly heated to the boiling point, but the boiling must not continue. If it is too rich, it may be diluted with from one to two pints of boiling water to every gallon.

Stock soup may be made the base of a variety of soups. It is also valuable and preferable to water for making meat gravies, stews, hash, etc. It is recommended for its simplicity and convenience.

### VEGETABLE SOUP (FROM STOCK).

1 gallon stock.        4 lbs. mixed vegetables (about).
Salt and pepper.

Prepare the vegetables as directed in Remarks on Soup, put them into a pot of boiling water slightly salted, and just enough to cover them, and boil until cooked. About ten minutes before the vegetables are cooked, put on the stock and bring it to a boil, then stir in the cooked vegetables, and, in order that they may not stick to the bottom, keep stirring the soup until it boils up; season lightly and serve. If rice is also used with vegetables, pick and wash it, then drain and put into a separate pot with boiling water, enough to cover it, with a teaspoonful of salt. Boil it twenty-five minutes, or until cooked; stir it and the vegetables, with the waters in which they were boiled, into the stock.

### TOMATO SOUP (FROM STOCK).

1 gallon stock.        6 lbs. fresh or canned tomatoes.
Pepper and salt.

Prepare the tomatoes as directed in Remarks on Soup. Stew the tomatoes until cooked; add a tablespoonful of salt; stir frequently to dissolve them and prevent scorching.

Stir the cooked tomatoes into the pot of stock, previously heated, and stir the whole until it comes to a boil. Season lightly and serve.

### BARLEY SOUP (FROM STOCK).

8 tablespoonfuls pearl barley.       1 gallon stock.
Salt and pepper to taste.

Wash the barley in cold water, then cover it with boiling water; let it boil up once and drain it; cover it again with boiling water and simmer two hours, then drain and add to the stock when boiling. Let it stand on the back of the range for ten minutes; then add salt and pepper and serve.

### DRIED BEAN SOUP (FROM STOCK).

2 quarts dried beans.       1 gallon stock.
2 pounds bacon.       1 gallon boiling water.
Salt and pepper to taste.

Wash the beans and soak them over night. In the morning drain the water off, and cover them again with the boiling water; add the bacon and boil gently two hours or more; now add the stock. Press the beans through a sieve, return them to the soup kettle, and bring to a boil; add salt and pepper, and serve with toasted bread.

### MACARONI SOUP (FROM STOCK).

4 ounces macaroni.              1 gallon stock.
Salt and pepper to taste.

Break the macaroni into pieces about two inches long; put it into a stewing pan and cover it with one quart of boiling water; boil it twenty minutes, drain, and cut each piece in two. Melt the stock, bring it to a boiling point; add the macaroni, let it simmer five minutes; add salt and pepper and serve.

A plate of cheese may be served with this if liked.

## SAGO SOUP (FROM STOCK).

4 ounces sago.                    1 gallon stock.

Salt and pepper to taste.

Wash the sago through several waters, then cover it with warm water and let it soak one hour. Melt the stock and bring it to the boiling point; drain the sago, and add it to the stock. Let it boil slowly half an hour, stirring very often to prevent scorching; add salt and pepper and serve.

## RICE SOUP (FROM STOCK).

1 gallon stock.                   ½ to ¾ pound rice.

Pepper and salt.

Prepare the rice as directed in Remarks on Soup; put it into a pot of boiling water, enough to cover it well; add two teaspoonfuls of salt. Boil gently for thirty minutes or until cooked. Stir the cooked rice, with the water it was boiled in, into the pot of stock, previously heated, and stir the whole until it comes to a boil; season lightly and serve.

## TOMATO AND RICE SOUP (FROM STOCK).

1 gallon stock.                        ¼ pound rice.

3 lbs. fresh or canned tomatoes.      Pepper and salt.

Prepare the tomatoes and rice as directed in Remarks on Soup. Cook the tomatoes and rice separately, as directed in the two preceding recipes. Stir in the cooked tomatoes, then the cooked rice, with the water in which it was boiled, into the pot of stock, previously heated, and stir the whole till it comes to a boil; season lightly and serve.

## VEGETABLE SOUP.

| 4 pounds fresh lean beef. | 1 gallon cold water. |
|---|---|
| 1 or 2 pounds soup bone. | Pepper and salt. |

4 pounds such vegetables as may be obtainable.

Time, five and a half to six hours.

Put the meat and bone into a pot with the water and one tablespoonful of salt, and cook as directed in Remarks on Soup. When the soup has boiled about four or four and a half hours, strain it through a colander, return it with the good meat to the pot, leaving out all bones, skin, gristle, etc.

Prepare the vegetables as directed in Remarks on Soup, put them into the soup, and let them boil gently until thoroughly done, stirring occasionally to prevent them from scorching or sticking to the bottom of the pot. When cooked take out the vegetables, mash and return them to the soup, boil one minute, season lightly, and serve. The vegetables can be varied according to season and opportunity, using onions, potatoes, carrots, turnips, parsnips, cabbage, green or canned corn, fresh or canned tomatoes, celery or celery seed, cauliflowers, okra, rice, pumpkins, squash, green peas, string beans, etc.

## TOMATO SOUP, No. 1.

| 4 pounds fresh lean beef. | 1 or 2 lbs. soup bone. |
|---|---|
| 1 gallon cold water. | 1 onion, sliced. |
| 6 lbs. fresh or canned tomatoes. | Pepper and salt. |

Time, five and one-half to six hours.

Put the meat and bones into a pot with the water, one tablespoonful of salt, and the sliced onions, and cook as directed in Remarks on Soup. One hour and a quarter before the soup is cooked strain it through a colander and return it with the good meat

to the pot, leaving out bones, skin, gristle, etc. Prepare the tomatoes as directed in Remarks on Soup.
Put the tomatoes into the soup directly after it is
strained; stir the tomatoes hard and frequently, that
they may dissolve thoroughly and not scorch. Boil
gently one hour. Season lightly and serve.

### TOMATO SOUP, No. 2.

| | |
|---|---|
| 3 pints cold water. | 3 lbs. fresh or canned tomatoes. |
| 1 onion, chopped fine. | 1 large spoonful sifted flour. |
| 1 pint boiled milk. | Pepper and salt. |

Piece of butter the size of an egg.

Time, one hour.

Mix the flour and butter together into a smooth
paste. Prepare the tomatoes as directed in Remarks
on Soup. Put the tomatoes, chopped onion, buttered flour, and a teaspoonful of salt into a pot with
the water. Boil gently for one hour, stir frequently
to dissolve the tomatoes and prevent scorching, then
stir in the milk (hot) and keep stirring till it comes
to a boil. Season lightly and serve.

### RICE SOUP.

| | |
|---|---|
| 4 pounds fresh lean beef. | 1 or 2 pounds soup bone. |
| 1 gallon cold water. | 1 onion, sliced. |
| ¼ to ¾ pound rice. | Pepper and salt. |

Time, five and one-half to six hours.

Put the meat and bones into a pot with the
water, one teaspoonful of salt, and the sliced onion,
and cook as directed in Remarks on Soup. Three-
quarters of an hour before the soup is cooked strain
it through a colander, return it with the good meat
to the pot, leaving out bones, skin, gristle, etc. Stir
the rice, previously prepared as directed in Remarks
on Soup, into the strained soup thirty minutes before
it is cooked; stir frequently to prevent the rice from
scorching or sticking to the bottom of the pot.
When cooked season lightly and serve.

## MUTTON OR LAMB BROTH.

| | |
|---|---|
| 4 lbs. lean mutton or lamb. | 1 gallon cold water. |
| 1 onion, sliced. | 2 gills rice. |

Pepper. salt, parsley, and thyme.

Time, four to four and one-half hours.

Cut the mutton or lamb into small pieces, put them into a pot with the water, tablespoonful of salt, and cook as directed in Remarks on Soup. One hour before the soup is cooked put in the sliced onion. Prepare the rice as directed in Remarks on Soup, and put it into the soup thirty minutes before the soup is cooked. After it is in stir it frequently to prevent it scorching or sticking to the bottom of the pot. When cooked season lightly and serve at once, as the broth is apt to burn.

One or two pounds of fresh or canned tomatoes may be added to it.

## DUMPLING BROTH.

| | |
|---|---|
| 1 knuckle veal. | 3 quarts cold water. |
| ½ cup flour. | ½ cup chopped suet. |
| ¼ teaspoon salt. | 1 tablespoonful grated onion. |

Bay leaf, parsley, and carrot.

Put veal in kettle with three quarts of water. Simmer two hours. Add sprig of parsley, carrot, and bay leaf (optional), and simmer one hour longer. Strain and stand away to cool. When cold take fat from top and turn soup carefully into the kettle, leaving all sediment behind, and place over fire to heat. Put suet in dish, add flour, mix, add salt and enough ice water to moisten; make into dumplings the size of a marble. When all are done place in soup, boil ten minutes, add grated onion and salt and pepper to taste. Serve while hot.

## OX-TAIL SOUP.

| | |
|---|---|
| 2 ox tails. | 1 tablespoon salt. |
| 1 large onion. | 1 tablespoon mixed herbs. |
| 4 quarts cold water. | 4 cloves. |
| 1 tablespoon beef dripping. | 4 peppercorns. |

Wash and cut up ox tails, separating at joints. Cut the onion fine and fry it in beef dripping. When browned slightly, draw it to side of pan and brown half the ox tails. Put fried onion and ox tails in soup kettle and cover with four quarts cold water. Tie herbs, cloves, and peppercorns in a strainer cloth and add to soup. Add salt and simmer three or four hours or until meat separates from the bone and gristly parts are soft.

Select nicest joints to serve with soup. Skim off fat and add more salt and pepper if needed. Strain and serve very hot. Vegetables may be served with this soup. If so, cut one pint mixed onions, carrots, turnips, and celery into small pieces or fancy shapes. Add them to liquor after straining and boil twenty minutes or until tender.

## CONSOMMÉ.

| | |
|---|---|
| 4 pounds beef. | 4 cloves. |
| 1 ounce suet. | 3 quarts cold water. |
| 1 small onion. | 1 small carrot. |
| Piece of celery. | |

Cut up four pounds lean beef into dice. Put one ounce suet and onion, sliced, into kettle and cook until brown. Add the meat and cook without covering thirty minutes. Add the cold water, cover kettle, and simmer for three hours. At end of time add the carrots, cloves, celery, and simmer one hour longer. Strain and stand away to cool. When cold remove all grease from top and turn into kettle. Boil one minute and strain through cheese cloth. Season and serve.

## TOMATO AND RICE SOUP.

| | |
|---|---|
| 4 pounds fresh lean beef. | 1 onion, sliced. |
| 1 or 2 pounds soup bone. | ¼ pound rice. |
| 1 gallon cold water. | Pepper and salt. |
| 4 pounds fresh or canned tomatoes. | |

Time, five and one-half to six hours.

Put the meat and bones in a pot with the water, one tablespoonful of salt and the sliced onion, and cook as directed in Remarks on Soup. One hour and a quarter before the soup is cooked strain it through a colander and return soup and good meat to the pot, leaving out bones, skin, gristle, etc. Prepare the tomatoes and rice as directed in Remarks on Soup. Put the tomatoes into the soup directly after it is strained, and the rice thirty minutes before the soup is cooked. Stir frequently that the tomatoes may dissolve thoroughly and the rice be prevented from scorching or sticking to the bottom of the pot. When cooked season lightly and serve.

## BEAN SOUP.

| | |
|---|---|
| 2 quarts beans. | 6 quarts cold water. |
| 1 pound salt pork. | Pepper. |
| 1 teaspoonful bicarbonate of soda. | |

Time, three hours.

Pick over the beans, wash, and soak them over night in cold water; scrape the pork clean and cut it into thin slices. Drain the beans and put them into a pot with the cold water and bicarbonate of soda. Cover the pot, heat gradually, and boil gently for thirty minutes; remove the scum as it rises. Turn off the water and replenish with six quarts of fresh boiling water. Cover, and boil slowly and gently for one and a half hours, stirring the beans frequently to prevent scorching, then put in the sliced pork. As soon as the beans become tender and crack, take out the pork and mash the beans into a paste with a wooden masher, while in the pot, or press them through a colander, using a wooden masher or heavy iron spoon. The skins of the beans will be left in the colander to be thrown away. Put the pork and beans back into the pot and complete the boiling. Season lightly and serve.

This soup can be made richer by adding a half pound of lean beef for every quart of water. It is put into the pot with the pork. Bean soup is apt to burn, and great care must be taken to prevent it by not exposing it to too great a heat and by frequent stirring.

If soda is not used a longer time will be required to make this soup.

### PEA SOUP.

| | |
|---|---|
| 2 quarts split peas. | 1 pound fresh lean beef. |
| 1 pound salt pork. | 6 quarts cold water. |

Pepper and salt.

Time, three hours.

Pick over the peas, wash, and soak them over night in cold water. Scrape the pork clean and cut it and the beef into pieces. Drain the peas and put them with the cut-up meats into a pot with the water. Cover the pot, heat gradually, and boil gently. Remove the scum as it rises; stir frequently from the bottom to prevent scorching. About the second hour, or when the peas have become soft, take out the meats and with a wooden masher mash the peas, then put the meats back into the soup and complete the boiling. When cooked season lightly and dish. Have ready some slices of fried bread cut into square pieces. Scatter them on the surface of the soup and serve. Do this quickly, as pea soup cools and thickens rapidly. Pea soup is apt to burn, and great care must be taken to prevent it by not exposing it to too great a heat and by stirring it frequently.

## OYSTER SOUP (COVE OYSTERS).

6 cans cove oysters.          ½ pound butter.

1 gallon milk.          1 pound rolled crackers.

Pepper and salt.

Drain the liquor from the oysters and pick them over. Put the milk and butter into a vessel and heat gradually to a boil. Stir in very gradually the liquor, then the rolled crackers. Let it boil up once, then stir in the oysters; let it remain two minutes. Season and serve at once.

Success in making oyster soup depends upon cooking it just enough. Too much cooking hardens the oysters, while if underdone it is not palatable.

## OYSTER SOUP (FRESH OYSTERS).

4 quarts fresh oysters.          1 pound butter.

2 gallons milk.          2 pounds rolled crackers.

Pepper and salt.

Drain the liquor from the oysters. Put the milk and butter into a vessel and heat gradually. When warm stir in the liquor; do this very gradually to prevent the milk curdling; then the rolled crackers. Let it come to a boil, then add the oysters. In four or five minutes, or when the edges of the oysters become curled, season and serve.

## MOCK OYSTER SOUP.

Mash one quart of canned tomatoes through a colander and boil them for about twenty minutes. Season well with cayenne pepper and salt. While the tomatoes are boiling add a half teaspoonful of bicarbonate of soda and let it ferment. Pour in a quart of milk and add two crackers rolled fine and two ounces of butter. Let it boil and serve.

## BEEF TEA.

| 1 pound lean beef. | 2 tablespoonfuls cold water. |
| | Salt. |

Time, three to four hours.

Cut the beef into small pieces, rejecting skin and fat. Put the meat and water into an open-mouth bottle or stone jar; close it with a cork. Set the bottle in a pot of cold water; heat it very gradually to a boil. Boil gently for three or four hours or until the meat is colorless. If it comes to a boil too quickly the glass bottle will crack. As the water evaporates replenish the pot with boiling water, taking care when it is put in not to strike the bottle. Exercise the most watchful care while cooking. If the bottle cracks remove it instantly from the pot and transfer the contents to a fresh bottle, first heating the bottle with hot water, and put it into the pot. When cooked strain the tea into an earthen vessel. Season with salt. Set it aside and when cold skim off any fatty particles. Serve hot or cold. If too strong for use dilute it with warm water.

### ONION SOUP.

(Sufficient for 22 men.)

| 5 pounds fat and bones. | 6 ounces salt. |
| 10 pounds onions. | 4 ounces sugar. |
| 1 head celery. | ½ ounce pepper. |
| 1 pound flour. | 3½ gallons water. |
| 4 pounds bread. | |

Chop up the bones and fat into small pieces; place them in the boiler with one gallon of cold water; boil well for one hour. Peel the onions, and cut off the tops and bottoms of the celery, or it will be bitter; place them in a net, and add them with the remainder of the water to the boiler, and boil. At the end of forty minutes (if very large, longer) take out the onions and celery and pulp them; replace them in the boiler with the seasoning and flour mixed, and boil for thirty minutes longer. Prepare the bread in dice, place it in the pail, pour the soup on it, and serve.

The remainder of the ration meat may be either baked, broiled, fried, or made into puddings or pies.

### KIDNEY SOUP.

(Sufficient for 22 men.)

| | |
|---|---|
| 2 ox kidneys. | 6 ounces salt. |
| 1 pound suet. | 5 ounces sugar. |
| 1 pound onions. | ¼ ounce pepper. |
| 3½ gallons water. | |

Chop up the suet and onions and place them in the boiler and let them fry; cut up the kidneys in small pieces about the size of a nut, place them in the boiler with the seasoning, let them fry for five minutes, then add the water, and let it simmer for two and a half to three hours. The kidneys when cut up should be shaken about with as much flour as will stick to them; this helps them to brown and improves the appearance of the soup. Two ounces of the sugar should be made into coloring, as the soup ought to be clear and of a nice brown color. A tablespoonful of celery seed, placed in a piece of cloth and boiled in it, is an improvement; also some chopped parsley. If it is required thick, one pound of flour must be added. Some carrots and turnips cut into small pieces, slightly browned and simmered in the soup, are a good addition.

### ST. PATRICK'S SOUP.

(Sufficient for 22 men.)

| | |
|---|---|
| 6 pounds meat and fat. | 1 large cabbage. |
| 6 pounds potatoes. | 1 pound flour. |
| 1 pound onions. | 6 ounces salt. |
| 1 pound celery. | 6 ounces sugar. |
| 1 pound turnip. | 6 tablespoonfuls vinegar. |
| 1 pound carrot. | 3½ gallons water. |

Cut the meat into pieces one inch square, the fat into smaller pieces; place them in the boiler; when warm add the vegetables (except the potatoes) cut very small, stir them round so that they do not burn; when they are on the point of doing so add the water by degrees; peel the potatoes, put them in a net, and place them in the boiler; when done take them out and mash them; after the soup has been boiling two hours add the potatoes, with the seasoning and flour mixed, and the vinegar; boil slowly for thirty minutes, keep stirring it, and serve.

## FRIED BREAD FOR SOUPS.

Cut stale bread into dice, and fry in boiling fat until brown. It will take about half a minute.

## REMARKS ON FISH.

Fresh fish are best when just taken from the water. They are fresh when the eyes are clear, the fins stiff, the gills red, and hard to open. Unless fish have been frozen or have inhabited muddy streams they should not be soaked. If frozen, soak them in ice-cold water to thaw. If they have inhabited muddy streams, after they have been cut up soak them in strong salt water. A fish or part of a fish of less than three pounds' weight except rockfish is too small for boiling. Exact time for boiling fish can not be given, as much depends upon the size and kind. A piece of fresh cod weighing three pounds will cook in from eighteen to twenty minutes. Salmon should be allowed a longer time, while six or seven minutes per pound will be enough for sheepshead, rockfish, etc. Mackerel need from ten to twelve minutes; herring and many other kinds of fish scarcely half so long. As a general rule fish with white flesh require less time for boiling than fish with dark flesh. It requires experience to know exactly how long to boil a fish, although it is claimed that by putting salt and vinegar into the water six minutes to the pound is enough for all kinds of fish, thick or thin. Care must be taken that the fish is not underdone, but if boiled too much or allowed to remain too long in the water it will be insipid. The fish is done when the meat separates easily from the backbone. Test with a fork.

### TO PREPARE FISH.

Scrape off the scales, remove the entrails, etc., thoroughly wash the fish inside and out in cold water, and wipe it dry immediately with a cloth, inside and out. If the pot is small for the fish, skewer the tail into the mouth, then tie or pin the fish up in a clean towel or cloth and it is ready for boiling.

### BOILED FISH.

Put the fish into enough boiling water to cover it about an inch, with two tablespoonfuls of salt and four tablespoonfuls of vinegar to a piece of fish of about five pounds weight. Simmer steadily until done. When cooked take up the fish, remove the cloth carefully, put the fish into a hot dish, pour a hot fish sauce over it (see Sauces for Boiled Fish), and serve, or send the sauce to table in a separate dish.

To boil the roes, wash and wipe with a soft cloth. Put them inside the fish, tied with a thread or light twine, and boil as above; or they may be boiled separately wrapped in a cloth.

### FRIED FISH.

Small fish should be fried whole. Large fish should be cut up. Clean and wipe the fish dry, rub it over with dry sifted flour, or better, dip it into well-beaten egg and then into bread crumbs or rolled cracker.

Put into a frying pan enough dripping to well cover the fish. When this is hot put in the fish and fry both sides a clear golden brown. Just as the fish is turning brown sprinkle it lightly with pepper and salt. When cooked serve in a hot dish. Roes may be prepared and fried as above.

## BAKED FISH.

Any fish may be baked, provided it is large enough to admit of being stuffed. A fish of five or six pounds when stuffed will take from forty to fifty minutes to bake.

To prevent scorching place over it a well-greased paper. Prepare a stuffing of bread crumbs, with sufficient butter, lard, or beef dripping to make the mixture moist. Season with pepper, salt, a little summer savory, thyme, or sage.

Clean and wipe the fish dry, put in the stuffing lightly, and sew up the opening. Lay the fish in a baking pan; rub it over with butter, lard, or beef dripping; dredge with flour, bread crumbs, or rolled cracker; spread on the upper side a few thin slices of raw onion and sprinkle them with salt and pepper; or instead of dredging lay thin slices or strips of fat salt pork or bacon on the sliced onion, and above the seasoning. Put into the pan a half pint of stock or beef dripping, taking care that a part of it gets under the fish to keep it from adhering to the pan. Bake in a hot oven. Baste very frequently and serve with a fish-gravy. (See Gravy for Baked Fish.) Tomatoes laid on the onions and above the seasoning add to the taste and flavor. It may be eaten cold.

## FISH OR CLAM CHOWDER, No. 1.

Use firm fish, such as fresh cod, catfish, etc. Do not cook the heads. Scrape, cleanse, and wash the fish. Cut it into small pieces, leaving out as many bones as possible. Cover the bottom of the pot with

slices of fat salt pork; place on that a layer of potatoes cut into small pieces; on the potatoes a layer
of chopped onions; on the onions a layer of tomatoes;
on the tomatoes a layer of fish; on the fish a layer
of crackers or biscuit, first made tender by soaking
in water or milk; then repeat the process, commencing with potatoes, until the pot is nearly full. Every
layer is seasoned with pepper and salt; use only
enough cold water to moisten and cook the mass.
Cover the pot closely, set it over a gentle fire, let it
heat gradually, and then simmer one hour. When
nearly done, stir it gently, finish cooking, and serve.
When cooked, if found too thin, simmer a little
longer. The tomatoes may be omitted. Clam
chowder is made as above, using clams instead of
fish.

A chowder may be made as above by using any
fresh meat instead of fish.

### FISH CHOWDER, No. 2.

| | |
|---|---|
| ½ pound salt pork. | 4 onions. |
| 6 medium-sized potatoes. | 3 pounds fish (about). |
| ½ pound crackers or biscuit. | |

Cleanse, remove the rind, and cut the pork into
thin slices; slice the onions. Put the pork and
onions together into a pot and fry them brown; then
season lightly with salt and plenty of pepper. Sweet
herbs may also be used for additional seasoning.
Slice the potatoes and lay them in cold water until
wanted. Scrape, cleanse, and wash the fish; cut it
into small pieces; soak the crackers in water or
milk until tender. When the pork and onions have
browned and been seasoned, add a layer of fish; on
the fish a layer of potatoes; on the potatoes a layer
of crackers; then repeat the process, commencing
with fish, in regular layers until the pot is nearly
full, or till the ingredients are used up. Each layer
is seasoned with pepper and salt. Use only enough

cold water to moisten and cook the mass. Cover the pot closely, set it over a gentle fire, let it heat gradually, and cook and serve as directed in Chowder, No. 1. Tomatoes may be added as one of the layers.

### TURBOT (FISH HASH).

(Turbot can be made from any kind of firm fish.)

| | |
|---|---|
| 6 pounds fish. | 1 quart milk. |
| 1 bunch parsley. | 4 ounces flour. |
| 3 slices raw onion. | 4 ounces butter. |
| 2 eggs, beaten. | A little thyme. |

Grated bread crumbs or rolled crackers.
Cheese, pepper, and salt.

Scrape, cleanse, and wash the fish, and boil it until done. Drain it and remove the skin. Cut the fish into inch pieces, leaving out the bones; season with pepper and salt. While the fish is cooking put into a pot the milk, parsley, thyme, onion, and a seasoning of pepper and salt. Let this come to a boil; then stir in gradually the flour, blended with cold milk, and keep stirring until it reaches the consistency of thick cream. Take it at once from the fire, stir in the butter, strain through a colander, and when the mixture is about milk warm, stir in the beaten egg and mix thoroughly. Put into a baking dish a layer of the sauce; on the sauce a layer of fish; on the fish a layer of sauce, and so on in successive layers till the dish is full, being careful to finish with a layer of sauce; over this last layer sprinkle the grated bread crumbs, and on these a little of the cheese to form a top crust; bake half an hour with a moderate heat. Serve hot in the baking dish.

### BOILED SALT CODFISH.

Soak the fish twelve hours in tepid water, or longer if necessary. Scale and cleanse it. See that no crystals of salt adhere to the under part of the fish; put it into a pot, first cutting it into slices; cover with cold water and set it on a rather slow fire; carefully remove the scum as it rises. When it comes to a boil, if not cooked, change the water and let it come to a boil again. Drain well. Separate the flakes, put it into a hot dish, pour over a sauce (see Sauces for Boiled Fish), and serve.

## CODFISH BALLS.

Prepare the fish as for boiling. Pick the fish into very fine pieces or shreds, carefully removing skin and bone. Put it on the fire in a pot of cold water; remove the scum as it rises; let it come to a boil slowly, then pour off the water and replenish with boiling water. Let it come to a boil again, then drain well. Have ready an equal bulk of hot mashed potato worked light with butter and milk; mix mashed potato and fish together while both are hot. It makes a great difference in the lightness of the balls if the mixing is done while fish and potato are both hot. Form the mixture quickly into balls or thick, flat cakes. Put into a vessel enough lard or beef dripping so that when melted it will immerse the balls; when this gets hot, drop in the balls and fry to a light brown. When one side is done turn the other. While mixing the fish and potatoes together, beaten egg may be stirred with the mixture to make the whole smooth; or, after being made into balls, each ball may be dipped into beaten egg before it is dropped into the fat.

## SALT CODFISH HASH.

One-third fish (cooked); two-thirds mashed potato worked light with butter and milk.

Chop the cooked fish fine; then mash and work it as fine as possible. This done, work the potato gradually and thoroughly into the fish; mix in enough milk to make the mixture as soft as mashed potato. While working the mixture, season it with butter and pepper; also salt if necessary. Put it into a pot and heat it, constantly stirring it. Put into a frying pan enough butter or beef dripping so that when melted it will just cover the bottom of the pan; when this is hot press the hash into it firmly and fry very gently; when the lower side becomes brown turn it out without breaking, into a hot dish, and serve.

### BOILED SALT MACKEREL.

Wash the fish and soak it, skin side uppermost, in cold water eight or ten hours. If very salty a longer time will be required to soak. Put the fish into a shallow pan, skin side uppermost; cover with cold water; boil gently. It should cook in fifteen or twenty minutes. When cooked take it up carefully; drain well; put it in a hot dish skin side down. Pepper and butter upper side, and serve.

### BROILED SALT MACKEREL.

Wash and soak the fish in cold water for twelve or fourteen hours. This amount of soaking will make it sodden; hang it up by the head to drip for eight or ten hours before cooking. Wipe it clean and heat the gridiron on a bed of live coals (wood coals are the best); then grease it well with a piece of salt pork or bacon; lay the fish on the gridiron, skin side uppermost. Broil brown; turn carefully; separate with a knife any part of it which sticks to the gridiron, and brown the other side. When cooked, take it up carefully, put it in a hot dish skin side down, distribute small lumps of butter on its upper side, sprinkle with pepper, put it in the oven for a few minutes to let the butter soak in, and serve.

## BAKED SHAD.

Scrape free from all scales, make a short opening down the belly, and take out the insides. Wash well, inside and out, and immediately wipe dry with a clean towel. Rub it well with salt. Make a dressing of one cup of stale bread crumbs, one tablespoonful of chopped parsley, a half teaspoonful of salt, and a little black pepper. Mix well and stuff the body of the fish and sew it up with soft yarn. Now score one side of the fish with a sharp knife, making the scores about one inch apart, and put a strip of salt pork in each gash. Place it in the bottom of a baking pan and dredge thickly with salt, pepper, and flour; cover bottom of the pan with boiling water and put into a hot oven. Bake fifteen minutes to every pound of fish, basting every ten minutes with the gravy in the pan. As the water evaporates, add more to again cover the bottom of the pan. Garnish with slices of lemon, fried potato balls, and parsley. When done, loosen it carefully and slide it into the dish.

### BAKED HALIBUT (CREOLE STYLE).

Get thick square piece of halibut or other fish if preferred. Wash and lay on baking dish. Season with salt and pepper. Chop piece of white garlic size of a bean and strew over fish, then pour on cup of fresh or canned tomatoes. Bake until the flakes separate. Dish without breaking.

### LITTLE PIGS IN BLANKETS.

Season large oysters with salt and pepper. Cut fat bacon in very thin slices, wrap an oyster in each slice, and skewer (toothpicks are the best things). Heat a frying pan and cook just long enough to crisp the bacon—about two minutes. Place on slices of toast, and serve immediately. Do not remove the skewers. The pan must be very hot before the "pigs" are put in, and then great care taken that they do not burn.

### GRAVY FOR BAKED FISH.

After the fish is taken from the pan put the pan on the fire, and stir into it gradually two table-spoonfuls of blended brown flour. Boil up once, season with pepper and salt, remove any black specks, and pour it over the fish.

### SAUCES FOR BOILED FISH.

#### Drawn-Butter Sauce.

| | |
|---|---|
| 1 pint boiling water. | 2 tablespoonfuls sifted flour. |
| 2 tablespoonfuls butter. | Pepper and salt. |

Put a saucepan on the fire; put in the butter and flour; mix them with a spoon (a wooden one is preferable) into a smooth paste; pour over very gradually the boiling water, stirring it well in. Boil up once, season, and serve. If an acid taste is desired, add a few drops of vinegar.

#### Pickle Sauce.

Add to a drawn-butter sauce two or more table-spoonfuls of minced pickled cucumbers.

#### Boiled-Egg Sauce.

Add to a drawn-butter sauce two minced hard-boiled eggs.

### REMARKS ON MEAT.

Good fresh beef presents the following characteristics: The lean, when freshly cut, is of a bright red color, easily compressed and elastic, the grain fine and interspersed with fat. The fat is firm and of a yellowish-white color; the suet firm and perfectly white. If beef is of inferior quality the lean is coarse, tough, and inelastic, and of a dull purplish color; the fat is scanty, yellow, and moist. The above remarks apply to mutton, except that in good mutton the fat is white. In unwholesome mutton the fat is decidedly yellow. If meat is frozen it should be thawed in cold water before it is cooked. This rule applies to all frozen meats, poultry, game, and fish. If meat is tainted, it is useless to attempt to disguise it; it should be thrown away.

Meat becomes tender and more digestible by keeping. If it is to be kept longer than ordinary it should be dredged with pepper. It should be wiped with a dry cloth as soon as it comes from the butcher.

Meat must not be placed in contact with ice. It should not be kept wrapped in paper, nor in anything that may impart flavor. Before putting raw or cooked meat into a refrigerator cover it with a clean cloth. The practice of taking the bones out of baking pieces and skewering is improper, as the escape of the juices is thereby facilitated. The time required for baking depends on the oven, the quality of the meat, its size and shape, and the time it has been killed; fresh-killed meat requires a longer time to cook. A longer time is required in cold than in warm weather.

The time may be generally stated at from fifteen to twenty minutes to the pound. If dripping from the baked beef is not used for gravy, strain it into a tin or earthen vessel, cover it, and put it in a cool place for future cooking. When congealed into a cake, if any sediment adheres to it, scrape it off. *Mutton dripping* can not be used for any kind of cooking, as it communicates a tallowy taste to everything cooked with it.

### BAKED BEEF.

Cleanse the meat; then place it in the pan with the fat and skin side up; put the pan into a hot

oven, and when the heat has started enough of the
oil of the fat commence to baste, which should be
performed quickly, closing the oven door as soon as
basting is done.  The basting should be repeated
often during the baking; when nearly done sprinkle
it with pepper and salt, and baste.  The meat should
be served on a warm platter.  (See Gravy for Baked
Meats.)

If the beef is not sufficiently fat and juicy to furnish material for basting, a tablespoonful or more
of stock, gravy, or beef dripping should be put into
the pan; putting water into the pan to baste with
is improper, as water can not be raised to as high a
temperature as fat and does not, therefore, serve as
well; besides this, when water is used, the beef is,
to a certain extent, stewed and not baked, and its
flavor is injured.  One or more onions sliced and
placed on the beef may be cooked with it.

Mutton, veal, and fresh pork may be prepared
and baked as above.  They must be well done to be
palatable.  Before putting pork into the oven, score
the skin into small squares.

As ordinarily cooked by the soldier, baked meats
are generally *overdone* and dry.  It has been sug-
gested that just before the beef is done it be covered
with a large pan to confine the juices which would
otherwise evaporate.

When cutting meats to cook, cut across grain of
muscle.  Never wash fresh meat before roasting;
scrape it if necessary to clean it.  If wet or moist,
dry thoroughly before cooking.

Do not place meat on ice but in a vessel on ice.
Do not use salt when basting, but salt the meat
when done.

### POT ROAST.

Trim off the rough parts of a nice brisket of beef,
and place in a kettle over a good fire.  Add one pint
of boiling water, cover, and cook slowly fifteen minutes to every pound.  Add salt when meat is half

done. After the water evaporates add no more, as there should be fat enough to finish cooking the meat. Serve with gravy made from the fat in the pot.

### BROILED FILLET.

Cut a fillet of beef into slices an inch thick. Moisten them with melted dripping or butter and let stand for half an hour. Then place them on a broiler and broil over a quick fire five minutes, turning them two or three times. Place them on a hot plate, season with salt and pepper, pour sauce around, and serve.

### POUNDED BEEF.

Cut the lean meat from a shin of beef weighing 10 pounds. Break up bone and lay in the bottom of the kettle. Place meat on bones, cover with cold water, and let it slowly come to a boil, removing scum as it rises. Peel two turnips and two onions, scrape one carrot, and place with beef after the broth is skimmed. (If available put in half a cup green sweet herbs and parsley.) Also add one level teaspoonful of salt. Cover kettle closely and boil six hours slowly. At end of six hours, take up meat, fat, and gristle, remove all bone, put into a colander, and rub through with a potato masher. Season highly and press firmly into a tin or earthen mold. Strain broth left and save it for soup, using first enough to moisten meat in mold. After pressing beef into mold and moistening with broth, put a weight on to keep it down and put away to cool. When beef is quite cold, turn out of mold and cut into thin slices.

### BROILED BEEFSTEAK.

#### In a frying pan.

The best pieces of beef for steak are the tenderloin, sirloin, and rib pieces. A steak should not be less than three-quarters of an inch nor more than an inch and a quarter thick. If beating is necessary, beat on both sides, but not enough to tear the beef and allow the juices to escape.

Cleanse the steak, but do not put it into water. Have the frying pan very hot and dry; put in the steak, cover it with a tin plate or pan, and turn the steak often, preferably with a pair of meat tongs. If a knife and fork are used, insert the fork in the outer or skin edge of the steak.

A steak an inch to an inch and a quarter thick will be cooked in twelve or fifteen minutes. When cooked put it on a hot dish and season with pepper and salt. The juices will then escape and furnish the gravy. Or, have ready in a hot dish a half teaspoonful of salt, a quarter of a teaspoonful of pepper, a piece of butter or beef dripping not quite the size of an egg; add two tablespoonfuls of boiling water. Mix well together. Put the steak into it and turn it over once so that both sides will be moistened with the gravy, and serve.

If this does not furnish enough gravy, add two or more tablespoonfuls of boiling water to the fat remaining in the pan, mix thoroughly, pour it over the steak, and let it mix with the other gravy.

Prepare and broil mutton chops, venison, and pork steaks as above.

Meat prepared in this way is quite equal to that broiled on a gridiron, and this method does not waste its juices.

### On a gridiron.

Prepare the steak as directed for broiling in a frying pan. Have ready a bed of live coals; wood coals are the best. Wipe the gridiron clean; put it over the bed of coals. As soon as heated put the steak on it; broil, turning often. If the fire smokes or blazes from the dripping fat withdraw the gridiron for a moment. It should cook in fifteen minutes.

After it is dished, season with pepper and salt. If gravy is desired prepare it as directed in recipe for Broiled Beefsteak in a Frying Pan.

Prepare and broil mutton chops, venison, and pork steaks as above.

### BEEFSTEAK SMOTHERED IN ONIONS.

Cut one dozen onions into slices, fry a quarter pound salt pork or bacon until all the fat is tried out, then take out the crackling; into this hot fat put the onions, fry and *stir* for twenty minutes over a good fire; add a teaspoonful of salt, a dash of black pepper, and one cup of boiling water; place over a moderate fire to simmer for half an hour; by this time the water should have entirely evaporated and the onions should be a nice brown. Have ready a broiled steak, place it in the pan with the onions, cover it over the top with some of them, and stand in the oven for five minutes. Then place the steak on a hot dish, heap the onions over and around, and serve.

The Welsh method is as follows: Broil the steak over a quick fire and butter it well. Then slice onions over it; after which chop them up fine on the meat. The onions impart their flavor to the beef, but are not eaten with it. It is important to chop them *on the steak*, otherwise the flavor is lost.

### BOILED FRESH BEEF.

Time, fifteen minutes to the pound, or longer, depending upon the shape and quality of the piece.

Cleanse the meat. Put it into a pot of boiling water, rather more than enough to cover it. Cover, bring the pot to a boil quickly, and let it boil for ten or fifteen minutes; then set it back on the stove to simmer until the meat is cooked. Remove the scum as it rises. The scum commences to rise just before boiling, and if it is not carefully taken off it will fall back, adhere to the meat, and injure and disfigure it. While boiling turn the beef several times. If the water needs replenishing use boiling water. A short time before the meat is done put into the pot one teaspoonful of salt for every five pounds of meat; one bay leaf to every pound of meat may be put into the pot of water with the meat. If carrots, turnips, or potatoes are to be cooked with the meat, prepare them as directed under Rules for Cooking Vegetables.

Put carrots and turnips, sliced, in the pot one to one and a half hours, potatoes twenty to thirty minutes, before the meat is cooked. When cooked take up the meat and vegetables, drain, and serve them separately or in the same dish, the vegetables around the meat.

Carrots alone are an excellent accompaniment to boiled beef. The vegetables may be boiled separately from the meat, but will not be as well flavored. The liquor may be served with the meat and vegetables, or used for making stock or soup, or for hashes, stews, gravies, etc., instead of water; if boiled in an iron pot and to be kept for any of the above uses, it must be poured into a tin or earthen vessel and kept in a cool place.

When cold, remove the fat from the top and save it for frying, etc.

### A LA MODE BEEF.

| | |
|---|---|
| 5 pounds round of beef. | 3 or 4 tomatoes. |
| ½ pound fat salt pork or bacon. | 1 carrot. |
| 6 cloves. | 2 onions. |
| 2 bay leaves. | 5 gills vinegar. |
| 2½ tablespoonfuls salt. | Clove of garlic. |
| 1¼ teaspoonfuls pepper. | Sprig of thyme. |
| A little parsley. | |

Time, five or six hours.

Scrape the pork and remove the rind. Cut the pork into strips of a size that can be easily inserted into the larding needle, about half an inch thick and not over four inches long. Insert the needle half its length into the meat, then load it with a strip of pork, pass the needle through, and leave the pork in the meat. Repeat this process until the meat is larded to the extent desired. If the piece of meat is too thick to run the strip of pork through, lard one side first, then the other. Lard the beef with or in the direction of the grain. If a larding needle is not to be had, make incisions in the meat with a narrow-bladed knife and press the strips of pork into the incisions, or thrust a steel through the meat and put the strips of pork into the holes. The pot in which the beef is to be cooked must not be too large or too small, but large enough to hold the meat without bending or folding it. It may be cooked in an earthen vessel.

Cut up the vegetables fine; put into the pot a pint of stock or gravy (stock is preferable); then spread over the bottom of the pot the seasoning, the cut-up vegetables, the rind, and any strips of the pork left from larding. Place on top of all the larded beef, pour over the beef the vinegar, then enough cold water to just cover the meat. Cover, simmer slowly for five or six hours, and turn the meat occasionally.

If there is any fear of the vegetables scorching, or sticking to the bottom of the pot, stir them gently. Do not allow the pot to stop simmering until the meat is cooked.

If the water gets low replenish carefully with boiling water. When done take up the meat and put it in a hot dish, then take up the vegetables, put them around the meat, strain the gravy, and skim off the fat. Return the gravy to the pot, let it boil up, then pour it over the meat and vegetables, and serve. If the gravy is too thick stir in some boiling water. If too thin, stir in a little blended browned flour, let it boil up once, season with pepper and salt if necessary, pour it over the meat and vegetables, and serve.

Another method may be used. Powder and mix together the seasoning, dip the strips of pork into vinegar and then into the seasoning, then lard the meat. Put any seasoning that is left into the pot. The seasoning may be varied and the larding omitted.

A beefsteak may be cooked as above, omitting the larding and reducing the amount of seasoning. Time, one hour.

### BEEF BOUILLI.

Take a piece of the round weighing four pounds. Tie it into a neat shape with strong muslin, put into a large stewing pan, and cover with boiling water. Stand over a moderate fire, skim carefully, and simmer forty-five minutes to every pound. When meat is half done, add large teaspoonful of salt, and one carrot, one turnip, and one onion sliced. Fifteen minutes before you dish it add two sliced potatoes.

When done dish the meat. Rub together one tablespoonful of suet and three tablespoonfuls of flour, and stir them into the boiling stew. Season to taste and serve in a tureen, reserving enough vegetables to garnish the meat.

### TO STEW FRESH BEEF.

| | |
|---|---|
| 4 pounds fresh beef, free from bone. | ½ pound onions. |
| 1 pound potatoes. | ¼ pound carrots. |
| 1 pound fresh or canned tomatoes. | Pepper and salt. |

Time, three hours.

It is not necessary to use the choice parts of beef for a stew.

Cut the meat into pieces about two inches square. Cut the vegetables into small pieces. Put the meat into a pot with enough cold water to cook it; add a tablespoonful of salt. Cover closely. Put the pot over the fire to simmer; skim carefully. When the stew has simmered for two hours put in the prepared vegetables; season with pepper and salt. Simmer one hour longer, stirring occasionally. When done serve in a hot dish. If it is desired to serve the potatoes whole, put them into the pot twenty or thirty minutes before the stew is cooked. If the water gets too low, replenish carefully with boiling water.

If the liquor of the stew is not sufficiently thick, stir into it two tablespoonfuls of blended browned flour. A bay leaf to every pound of meat may be put into the pot of cold water with the meat.

Stew mutton, lamb, veal, and fresh pork as above. The bones of mutton and veal, if small, need not be removed. Add thin slices of fat pork or bacon to a veal stew.

The onions may be fried brown before they are put into the stew.

Too much water is commonly used in making stews. They should be thick rather than thin.

## TO MAKE A BEEF PIE.

Fresh beef, potatoes, onions, tomatoes, pieces of butter or beef dripping the size of a hazelnut; pepper and salt on every layer.

Cut the meat into two-inch pieces, removing gristle, bone, and any superabundance of fat. Cut the potatoes into slices a quarter of an inch thick, rinse in cold water, and parboil them. Chop the onions fine. Slice the tomatoes. Roll the pieces of butter or dripping in sifted flour. Put the meat and one or two teaspoonfuls of salt into a pot of cold stock or water, just enough to cover the meat. Cover closely; remove the scum as it rises; simmer steadily until half done. Remove it from the fire. Take up the meat and strain the gravy; keep both warm. Line a baking dish or pan with a paste (see Pie Crust), first greasing the sides and bottom.

Put in a layer of the semi-stewed meat, on the meat a layer of chopped onion, on the onion a layer of sliced tomato, on the tomato a half dozen or more pieces of floured butter or dripping, on these a layer of potato, on the potato a layer of meat, and so on in successive layers.

Pour over all the strained gravy. If the floured butter or dripping is not used the gravy must be thickened with blended browned flour. Wet with cold water the upper edge of the lower crust; lay on the top crust; trim the paste around the edge of the dish; pinch the edges of the lower and upper crusts together. Make a slit in the center of the top crust. Put the pie into the oven and bake. Keep a moderate heat. It will bake in from one to one and a half hours. If, after baking some time, there is fear of the crust burning, cover it with a tin pan, removing the cover in time to allow the crust to brown; serve in the dish in which it was baked. A bay leaf for every pound of meat may be added when the meat is put in to stew.

Instead of semi-stewing the meat, it may be browned in a frying pan in hot beef dripping or lard. If, when the dish is full, there is not sufficient gravy, use stock or water. The bottom and side crust may be omitted, or the bottom and sides may be lined with crackers or slices of bread previously dipped in stock gravy or water.

Lamb, veal, pork, venison, or any sort of fresh meat may be made into a pie. Use thin slices of pork, bacon, or ham in veal pie, putting them in next to the veal.

Meat pies may also be made, as above, from any kind of cold cooked meats, using stock or gravy in preference to water.

### BAKED BEEF HEART.

Cut across the base of the heart and remove the valves and all tough fibrous tissue. Prepare a stuffing as follows : Mix thoroughly into some grated bread crumbs one small onion parboiled and minced, a half teaspoonful of sage, pepper and salt, and enough butter, beef dripping, or lard to moisten the mixture. Soak the heart in cold salt water for two hours, then wash it thoroughly in cold water. Put it into a pot of cold water, enough to cover it, add two teaspoon-fuls of salt, cover, and boil for ten minutes. Remove the scum as it rises; take out the heart, pepper and salt the cavities, put in the stuffing, secure it with cross-stitches, put it into a baking pan, spread it over with beef dripping, and sprinkle it with pepper and salt. Pour into the pan about a pint of boil-ing-hot stock, gravy, or beef dripping. Bake in a moderate oven, allowing twenty minutes to the pound. Baste frequently. Be careful that it does not burn. Serve while hot, as it cools rapidly; serve with a gravy from recipe for Gravy for Baked Meats. Veal heart should be thoroughly washed but not soaked nor parboiled. In other respects it is pre-pared and baked as above.

### POTATO PIE.

(Sufficient for 22 men.)

| | |
|---|---|
| 16½ pounds meat. | 1 pound onions. |
| 20 pounds potatoes. | 3 ounces salt. |

¼ ounce pepper.

Cut up and stew the onions with jelly from the meat added; boil or steam the potatoes, and mash them; grease the inside of a baking dish; line the sides with a portion of the mashed potatoes; place the meat and cooked onions in the center; season with pepper and salt; cover over with the remainder of the mashed potatoes, and bake till the potato cover is brown. As the mashed potatoes absorb the moisture of the meat and render it dry, about two pints of gravy prepared from the liquor in which the onions were cooked should be poured into the pie after it is taken out of the oven.

## TURKISH PILLAU.

### (Sufficient for 22 men.)

| | |
|---|---|
| 16½ pounds meat. | ½ ounce cayenne. |
| 4 pounds rice. | 1 bunch sweet herbs. |
| 1 pound onions. | ½ pound flour. |
| 3 ounces salt. | 3 quarts water. |

Cut the meat from the bone and into pieces against the grain, of two ounces each; put some fat into the boiler; mix two ounces of the salt and flour together; rub the pieces of meat with it, the fat being melted; place the pieces of meat in the boiler, and stir them round, so that they get brown; when nearly brown add the onions sliced; let the whole fry for five minutes, then add the water, herbs, and cayenne, and simmer gently for one hour and a half.

The rice in the meantime should have been well washed and soaked, and then put into a boiler with plenty of water, and boiled for twenty minutes or longer; when done, make a border round the dish with the rice, and place the meat and sauce in the middle; place the whole in the oven for a few minutes, and serve.

If two boilers can not be had, take out the meat, and keep it warm whilst the rice is boiling.

The above ingredients are enough for two large round tins.

## CRIMEAN KEBOBS.

### (Sufficient for 22 men.)

| | |
|---|---|
| 16½ pounds meat. | 1 ounce pepper. |
| 1 pound flour. | 2 ounces salt, mint, and parsley. |
| 1 pound bread. | 1½ pints vinegar. |
| 1 pound onions. | 2 quarts water. |

Cut the meat from the bone and into pieces of about half an inch thick and three inches square; beat it well. Boil the onions, strain, and chop them up;

chop up the mint and parsley, and mix the whole with half the pepper and salt. Make a stiff batter of flour and water; make the bread into crumbs, add it to the batter with the remaining pepper and salt. Now rub the mixture of onions, etc., on the pieces of meat, or, if preferred, press the pieces on the mixture so that some adheres, then dip them into the batter, and run them as they are done upon a small spit, or bit of wire, two pieces of lean to one of fat, and place them in a *quick* oven; they will take from twenty to thirty minutes; make a gravy from the bones and cuttings, to which add the vinegar, and also the mixture and batter that may be left. Serve very hot.

### BOMBSHELLS.

(Sufficient for 22 men.)

| | |
|---|---|
| 16½ pounds meat. | 3 ounces salt. |
| 6 pounds flour. | 1 ounce pepper. |
| 1 pound onions. | Sweet herbs. |

Water.

Cut all the meat from the bone and sinews, reserving 1½ pounds of fat for the paste. Chop up the meat like sausage meat with the onions and herbs shred fine; season with one-half the salt and pepper. (In India it is the custom to mix spices, capsicums, fruit, etc., with the meat.) Make the paste as follows: Place on the table the flour, make a hole with the hand in the center, in which place the chopped fat and the remaining salt and pepper, then put some water in the hole; gradually stir the flour into it until it is all moistened and forms a stiff paste; work and roll it well for two minutes; let it remain as a ball for ten minutes, then roll it out to the thickness required. Have some very clean pudding cloths ready; their size must depend on the size of the shell; divide the paste according to the size, for either 12 or 32 pounders; form it into

a ball, and roll it out round; divide the chopped
meat and place it in the paste; add a little water;
gather it round like a dumpling; bring the cloth
around it, and tie it *lightly*, and boil according to
size: a 12-pounder, for one person, one and three-
quarter hours; 32-pounder, for two, two and a half
hours. The bones and cuttings must be made into
a gravy, and served separate. The meat must be
made into balls the size of bullets, and placed in it.

The cloth, before being used, should be dipped
into boiling water, wrung out, and some flour
dusted over the part the pudding will occupy.
This prevents the pudding from sticking to the
cloth. Some salt should be put into the water the
puddings are boiled in. This applies to all boiled
puddings or dumplings made with flour and dripping or suet.

### STEWED BEEF HEART.

| | |
|---|---|
| 1 beef heart. | 1 lb. potatoes, sliced thin. |
| 2 medium-sized onions, sliced thin. | 1 pinch cayenne pepper. |
| 2 bay leaves. | Little chopped parsley. |

1 head celery chopped fine, or 1 level teaspoonful celery seed.
3 tablespoonfuls tomato catsup, or ⅓ lb. fresh or canned tomatoes.
Butter or beef drippings the size of an egg.

Cut the heart into small pieces, and remove all
tough, fibrous tissue. Wash thoroughly in cold,
salt water. Put the pieces into a pot of cold water
enough to cover them; add two teaspoonfuls of salt;
cover closely; stew gently for ten minutes; remove
the scum as it rises. Take out the meat with a
skimmer, pour off and strain the liquor, wash out
the pot, return the strained liquor, together with the
heart, the potatoes, onions, tomato catsup, celery,
cayenne pepper, butter, and bay leaves; stir them
well together; cover; stew gently until quite tender, stirring occasionally. When cooked season
with pepper and salt, and serve. If necessary to

replenish the water add boiling water. If necessary to thicken the liquor proceed as directed in to Stew Fresh Beef. Veal heart is prepared and stewed in the same way.

## BOILED FRESH BEEF TONGUE.

Soak the tongue one hour in cold water; rinse in fresh cold water; put it into a pot of cold water enough to cover it; add two tablespoonfuls of salt and two bay leaves; cover; boil slowly; turn the tongue once or twice; remove the scum as it rises; boil until so tender that a broom straw will easily penetrate it. If necessary to replenish, use boiling water. When cold enough to handle peel off the thick skin carefully; serve hot or cold. If to be eaten cold, let the tongue remain in the liquor until cold. A boiled tongue, after it is peeled, may be prepared according to the following directions: Put a piece of butter or beef dripping the size of an egg into a pot and brown it slightly; move it about quickly so as to melt it as fast as possible and prevent it blackening; put the tongue into the browned butter or dripping; turn it over quickly until both sides are slightly browned; add about a pint of stock or gravy, two or three whole cloves, two medium-sized onions parboiled and sliced, and a seasoning of pepper and salt; cover; simmer from a half to three-quarters of an hour; take up the tongue, put it in a dish, and set it aside to keep warm; thicken the gravy with blended browned flour, let it boil up once, pour it over the tongue, and serve.

## FRIED LIVER.

Liver to be good should be fresh, uniform in appearance on the surface—that is, not streaked or spotted; firm; of a bright-red color when cut, and free from nodules. It must be thoroughly done to be palatable.

Cut the liver into slices a quarter of an inch thick, and soak it one hour in cold, salt water; rinse well with warm water, wipe it dry, and dip each slice into flour seasoned with pepper and salt; put into a frying pan enough lard, beef dripping, or bacon fat so that when melted it will just cover the bottom of the pan; when this is hot put in the liver and fry both sides a deep brown; then dish; pour the grease remaining in the pan over the liver, and serve; or make a gravy as follows: Put into the pan a lump of butter or beef dripping, the size to be determined by the quantity of gravy wanted, with a half pint or more of boiling water and pepper and salt to suit taste; mix them well; stir in gradually two or more tablespoonfuls of blended browned flour; let it boil up once; pour it over the liver, and serve.

If the fat remaining from the frying is burnt, throw it away and wash out the frying pan before proceeding to make the gravy. Fried bacon may be served with the liver, frying the bacon first, using the fat for frying the liver. Fried onions may be served with liver.

### MARROW BONES.

Have the bones neatly sawed into convenient sizes and cover the ends with a small piece of common crust made with flour and water, over this tie a floured cloth, and place them upright in a saucepan of boiling water, taking care there is sufficient to cover the bones. Boil two hours, remove the cloth and paste, and serve with dry toast.

### COOKED SALT BEEF.

Salt beef before being cooked should be well washed, and then, when practicable, soaked in cold water for twenty-four hours, changing the water three times.

## BOILED SALT BEEF.

The meat should be placed in a pot of cold water and made to boil quickly. As soon as the water boils the meat must be taken out and the water replaced with fresh cold water; boil it according to quality and size of pieces until thoroughly cooked.

## BAKED SALT BEEF.

Prepare the meat as above, make a paste of flour and water, cover the meat with it, and bake in a slow oven twenty minutes for every pound of meat.

## STEWED SALT BEEF.

Prepare the meat as above, and cut into slices; have some chopped greens or soaked desiccated mixed vegetables, and put them with the meat and a little water in a stew pan; season, and stew gently for two hours.

## BOILED CORNED BEEF.

The time required for cooking corned beef depends upon the quality of the meat and the size of the piece. It is done when the bones become loose in the meat.

Wash the meat thoroughly in cold water, changing the water two or three times. Put it into a pot of cold water, enough to cover it. Cover; boil steadily and gently until tender; remove the scum as it rises. While boiling turn the beef several times. If the meat is to be served hot drain it, but if it is to be served cold, let it cool in the liquor in which it was boiled; keep the pot covered. When cold take the meat out and place it between two dishes, with a heavy weight on the upper dish; leave it for one hour or until the liquor is pressed out of the meat. Empty the liquor as it escapes.

Many vegetables, such as cabbage, carrots, turnips, and potatoes are improved in flavor if boiled with corned beef. The liquor may in cold weather be kept a day and used to boil vegetables. If it has been boiled in an iron pot it should be poured off into a tin or earthen vessel and kept in a cool place.

## CORNED BEEF AND CABBAGE.

Wash meat in cold water. Put it in a large kettle and cover with cold water. Simmer gently for two hours. In meantime, remove the outside leaves from a hard white head of cabbage, cut it into quarters, and soak in cold water for one hour. After the meat has been simmering two hours, add cabbage and simmer one and one-half hours longer. When done put the meat in the center of a large dish with the cabbage around it. May be served with tomato or horse-radish.

## NEW ENGLAND BOILED DINNER.

Remove bone from eight pounds of corned beef (cut from round), tie meat closely, put in deep pot, cover with water, add one teaspoonful salt, one-half salt spoonful pepper, and boil quickly, removing all scum. When no more scum rises, put in following vegetables, peeled and cut in slices two inches thick:

| | |
|---|---|
| 2 carrots, 4 beets. | 1 yellow turnip. |
| 4 white turnips. | 1 large head celery, cut |
| 6 small onions. | in 2-inch lengths. |

Simmer slowly two hours. Place meat, when done, in center of platter, arrange vegetables around, and pour a little of the gravy over all. More gravy may be served in boat, with a dish of boiled potatoes.

## BRINE TO CORN MEATS.

| | |
|---|---|
| 16 gallons water. | 16 quarts salt. |
| 1 pound saltpeter. | 3 pounds best brown sugar. |

Boil the whole together for ten or fifteen minutes, stirring it well. Remove the scum as it rises. When

cold it is ready for use. Cleanse the meat, put it
into the brine, place a weight on it to keep the meat
submerged. The weight must be of such a kind
that the salt will not act on it.

The meat will be cured in eight days. When the
brine has been used for four picklings, boil and skim
it again. When cold it is fit for use. This may be
repeated three times before fresh brine is needed.
Brine is fit for use so long as it will bear up an egg
or a potato.

### BROWNED FLOUR.

Useful to thicken gravy and darken it. Set flour in
a hot oven or over a moderate fire, and stir continually
until it is parched brown. Do not scorch it. Keep
in a closely corked bottle or jar for future use.
When to be used it should first be blended with a
little stock, beef dripping, or water.

### GRAVY FOR BAKED MEATS.

Having removed the joint, put the pan on the fire,
remove the floating grease and save it as dripping;
pour into the pan from a half pint to a pint or more
of boiling water. Mix well; then stir into the mixture quickly two or more tablespoonfuls of blended
browned flour; boil up once; season with pepper and
salt, and serve. If the gravy is preferred with the
grease in it omit the skimming.

### GRAVY.

Place the required quantity of stock in a stew pan,
bring the contents to a boil, make the thickening
by mixing four ounces of flour for each gallon of
gravy required with cold water, or stock, into a
smooth batter, add the thickening, keeping it well
stirred to prevent it burning; allow it to simmer
gently for thirty minutes, add the bay leaves or
mixed herbs and seasoning according to taste, and
allow the leaves to remain for a few minutes, remove

them, and color the gravy by adding a small quantity of caramel made as follows:

Place four ounces of sugar in a small stew pan, place it on the fire, and allow it to remain until the sugar is of a very dark color, when it will be seen to boil or bubble; add about one and one-half pints of water and simmer for a few minutes, allow it to partly cool, and place in a bottle ready for use.

### ONION JUICE FOR MEAT DISHES.

Take outside skin from a large onion and then trim off the bottom. Press the onion firmly against a large grater and quickly draw it up and down, allowing the juice to drop from one corner of the grater.

### TO THICKEN GRAVIES.

To one-half quart of flour add one quart cold water, a little salt and pepper, and stir to a batter. Remove the meat and vegetables (to keep hot) and put the pan on the fire. Stir into your gravy the batter, boil ten minutes, and serve.

### TO COLOR SOUPS, GRAVIES, STEWS, ETC., TO A RICH BROWN.

Take a few handfuls of sugar, or flour, and put into a pan or ladle, lay close to the fire and stir until it browns or darkens to a rich brown, dark, but do not burn black. Into this stir some hot gravy until dissolved, then to your gravy, soup, or stew add this liquid until the color suits you.

Time for making this, about ten minutes.

### CREOLE SAUCE.

| | |
|---|---|
| Juice of 1 lemon. | 3 tablespoonfuls powdered sugar. |
| 1 teaspoonful mustard. | 3 tablespoonfuls tomato catsup. |

Heat all to near the boiling point and use hot with meats.

## SAUCE FOR BOILED MUTTON.

Rub togetl.  er in a pan two tablespoonfuls of flour and butter or beef dripping twice the size of an egg; season with pepper and salt to suit taste.  Put the pan over the fire; stir gradually into the pan one pint of boiling water or liquor in which the mutton was boiled; mix in a half cupful of chopped, pickled cucumbers or green nasturtium seed and three tablespoonfuls of vinegar.  Stir well, let it boil one minute, and serve in a separate dish.

## BROWN SAUCE.

Slice one-fourth pound bacon, put it into a frying pan, and try out all the fat.  Take bacon out, add one tablespoonful flour, and stir until smooth; add one-half pint stock; stir constantly until it boils; add tablespoonful Worcestershire sauce; salt and pepper to taste; serve.

## CURRANT-JELLY SAUCE.

Make brown sauce and add to it four tablespoonfuls of currant jelly.  Let it boil up once and it is ready for use.  May be served best with game.

## BAKED HASH.

From cold cooked fresh beef, veal, or mutton. These meats may be used singly or together.

Four pounds of meat free from bone; two onions; two cupfuls of bread crumbs; butter, beef dripping, or lard twice the size of an egg (melted); eggs in the following proportions: two for two pounds of meat, three for four pounds, four for six pounds, and so on; enough milk, stock, or water to make the mixture moist; pepper and salt.

To highly season the hash add thyme, sweet marjoram, summer savory, or *chile colorado*.  If an acid taste is desired, mix in three or more tablespoonfuls of lemon juice or vinegar. Parboil the onions, mince them and the meat together, beat the eggs, put the minced meat and onions into a vessel; mix well with them the bread crumbs, the melted butter or dripping, the beaten eggs, the milk, and lastly, the seasoning. Put the mixture into a greased baking pan, smooth off the top, and bake it for fifteen or twenty minutes or to a light brown; serve in the baking pan. The eggs may be omitted. The onions may be minced and fried a light brown instead of being parboiled.

## WET HASH.

From cold cooked fresh beef, veal, or mutton. These meats may be used singly or together.

Four pounds of meat, free from bone; one large onion; two pounds of boiled potato; the meat cut into half-inch pieces; the onion parboiled and minced; the potato chopped into very small pieces; mix all together; season with pepper and salt. Put the mixture into a pot; stir into it about a quart of hot stock, gravy, beef dripping, or water; stock is preferable. Stir well together; cover; simmer for thirty minutes, or until the meat is quite tender, frequently stirring it. When the hash is done, pour it into a dish containing toasted or fried bread, and serve. If there is no stock, gravy, or beef dripping on hand, in preference to water take the bones of the cooked meats, crack them open, put them into a pot with enough cold water to cover them; put in a little salt; cover; boil steadily for half an hour; remove the scum as it rises; take up the bones and strain the gravy remaining and put it into the hash. If potatoes are not used in the hash, stir into it three or four tablespoonfuls of blended browned flour, let it boil up once, and serve. Instead of parboiling the onion, it may be minced and browned in the pot before putting in the other ingredients.

## DRY HASH.

From cold cooked fresh or corned beef, veal, or mutton. These meats may be used singly or together. Four pounds of meat, free from bone and gristle; one large onion, parboiled; two pounds of cooked potato; the meat, potato, and onion minced. Mix all together; season with pepper and salt. Stir into the mixture about a pint or enough hot stock, gravy, beef dripping, or water to well moisten it; stock is preferable. Mix well; put into a frying pan enough lard or beef dripping so that when melted it will cover the bottom of the pan; when this is hot put in the hash; stir it for a few minutes, then let it fry until it becomes brown on the lower side; turn it out, without breaking, into a hot dish, and serve; or, after the hash has been stirred in the pan, empty it into a greased baking pan, smooth the top of the hash, and bake until it is browned on top; serve in the baking pan. If the hash is to be made of corned beef alone, very little, if any, salt for seasoning will be needed. Instead of parboiling the onion, it may be minced and fried to a light brown.

### PEMMICAN.

Meat, without fat, cut in thin slices, dried in the sun, pounded, then mixed with melted fat, and sometimes dried fruit, and compressed into cakes, or in bags. It contains much nutriment in small compass, and is of great use in long voyages.

Pemmican may be made of the lean portions of venison, buffalo, beef, etc., and may be cooked the same as sausage, or eaten simply as dried beef. A little salt added would make it more palatable to the civilized taste.

### REMARKS ON PORK.

Young pork has a thin skin, easily indented, and the lean will break by pinching. If fresh, the meat is smooth and dry, but if damp and clammy it is not good. If the fat contains small kernels, the meat is diseased and should not be eaten.

Pigs fed entirely on slop make bad pork; they should be kept up for at least two months before they are killed, and fed principally with grain. Fish should not be fed to them while fattening, as it gives a bad odor and flavor to the meat.

### BAKED FRESH PORK.

See recipe for Baked Beef.

### ENGLISH PORK PIE.

Make pie crust (not too rich) and put around sides of a deep pie dish. In bottom and above place layers of thin sliced bacon, sliced potatoes, onions, sliced or chopped and lean fresh pork cut in small pieces. Season with salt, pepper, and sage. Fill dish with any good gravy left from roasts and water thickened for occasion. Cover with crust and bake one and one-half hours. Cover pie with thick brown paper if it gets too brown.

### FRIED SALT PORK.

Cut the pork into thin slices; soak it in cold water one hour or longer; drain and wipe it dry. Have the frying pan very hot and dry; put the sliced pork into the pan and fry brown on both sides. Season with pepper, and serve. Previous to frying, the pork may be dipped into grated bread crumbs or rolled cracker; in this case the pan should be greased.

### BOILED SALT PORK.

Soak the pork over night in cold water; rinse and put it into a pot with enough cold water to cover it. Cover; boil steadily until cooked, the time depending upon the quality of the pork, and whether it is thick or thin. Remove the scum as it rises. While boiling turn the pork several times. As the water evaporates, replenish with boiling water. While cooking, the pork must be kept covered with water; when cooked drain and serve.

Many vegetables, such as turnips, cabbages, potatoes, and greens, may be boiled with pork.

A cake of fat will form on the surface of the water in which the pork has been cooked, when it becomes cold. This should be saved for cooking purposes.

### BAKED PORK AND BEANS.

| | |
|---|---|
| 2 quarts beans. | 3 pounds salt pork. |
| 1 teaspoonful bicarbonate of soda. | |

Time to bake, six to eight hours.

Pick over the beans, wash, and soak them over night in cold water; soft water is preferable. Parboil the pork and cut it into thin slices. Drain the soaked beans; put them into a pot with enough fresh cold water to cover them plentifully; put in the soda. Cover; boil for fifteen or twenty minutes; remove the scum as it rises; pour off the water; replace with boiling water; cover; boil steadily until tender; drain and season with pepper. If the pork is freshly cured, add salt. Put one-half of the beans in a deep baking pan; lay over them the sliced pork, then cover the pork with the other half of the beans. Pour over from a half pint to a pint of boiling water, and bake with a uniform heat. Every hour add from a half to a cupful of boiling water. If the beans show signs of burning, cover them with a tin pan and remove it in time to allow the top to brown. Serve hot or cold. Cold beans may be made into a salad. If preferred, the beans and pork may be put into the dish in layers, finishing with a layer of pork.

A tablespoonful of molasses, or an equivalent of sugar, to the quart of beans may be added when the beans are put into the baking pan.

When cooked the beans should be comparatively dry.

## TO MAKE SAUSAGE MEAT.

| | |
|---|---|
| 14 pounds lean fresh pork. | 6 pounds fresh pork fat. |
| 4 ounces powdered sage. | 2 ounces fine salt. |
| 2 ounces sugar. | ¼ ounce cayenne pepper. |
| 1 ounce powdered black pepper. | |

Remove the skin, sinews, and gristle from the fat; chop the lean and fat as fine as possible. Mix them well together. Mix the seasoning together, and then into the meat. Pack it firm in stone jars. Pour melted lard over the meat and cover the vessel. Or pack it into stout muslin bags, dip them into melted lard, and hang them up. Sausage meat should be kept in a cool, dry place. It is better fresh made; if it is to be kept a length of time, the sage should not be put in until it is to be cooked. The proportion of fat and lean may be varied.

## FRIED SAUSAGE MEAT.

Make it into cakes about three inches in diameter and about three-quarters of an inch thick. Have the frying pan hot and dry; put in the cakes and fry until brown on both sides.

Sausage meat in skins may be boiled.

## BREAKFAST SAUSAGE.

| | |
|---|---|
| 2 pounds lean pork. | 1 teaspoonful salt. |
| 1 teaspoonful powdered sage leaves. | 1 salt spoonful black pepper. |

Chop meat very fine, add to it the salt, pepper, and sage, mix all thoroughly and form into small cakes. Put an even tablespoonful of dripping into a frying pan, and when hot cover the bottom of the pan with sausage cakes. Fry until nicely browned on one side, then turn and brown the other. Serve plain.

## FRIED BACON.

Prepare and cook as directed in Fried Salt Pork.

## BOILED BACON.

If the fat of bacon is yellow, the meat is rusty or tainted. If the lean has brownish or blackish spots, it is not good.

Scrape and trim the bacon, wash well, and soak it in plenty of cold water for two or more hours, changing the water once or twice. If the bacon is very salty and hard, soak it all night, changing the water late in the evening and again early in the morning. Wash the bacon in fresh cold water; put it into a pot with enough cold water to cover it well; cover; let it come to a boil slowly, and thereafter boil steadily until tender; remove the scum as it rises; skim off the fat and save it for cooking purposes. While boiling, turn the bacon several times. As the water evaporates, replenish with boiling water. When the bacon can be easily pierced with a fork in the thickest part it is done. Take it up, drain, remove the skin, and serve. If greens are to be cooked with bacon, do not skim off all of the fat; leave enough to season the greens.

## BOILED HAM.

Time, twenty to thirty minutes to the pound.

From one to three pints of vinegar, depending on the weight of the ham. Soak an old ham over night in cold water; if very hard, twenty-four hours; freshly cured, for ten or fifteen minutes; then scrape, trim, and wash it in cold water. Put it into a pot with enough cold water to cover it; cover; boil gently for thirty minutes; remove the scum as it rises; pour off the water; refill with enough boiling water to cover the ham; add the vinegar; cover; boil gently until done, turning the ham several times. When cooked take it up; when cool enough to handle,

peel off the skin.  Be careful not to tear off the fat.
Rub into the fat some brown sugar; then stick
whole cloves, about two inches apart, into the
sugared fat; put the ham into a dry baking pan;
put it into the oven, and bake it in a moderate heat
from half an hour to one hour, or until it becomes
a light brown.*

Eat it hot or cold.  If to be eaten cold set it aside
and do not cut it until it is thoroughly cold.  It
will add to the appearance of the ham to sprinkle
over it some grated bread crumbs or rolled cracker
before sticking it with cloves.  Ham for boiling
should be from six months to two years old.  If
newer it should be broiled, fried, baked, or may be
boiled.

### BROILED HAM.

Old hams, if soaked over night and then boiled
for a short time (sufficient only to soften them) are
better for broiling or frying than the dry ham without previous preparation.

Prepare the ham as directed for Frying.  Wipe
the gridiron clean and heat it.  Put on the sliced
ham and broil both sides brown.  Put it into a hot
dish containing a little melted butter seasoned with
pepper; turn the ham over once to butter both sides.

### FRIED HAM AND EGGS.

Cut the ham into slices about a fourth of an inch
thick, trim off the rind, put the sliced ham into a
pan.  Cover with boiling water and soak for a half
hour.  If the ham is old and very salty soak it
several hours in cold water before using the boiling
water.  Wipe it dry.  Have the frying pan hot and
dry.  Cover the bottom of the pan with ham and
fry brown on both sides.  When cooked take it up
and set it aside in a hot dish to keep warm.

* The above is practically the recipe known as the "General Scott."

## PLAIN BACON (NEW ORLEANS STYLE).

Fry bacon crisp in hot dripping in the same manner as doughnuts.

## FANCY BACON (NEW ORLEANS STYLE).

Roll very thin slices of breakfast bacon in fritter batter or bread crumbed with egg, fry in boiling dripping or lard, and serve on toast or fried mush.

## BROILED BACON (NEW ORLEANS STYLE).

Broil and put in hot oven; serve immediately.

## FRIED LIVER (BEGUÉ STYLE).

Cut liver half an inch thick, put in platter, sprinkle with sufficient salt, pepper, and a little flour, fry in hot dripping or lard, the same as doughnuts, turning pieces over two or three times, and serve hot.

## BOILED MUTTON.

Time, fifteen minutes to the pound, or longer, depending on the quality and shape of the piece.

Cleanse the mutton. Put it into a pot of boiling water rather more than enough to cover it. Cover; boil gently until cooked. Remove the scum as it rises. While boiling turn the mutton several times. If the water needs replenishing, use boiling water, and add it carefully. When cooked serve with sauce for boiled mutton. One bay leaf for every two pounds of mutton may be put into the pot with the mutton. The liquor may be served with the mutton or made into stock or soup, or it can be saved for hashes, stews, gravies, etc., instead of water. If boiled in an iron pot, and to be kept for any of the above uses, pour it into a tin or earthen vessel and keep it in a cool place. If, when cold, there is a layer of fat on top remove it, *but do not use it for cooking.*

Many vegetables, such as carrots, turnips, and potatoes, are improved in flavor when boiled with mutton.

## MUTTON POT PIE.

Take piece of mutton from the neck, cut into small pieces, stew slowly for two or three hours, and season with pepper and salt. Half an hour before serving drop dumplings into the water, made by adding two teaspoonfuls of baking powder to a pint of flour and stirring in water until as stiff as biscuit dough. Do not uncover the pot when boiling.

## IRISH STEW.

(Sufficient for 22 men.)

| | |
|---|---|
| 16½ pounds meat. | 6 ounces salt. |
| 16 pounds potatoes. | 1 ounce pepper. |
| 4 pounds onions. | ½ pound flour. |

Cut the meat away from the bone, and then into pieces of one-quarter pound each; if a loin or neck of mutton, cut it into chops; if a shoulder disjoint it, and cut the blade bone into four pieces; if a leg, cut the meat into slices ¾ inch thick; rub the meat with the salt, pepper, and flour, and place it in the boiler with some fat, brown it on both sides, then add the onions whole, and then the potatoes, and enough water to cover the potatoes; stew gently for two hours; keep the fire down during the cooking and the boiler well covered.

## HOT POT.

| | |
|---|---|
| 2 lbs. cold cooked mutton. | 2 large onions. |
| 6 medium-sized potatoes. | 1 quart water or stock. |
| 1 tablespoonful chopped parsley. | |

Cut the mutton into pieces one inch square. Pare and cut four potatoes into dice, also onions. Put a layer of the mutton in the bottom of a baking dish, then a layer of potatoes, sprinkling of

onion, parsley, salt, and pepper. Continue these
alternations until all is used. Cut the remaining
two potatoes into three slices each; cover these over
the top, add the water or stock, and bake in a
moderate oven two hours; serve.

## LAMB.

Lamb, like mutton, should be of a bright red
color with white fat. It is in season from April to
September, but is best when two months old. It
will not keep like mutton and should be used at
least within three days after killing. Like veal it
is unwholesome if not cooked thoroughly. The
better way of cooking is to roast or bake it. The
loin may be cut into chops and cooked the same as
mutton chops.

## MINT SAUCE.

Chop one bunch mint (ten stalks) very fine. Mix
it with one large teaspoonful sugar. Add one-half
teaspoonful salt and two dashes black pepper. Rub
well, adding four tablespoonfuls vinegar, gradually,
and serve with roast lamb.

## TO BAKE OR ROAST A QUARTER OF LAMB.

Wipe the meat with a damp towel, place it in a
baking pan, and dredge it with pepper. Put one
teaspoonful of salt in bottom of the pan, add one
cup of water to baste with at first. When that
evaporates use its own drippings. Lamb must be
basted every ten minutes, and baked fifteen minutes
to the pound in a very hot oven. Mint sauce, green
peas, and asparagus tips should be served with
spring lamb.

## VEAL.

Veal is divided, the same as mutton, into fore
and hind quarters: the fore quarter is divided into
loin, breast, shoulder, and neck. The hind into leg

and loin.   Chops are cut from the loin, and the leg
is used for cutlets and fillets.   The fillet is a solid
piece cut from the leg, also called a cushion, and
does not correspond with the fillet of beef.   Do
not buy veal that is too young, as it is not only
unwholesome but dangerous.   It may be known by
the small and tender bones; the flesh has a bluish
tinge and a soft, flabby appearance.   A calf should
not be killed until it is two months old; then the
flesh is firm, with a pinkish tinge, and the bones are
hard.   The loin, shoulder, fillet, and breast are
used for roasting.   The knuckle, which is the lower
part of the leg after the cutlets are taken off, and
the neck are used for soups, stews, and pies.

### ROAST LOIN OF VEAL.

Wipe the loin, place in a baking pan, dredge it
with pepper, add a teaspoonful of salt and a cup of
water to the pan, and place in a very quick oven for
fifteen minutes.   Then cool the oven somewhat by
closing the drafts, and roast slowly fifteen minutes
for every pound of veal, basting frequently, at first
with the water in the pan and afterwards with its
own gravy.

Veal must be well done to be eatable.   When
done make a gravy the same as roast beef.

### VEAL POT-PIE.

Take two pounds veal (rib piece is good), cut in
small pieces, and place in pot (having placed small
plate in bottom to prevent meat from burning).
Put in two quarts water, hot or cold.   Boil one and
one-half hours.   Make one quart flour into biscuit
dough and one-half hour before serving drop in
small lumps of the dough.   Be sure there is water
enough to cover meat entirely when dumplings are
put in and cover closely for twenty minutes.   Potatoes may be cooked with it if desired.

Twelve or fourteen hours should elapse between the time of killing and cooking poultry; but it must be picked and drawn as soon as possible.

## TO SELECT POULTRY.

Turkey cannot be too fat; the broader the breast and the shorter the neck the better. The skin must be uniform in appearance and white. A young turkey has a smooth leg and a short spur, eyes bright and full, and, if fresh, the feet are flexible. The absence of these signs denotes age or staleness.

**Chickens.**—The skin of a chicken should be a clear white and easily torn, the fat pale yellow, and the flesh white. If the rump is hard and stiff it is fresh, if soft it may be tainted.

**Ducks.**—If the duck is young the lower part of its legs is soft, the web is also soft, and the lower mandible will not sustain the weight of the bird. This rule applies to all birds. If the breast of the duck is hard it is fresh enough.

**Geese.**—A young goose has much down, the bill yellow, and the legs soft and of a yellow color. An old goose has little down, the skin is thick and tough, and the legs are reddish and rough. When fresh the legs are soft and the feet pliable.

## TO PREPARE POULTRY.

Cut off the neck within an inch or two of the body, and the legs at the first joint. Make a lengthwise incision under the rump large enough to easily draw the bird, which must be done carefully, exercising particular care not to rupture the gall bladder; carefully pick the bird and singe with a piece of lighted paper, or, better, over an alcohol flame.

9281——8

## BAKED TURKEY.

Tame and wild turkeys are prepared and cooked alike. The time for cooking is from fifteen to twenty minutes to the pound, but this depends much upon the age of the bird; it must be well done to be palatable. Success lies in cooking it long enough, and frequent basting

Put the turkey into a pan of cold water; rinse it inside and out in three or four waters; in the last water but one dissolve a teaspoonful of bicarbonate of soda. Fill the body with this water; shake it well; pour it off and rinse with fresh water; wipe it dry inside and out; rub the inside with pepper and salt. Prepare a *dressing* as follows: Mix into enough grated bread crumbs to fill the craw and body of the turkey, a half teaspoonful of pepper, one teaspoonful of salt, one teaspoonful of summer savory, thyme, or sage with sufficient butter, beef drippings, stock, or lard to make the mixture slightly moist.

Mix all thoroughly and stuff the craw and body with it; tie a string tightly about the neck; sew up the incision; tie down the wings and legs, then lay it on its back in the baking pan; wet the skin, season it with pepper and salt, and dredge it with flour. Distribute on the upper side small pieces of butter; put into the pan about a pint of boiling stock or a quarter of a pound of butter; bake with a brisk fire, to a rich brown. Baste frequently, at least every ten minutes. If it browns too rapidly lay a sheet of white paper over it until the lower part is done. When the turkey is browned on the breast turn it over in the pan while in the oven.

Pepper, salt, and dredge the back with flour, and bake until browned, basting as above. When baked remove the strings from the neck and body; put it into a hot dish and serve with a *gravy* prepared as follows: Cleanse the gizzard, liver, and heart of the turkey thoroughly in cold water; mince them: put them into a pot with enough cold water to cover them. Stew gently until tender, and keep warm. When the turkey is removed from the pan, add the giblets with the water in which they were stewed to the dripping remaining in the pan; put the pan on the fire; thicken with one or two tablespoonfuls of blended browned flour, stirring it in gradually; let it boil up once, season with pepper and salt, pour it into a separate dish, and serve.

Prepare and bake duck, goose, pigeon, grouse, partridge, chicken, etc., tame or wild, as above, except that the stuffing for ducks and geese must be made of mashed potato, instead of bread crumbs, with one or more parboiled onions finely chopped and mixed into the potato.

Some prefer to omit the dressing from the body in order that the bird may be more thoroughly cooked. The stuffing omitted from the body may be made into cakes and fried. Turkey may be stuffed with sausage meat, fresh oysters, or roasted chestnuts.

## REMARKS ON GAME.

The entrails should be taken out as soon as the game is killed. If the meat is not to be cooked at once hang it up in a cool dry place. Birds should be kept in their feathers and animals in their skins.

Bear and buffalo meats are better cooked by baking than in any other way. Prepare, cook, and serve bear and buffalo meat like fresh pork or fresh beef.

Clean, prepare, and cook birds as directed for poultry.

## BAKED VENISON.

Time, fifteen to twenty minutes to the pound.

Trim the meat, wash it in tepid water, and wipe it dry. Rub it over with fresh butter, beef dripping, or lard; then cover it over with a thick paste of flour and water about a half inch thick, closely molded to the meat with the hand.

Put it into a baking pan with about a pint of boiling stock, gravy, or beef dripping, and bake. Baste it frequently, at least every ten minutes. Thirty minutes before the meat is cooked remove the paste cover. When cooked serve it in a hot dish with a *gravy* made as follows: About two hours before the meat is baked put into a pot of cold water sufficient to cover them the scraps trimmed from the meat or one or two pounds of raw venison cut into pieces; season with cayenne pepper, salt, cloves, and nutmeg. Cover and let it simmer; remove the scum as it rises. When it has simmered to about one-half the quantity of water used take it from the fire and strain the gravy. After the meat is removed pour the gravy into the baking pan, and stir into it one or two tablespoonfuls of blended browned flour; let it boil up once, and serve in a separate dish. Instead of covering the venison with a paste there may be laid over it thin slices of fat salt pork or bacon. In this case cook the same as fresh beef and serve with a gravy made as directed in recipe for Gravy for Baked Meats.

### BAKED RABBIT.

The cleft in the lip of a young and fresh rabbit is narrow, the ears so tender they can be easily torn; claws smooth and sharp. Old rabbits are the reverse of this.

Remove the head; skin and draw the rabbit; soak it in cold salt water for one hour and longer if necessary, changing the water; wash in fresh cold water; wipe it dry. Stuff it with a dressing made of bread crumbs, the heart and liver (previously parboiled in a small amount of water), fat salt pork, a small onion minced and mixed together, seasoned with pepper, salt, and mace, and slightly moistened with the water

in which the heart and liver were parboiled; sew up
the opening closely; lay it in a baking pan, back
uppermost; rub it over with butter or beef dripping,
dredge it with flour, then lay on thin slices of fat
pork. Pour into the pan a pint or more of boiling
stock or beef dripping, and bake with a moderate
heat. Baste every few minutes. When it is browned
turn it over in the pan, baste it, dredge with flour,
and continue baking until browned. It should bake
in one hour. Serve in a hot dish with a gravy prepared as directed in recipe for Gravy for Baked
Meats.

### STEWED RABBIT.

| 1 rabbit. | 1 small onion. |
| ½ pound fat pork. | Mace, nutmeg, pepper, and salt. |

Prepare and clean the rabbit as directed for baking,
cut it into pieces, and wash it again in cold water;
mince the onions; cleanse the pork and cut it into
small pieces. Put the rabbit into a pot with a little
over a pint of cold water, together with the onion,
pork, and seasoning; cover; simmer until tender,
stirring it occasionally. When cooked take it up
and set it aside to keep warm. Leave the gravy
in the pot and add to it a cup of boiling milk or
water. Stir in gradually one well-beaten egg; then
one or two tablespoonfuls of blended flour. Boil
one minute, pour it over the rabbit, and serve.

It may be served by pouring it into a dish containing toasted or fried bread.

### FRIED RABBIT.

Unless the rabbit is tender it is not suitable for
frying.

Prepare and clean the rabbit as directed for baking. Cut it into pieces and wash it and dip each
piece into beaten egg and then into rolled cracker.
Put into a frying pan enough lard or beef dripping so

that when melted it will cover the bottom of the pan about a quarter of an inch deep. Put in the rabbit, season with pepper and salt, and fry brown on both sides. When cooked dish the rabbit, set it aside to keep warm, and make a *gravy* as follows: Put into the pan a small parboiled onion, minced, and one cup of boiling water. Stir in gradually one or two tablespoonfuls of blended browned flour. Stir well and let it boil one minute. Season with pepper, salt, mace, and nutmeg. Pour it over the rabbit, and serve.

## VEGETABLES.

Peas and beans are the most nutritious of all vegetables and contain as much carbon as wheat and almost double the amount of nitrogen (muscle-forming food).

Cabbage leaves are rich in gluten and therefore nutritious. The mushroom also is said to contain fifty-six per cent of gluten, and dried cauliflower more than either.

Spinach has a direct effect on the kidneys. The common dandelion, used as greens, is excellent for the same trouble. Asparagus purges the blood. Celery acts admirably upon the nervous system, and is a cure for rheumatism and neuralgia. Tomatoes act upon the liver. Beets and turnips are excellent appetizers. Lettuce and cucumbers are cooling in their effects upon the system. Onions, garlic, leeks, olives, and shallots possess medicinal virtues of a marked character, stimulating the circulatory system, and the consequent increase in the saliva and the gastric juice promotes digestion. Red onions are an excellent diuretic, and the white ones are recommended to be eaten raw as a remedy for insomnia. A soup made from onions is regarded as an excellent restorative in weakness of the digestive organs.

French cooks generally use carbonate of ammonia to preserve color of vegetables. A small quantity (little pinch) is mixed in water in which they are to be boiled. Ammonia evaporates in boiling, leaving no ill effects. It also prevents the odor of boiling cabbage.

A little baking soda softens water and is good for freshening and making tender green vegetables that are a little old, or not quite fresh. Boil fresh, young vegetables in hard water. A little salt will harden water at once.

If onions are peeled under water the eyes will not suffer with tears.

## RULES FOR COOKING VEGETABLES.

Summer vegetables should if possible be cooked on the same day they are gathered. Vegetables must be picked over, all decayed or unripe parts removed, then washed thoroughly in cold water. When they are to be boiled they should be put into enough boiling salt water to cover them and boiled steadily until done.

If the pot should need replenishing, boiling water should always be used. The vessel must be kept covered. Old and strong vegetables should be boiled in two or more waters. They must be thoroughly done, but if boiled too much they become watery. When the vegetables are cooked they should be thoroughly drained and served in hot dishes.

If the water boils a long time before the vegetables are put in, it loses all its gases, and the mineral ingredients are deposited on the bottom and sides of the kettle so that the water is flat and tasteless, and the vegetables will not look green nor have a fine flavor. The following is a time-table for cooking:

## TIME-TABLE FOR COOKING VEGETABLES.

Potatoes, old, boiled _____30 minutes.
Potatoes, new, baked_____45 minutes.
Potatoes, new, boiled _____20 minutes.
Sweet potatoes, boiled_____45 minutes.
Sweet potatoes, baked_____1 hour.
Squash, boiled _____25 minutes.
Squash, baked _____45 minutes.
Shell beans, boiled _____1 hour.
Green peas, boiled _____20 to 40 minutes.
String beans, boiled_____1 to 2 hours.
Green corn _____25 minutes to 1 hour.
Asparagus _____15 to 30 minutes.
Spinach _____1 to 2 hours.
Tomatoes, fresh_____1 hour.
Tomatoes, canned_____30 minutes.
Cabbage _____45 minutes to 2 hours.
Cauliflower _____1 to 2 hours.
Dandelions _____2 to 3 hours.
Beet greens_____1 hour.
Onions _____1 to 2 hours.
Beets _____1 to 5 hours.
Turnips, white_____45 minutes to 1 hour.
Turnips, yellow_____1½ to 2 hours.
Parsnips_____1 to 2 hours.
Carrots _____1 to 2 hours.

Nearly all these vegetables are eaten dressed with salt, pepper, and butter, but sometimes a small piece of lean pork is boiled with them, and seasons them sufficiently.

## REMARKS ON POTATOES.

As a general rule, the smaller the eye the better the potato. When full in the eye they are either of an inferior quality or about to sprout. Rather small and medium-sized potatoes are to be preferred.

Potatoes should be stored in a cool, dry, and dark place. They should be sorted often, the bad ones removed, and the sprouts rubbed off.

Paring potatoes before boiling them is wasteful and should only be resorted to late in the spring, when the potato has commenced to sprout. If pared they should be laid in cold water for a half hour before cooking.

Potatoes should be of a uniform size that they may be cooked in the same time. If they are of unequal size cut the large ones.

The potato being composed largely of starch, cooking breaks the cells and sets the starch free. If the potato is removed from the heat and moisture as soon as this occurs it will be dry and mealy, but if it is allowed to boil or bake even for a few moments the starch will absorb the moisture and the potato will become soggy and have a bad flavor.

## BOILED POTATOES.

Time, twenty to thirty minutes.

Wash the potatoes, and cut out the eyes and any black specks. Nick or cut off a piece of the skin at the pointed or eyed ends. Put them into a pot of boiling salt water, enough to cover them. Cover; simmer steadily until a fork will easily pierce the largest. If cooked too much they become watery.

When cooked drain them thoroughly, and set the pot uncovered near the fire for five minutes to dry the potatoes, shaking them two or three times during this period.

If desired to serve the potatoes mashed, peel and mash them thoroughly, and work in pepper and salt to taste, a tablespoonful of melted butter or dripping to every dozen of potatoes, and sufficient hot milk or water to make the mass about the consistency of soft dough. They should be mashed in a tin, wood, or earthen vessel, as iron discolors them. When thoroughly mixed, beat them with a large fork and pile them up lightly in a hot dish or shape the surface into a smooth mound; or, before serving, set the dish in the oven and let the top brown.

It is claimed that old potatoes cook best if put in *cold* water and allowed to boil. New potatoes should be put in boiling water.

### BAKED POTATOES.

Time, twenty-five to thirty minutes.

Wash the potatoes and wipe them dry. Nick or cut off a piece at the pointed or eyed end. Put them into the oven; avoid if possible their touching one another. Bake in a uniform heat; turn each potato frequently.

Potatoes should be pared when baked with meat. Lay them in the baking pan around the meat: sprinkle them lightly with salt; baste them when the meat is basted. They take from fifty to sixty minutes to bake. Serve with the meat or separately. They may be boiled in their skins, peeled, and laid in the baking pan with the meat twenty-five or thirty minutes before it is done.

Potatoes may be baked in their skins in hot ashes.

### STEAMED POTATOES.

Wash potatoes well, and place in steamer or colander over a kettle of boiling water. Cover and steam until you can pierce with a fork. It takes a little longer to steam than boil, but the potato, being naturally watery, should never be cooked by boiling, if you have conveniences for steaming. When done, remove skins quickly and serve in an uncovered dish.

### FRIED COOKED POTATOES.

Peel and slice cold cooked potatoes. Do not slice them too thin. Put into a frying pan enough lard or beef dripping so that when melted it will just cover the bottom of the pan. When this becomes hot put in the potatoes; season with pepper and salt. Fry gently until they become hot, stirring them frequently.

## FRIED RAW POTATOES.

Wash, pare, and slice the potatoes very thin. They will hold the shape better if cut lengthwise. Lay them in ice-cold water for ten or fifteen minutes. Drain and spread them on a dry cloth; cover with another dry cloth and press gently to dry each slice.

Have brisk, but not a fierce fire. Put into a frying pan enough lard or dripping so that when melted it will float the potatoes; when this becomes boiling hot drop in the sliced potatoes, a few at a time, so as not to chill the fat. Fry to a light brown; turn if necessary.

When cooked, take them up with an egg-beater or skimmer; put them into a colander and shake them an instant to free them from grease. Put them into a hot dish and season with salt.

## BOILED SWEET POTATOES.

Prepare and boil as directed for Potatoes. When cooked, take them out of the pot and dry them in the oven for five minutes.

**To fry cooked Sweet Potatoes.**—Slice them lengthwise and fry as directed for Potatoes.

## BAKED SWEET POTATOES.

Prepare and bake sweet potatoes as directed for Potatoes. They are cooked when mellow throughout. Test by gently pressing them.

If the potatoes are old and watery, peel, parboil, and drain them; put them into a baking pan with a little butter or beef dripping; sprinkle them with pepper and salt, and bake. They are cooked when a fork will easily pierce the largest.

## FRIED ONIONS.

Peel, slice, and fry the onions brown in butter, beef dripping, or lard; season with pepper and salt. Stir constantly or they will burn.

## BAKED ONIONS.

Boil the onions; put them in a baking pan: place on top of each onion pepper, salt, and a piece of butter or dripping; put into the pan a little of the water in which the onions were boiled, and bake quickly until browned; baste frequently, and serve very hot.

## BOILED ONIONS.

Onions should be as uniform in size as possible, and should not be boiled in an iron vessel.

Peel the onions and lay them in cold salt water for fifteen minutes. Put them into a pot of boiling salt water—enough to cover them. Cover; boil gently or they will break. They are cooked when a straw can pierce them. When cooked drain and season with butter or dripping, pepper, and salt. The strength of the onions may be reduced by boiling them in two or more waters.

## STEWED ONIONS.

Boil and drain the onions. Prepare a sauce as follows: Melt a piece of butter the size of an egg; as soon as it bubbles stir in gradually two tablespoonfuls of flour; keep stirring it until it is cooked; then add about one-half pint of thin cream or milk and a seasoning of pepper and salt. Stir it until it is perfectly smooth; take it from the fire and pour it over the onions and simmer a few minutes.

Young onions should be used for this dish. If the onions are strong they should be boiled in two or three waters.

## BOILED OKRA.

The okra should be tender. Wash it and cut off a small piece from each end. Put it in cold water for fifteen or twenty minutes; drain and put it into a pot of boiling salt water—enough to cover it; cover and boil until soft; drain and season with butter, pepper, and salt; or it may be served with a sauce made as directed for Stewed Onions.

## BRUSSELS SPROUTS.

Wash and cut off lower part of stems. Lay in cold water, slightly salted, one-half hour. Cook quickly in boiling water, with a little salt, fifteen minutes (or until tender). Drain well and heap upon dish, with pepper.

## BOILED PARSNIPS.

Time, thirty minutes to one and one-quarter hours.

Wash the parsnips; if young, scrape them; if old, pare and soak them in cold water for half an hour; if large, cut them across in two or three pieces. Put them into a pot of boiling salt water—enough to plentifully cover them. Cover; boil steadily until tender; drain and slice lengthwise. Season them with butter, pepper, and salt, or a drawn-butter sauce. If boiled with meat, the butter and sauce may be omitted.

Boiled parsnips may be placed in a baking pan with baked meat, sprinkled with pepper and salt, and browned, basting them when the meat is basted.

Boiled parsnips may be mashed and served like Irish potatoes.

## STEWED PARSNIPS.

Boil and slice the parsnips thin. Put them into a pot with enough stock, or the liquor from boiled fresh beef, to about half cover them. Season with

pepper, salt, and mace, or grated nutmeg.  Cover;
stew gently for fifteen minutes, stirring frequently.

### FRIED PARSNIPS.

Boil the parsnips until tender; scrape off the skin
and cut them lengthwise into slices one-quarter
inch thick.   Dip each slice into beaten egg or flour.
Put into a frying pan enough lard or beef dripping so
that when melted it will just cover the bottom of the
pan.   When this becomes hot put in the parsnips
and fry brown on both sides.   When cooked take
them up, drain off the grease, season with pepper,
and serve.   They may be fried without the egg or
flour.

### PARSNIP CAKES.

Scrape, wash, boil, and mash the parsnips.   When
cold, season with salt and pepper and, flouring your
hands, form into cakes; roll in flour and fry in boiling dripping; drain dry and serve in a hot dish.

### BOILED GREEN PEAS.

Time, fifteen to twenty-five minutes.
The pot in which peas are to be cooked must be
clean and free from odor.
Shell the peas and soak them in cold water (ice
water is preferable) for ten or fifteen minutes, drain,
and put them into a pot of boiling salt water; cover;
boil until tender.   When cooked, drain dry; season
with butter, pepper, and salt.   If the peas are old
and tough, there may be put into the pot with them
a small quantity of bicarbonate of soda.   It will
make the peas tender and freshen their color.   A
sprig of mint may be boiled with the peas.   It should
be removed when the peas are drained.
If peas are not really in season it is more satisfactory to use canned peas, and French peas are the
best.

## BOILED PUMPKIN OR WINTER SQUASH.

Wash, pare, and cut the pumpkin or squash into pieces and remove the seeds. Soak it in cold water for two hours, then put it into a pot of boiling salt water; cover, and boil until tender throughout. When cooked drain thoroughly and mash it through a colander; season with butter, pepper, and salt. If the pumpkin or squash is too hard to be easily pared, it may be first parboiled.

## BAKED WINTER SQUASH.

Small Hubbard squash is best. Saw the squash in halves; scrape out soft part and seeds; put the halves in oven and bake three-fourths of an hour, or until tender; serve in shell, helping from them.

## BAKED PUMPKIN OR WINTER SQUASH.

Cut the pumpkin or squash into slices and remove the seeds. Put it into a broad, shallow baking pan, with a very little water; put it in the oven and bake with a gentle heat. It requires a long time to bake, and should be done dry. When baked, season with butter, pepper, and salt. The slices may be pared and put into the baking pan in layers.

## BAKED PUMPKIN.

Cut the pumpkin in halves, then quarters; remove the seeds, but not rind; place in baking pan with the rind down, and bake in a slow oven until tender when pierced with a fork. When done serve in rind, helping it by spoonfuls, as you would mashed potatoes.

## BOILED SUMMER SQUASH, OR CYMLING.

Wash the squash, or cymling, and if the rind is tender enough to be easily pierced with the finger nail, cut it up without paring, removing the seeds.

If the rind is hard, pare thinly. Soak it in cold water for fifteen or twenty minutes; then put it into a pot of boiling salt water; cover, and boil until tender throughout. When cooked, drain thoroughly and mash it through a colander; season with butter, pepper, and salt.

### BOILED CABBAGE.

If the cabbage is large, quarter it; if small, cut it into halves. Remove the outer and all bad leaves; examine carefully for insects; wash, and soak it in cold water for half an hour.

Put it into a covered pot with plenty of boiling salt water; cover. If the cabbage is old, pour off the water after it has boiled for ten or fifteen minutes and replace with fresh boiling water; add salt, and boil until tender. When the stalk is tender, it is cooked. When cooked, drain and press out the water, and season with butter, pepper, and salt. Omit the butter if the cabbage is boiled with meat.

The odor of cabbage may be lessened by putting in the pot pieces of charcoal, or boiling in equal parts of milk and water, and the flavor is thereby improved.

A cabbage may have the central part cut out and filled with mixed vegetables, enveloped in a cloth, and boiled as above.

### FRIED COOKED CABBAGE.

Chop the cabbage. Put into a frying pan enough lard or beef dripping so that when melted it will just cover the bottom. When this becomes hot put in the cabbage; stir frequently to keep it from burning. When the cabbage is hot serve it.

### STEWED CABBAGE.

Boil the cabbage and cut it up fine; put it into a pot with two or three ounces of dripping or butter, three or four tablespoonfuls of vinegar, and a half pint of stock or broth, salt, black and red pepper. Cover, and simmer for fifteen minutes, stirring frequently.

## BOILED CAULIFLOWER.

Time, fifteen to twenty minutes.

Trim the cauliflower by removing the outside leaves and cutting off the stalk. Put it into cold water for half an hour; then into a pot of boiling salted water—enough to cover it, and boil until tender. Be careful to take it up as soon as tender, and drain.

A drawn-butter sauce may be poured over it, or a sauce made as directed for stewed onions. One cupful of grated cheese to a pint of sauce may be melted into the sauce.

## BOILED CARROTS.

Time, thirty minutes to one and one-half hours.

Trim off the roots, wash well, and scrape off the skin. If they are young do not remove the skin until they are cooked. If the carrots are large, split or quarter them lengthwise, or cut them across in two or more pieces. Soak them in cold water for thirty minutes; put them into a pot of boiling salt water—enough to plentifully cover them. Boil steadily until tender. When cooked, drain or dry them in a cloth, and season with butter, pepper, and salt. Tomato catsup may be added as a seasoning. If they are boiled with meat, butter may be omitted.

## STEWED CARROTS.

Boil the carrots, cut into thin slices, and keep them warm. For about a quart of carrots, put into a pot a pint of stock or liquor from boiled fresh beef or mutton; put it on the fire, add a piece of dripping or butter twice the size of an egg, season

9281——9

with pepper and salt, and stir in two or three table-spoonfuls of blended flour; stir slowly until it comes to a boil, then put in the carrots; cover and stew gently for fifteen minutes, stirring frequently. If water is used instead of stock, double the quantity of butter or dripping.

### RAW CUCUMBERS.

Cucumbers should be as fresh from the vine as possible, and eaten within twenty-four hours after they are gathered. Pare and slice the cucumbers thin and sprinkle them plentifully with salt, and let them remain for a half hour. Then rinse off the salt with cold water, drain, and put lumps of ice on top or lay them in ice water for one-half hour or longer. This will crisp them. Just before they are served drain them dry. Season with pepper, salt, and vinegar. Add olive oil if desired.

Thin slices of raw onions may be mixed with the cucumbers.

### STEWED CUCUMBERS.

Pare and cut the cucumbers lengthwise into slices one-quarter inch thick. Put them in cold or ice water for one hour, then drain them. Put into a pot one or more tablespoonfuls of dripping or but-ter and enough stock or boiling water to prevent the cucumbers from burning. Season with pepper and salt, mace, or grated nutmeg; put in the cucum-bers, cover, and stew gently for thirty minutes, fre-quently stirring to prevent burning. When the stew is done, pour over it one-half cupful of milk previously thickened with flour and water and sea-soned with pepper, salt, mace, or grated nutmeg.

Let it boil up once, constantly stirring; then add the juice of half a lemon or a teaspoonful of vinegar.

### FRIED CUCUMBERS.

Pare and cut the cucumbers lengthwise into slices not quite one-half inch thick. Put them in cold or ice water for one hour.  Wipe each slice dry with a soft cloth, sprinkle with pepper and salt, and dredge them with flour.  Put into a frying pan enough butter, beef dripping, or lard so that when melted it will just cover the bottom of the pan.

When this becomes hot, put in the cucumbers and fry both sides a light brown.

### BOILED GREEN CORN.

Time, thirty to forty minutes.

Corn for boiling should be full grown, but young and tender.  Sugar corn is the most desirable. When the grains become hard it is too old for boiling.  Test by piercing the grain, when the milk should escape in a jet.  Clean by stripping off the outer layer of shucks, turn back the inner shucks, pick off the silk, bring back the inner shucks over the grains, tie the ends.  This process preserves the sweetness of the corn.

Put the corn into a pot of boiling salt water— enough to cover it.  Cover and boil long enough to cook.  Any exposure to heat after this is accomplished injures the corn.

When cooked, cut off the stalk close to the cob and remove the shucks.

Cold boiled corn may be cut from the cob and fried, or fried mixed with mashed potato.

Green corn may be cooked in the shuck in hot ashes.  Time, about one hour.

### STEWED GREEN CORN.

Cut the corn from the cob by passing a sharp knife lengthwise through the center of each row of grains; then with the back and pointed end of the knife scrape the grains free from the hull.  Put it into a pot, barely covering it with cold milk; season with butter and salt, and, if common field corn, sugar.  Cover and stew gently until very tender.

Stir frequently to keep it from burning. When cooked season with pepper.

Stock or the liquor from boiled fresh beef may be substituted for milk.

## BOILED BEETS.

Time, from one to three hours.

Winter beets should be soaked over night in cold water. Wash the beets; do not scrape or cut them. If a knife enters them before they are boiled they will lose much of their color and quality. Put them into a pot and cover plentifully with boiling water. Cover and boil steadily until tender. When cooked, put them into cold water and rub off the skins. This should be done quickly. If large, slice them; if young, split them lengthwise. Put them into a hot dish and season with pepper, salt, and butter.

Or, after they are sliced, mix one large spoonful of melted dripping or butter with four or five of vinegar and a seasoning of pepper and salt; let it boil up once and pour it over the beets. Beets may may be sliced and served with vinegar.

Beets may be baked, turning them three or four times. Time for baking, four to six hours.

## BOILED STRING BEANS.

Time, about thirty minutes.

String the beans carefully and cut each pod cross-wise in two or three pieces; wash and soak them in cold water for fifteen or twenty minutes; drain and put them into a pot of boiling salt water—enough to cover them; cover, and boil until tender. When cooked, drain and season with butter, pepper, and salt.

String beans may be boiled with bacon; in this case the butter and salt may be omitted.

## BOILED LIMA BEANS.

Time, thirty to forty minutes.

Shell the beans and put them in cold water for fifteen minutes; drain and put them into a pot of boiling salt water— enough to cover them; cover, and boil until tender. When cooked, drain them in a colander and season with butter, pepper, and salt.

## STEWED LIMA BEANS.

Boil a pint of shelled beans until tender, with three slices of onion, and drain. Put into a pot a piece of dripping or butter the size of an egg. When the dripping or butter becomes hot, put into it an even tablespoonful of minced onion and fry it; then put in the beans; add hot stock or water enough to half cover the beans; stock is preferable. Cover closely and simmer fifteen minutes.

Just before dishing them, stir in a handful of minced parsley. Do not allow the parsley to boil, as boiling spoils its color.

## LIMA BEANS (DRIED).

Soak one pint of beans in water over night. In the morning drain off the water and cover with fresh warm water. Two hours before dinner drain again, cover them with boiling soft water and drain again after boiling them thirty minutes. Cover them once more with boiling water and boil until tender. Add a teaspoonful of salt after they have been boiling an hour. When done drain and dredge with a tablespoonful of flour. Salt and pepper to taste.

## BOILED GREENS.

Spinach, young beets, turnip tops, mustard, nettle, narrow dock, lambs' quarters, dandelion, mountain cowslip, kale, cabbage, poke, sprouts, etc.

Pick the greens over carefully; wash in three or four waters, and soak them in cold water for thirty minutes; drain well and put them into a pot of boiling salt water, enough to cover them. If the greens are light, such as spinach, etc., press them down until the pot is full. Cover and boil steadily until tender.

When cooked, drain in a colander and press out the water. Season with butter, pepper, and salt.

If the greens are young they should cook in twenty minutes; if they are old, add to the water a small quantity of bicarbonate of soda; boil them for ten or fifteen minutes; turn off the water and replenish with boiling water; add a little salt. Poached egg or hard-boiled egg sliced may be placed on top of the greens when served.

Greens may be boiled with salt pork, corned beef. bacon, or ham, putting them into the pot in time to be done with the meat. They may be served separately or with the meat.

### STEWED TOMATOES.

Peel by pouring boiling-hot water over them, when the skin will easily come off. Cut up the tomatoes, rejecting the unripe and hard parts; put them into a pot, preferably tin or porcelain lined; season with butter, pepper, and salt, and, if the tomatoes are very acid, enough sugar to partially counteract the acidity, but not enough to sweeten them. Cover, and stew gently for three-quarters of an hour, frequently stirring. The stew can be thickened with bread crumbs or rolled cracker. Minced onion cooked with the tomatoes improves the flavor of the stew; or the minced onion may be fried and then cooked with the stew. A mixture of equal quantities of tomatoes and young corn, cut from the cob, may be cooked as above.

## BAKED TOMATOES, No. 1.

Wash, peel, and slice the tomatoes; season them with butter, pepper, and salt, and mix thoroughly with enough bread crumbs or rolled cracker to absorb the greater portion of the juice; put the mixture into a baking dish, and bake for three-quarters of an hour or one hour, and serve in the baking dish. Minced onion, raw or fried, may be added to the seasoning.

## BAKED TOMATOES, No. 2.

Cut a disk from the stem end of the tomato, take out the core and stuff it with a mixture of bread crumbs, butter, salt, and minced onion, and bake with a moderate heat for one hour.

## BOILED TURNIPS.

Time, twenty minutes to an hour.

Wash the turnips; if young, peel them, and if old, pare thickly. Slice or cut them into pieces of uniform size. Soak in cold water for thirty minutes; put them into a pot with enough boiling salt water to cover them plentifully. Cover; boil steadily until quite tender. Drain thoroughly; season with butter, pepper, and salt. If they are boiled with meat, butter may be omitted.

Young turnips may be served whole, with a drawn-butter sauce. Boiled turnips may be mashed and served like Irish potatoes.

## SUCCOTASH.

Succotash is made with green corn and beans, the proportion being two-thirds corn to one-third beans. String beans may be used. Cut the corn from the cob and shell the beans. If string beans are used, string and cut them into half-inch pieces. Put them into a pot of boiling salt water—enough to cover them. Cover and stew gently until tender, stirring frequently. When cookèd, drain. To two quarts of succotash add about one-half pint of milk, then stir in a piece of butter or dripping about the size of an egg, and one or more tablespoonfuls of blended flour. Stir it constantly until it boils up once. Season with pepper, and also salt, if necessary.

Succotash may be made of dried beans and dried corn. They must be soaked over night in hot water.

## SAUERKRAUT.

The cabbage must be firm. Trim, pick over, wash, and shred it fine with a very sharp knife. The stalk should not be used. Line the bottom and sides of a barrel, keg, or crock with cabbage leaves, and put into it a layer of the cabbage three or four inches deep; pound this down well with a wooden pounder, then sprinkle over it a small handful of salt, preferably table salt, then cabbage, then pound, then salt, and so on, until four layers are put in. Cover the cabbage with a board cut to fit loosely on the inside of the barrel. Pound hard on the board until the cabbage is a compact mass. Take off the board and repeat the process until the barrel is full. Cover it with cabbage leaves, the leaves with a piece of clean cloth, on the cloth lay the board, and on this put a heavy weight to keep down the mass. Set it away in a cool, dry place to ferment. As soon as the sauerkraut commences to effervesce, the covering of leaves should be thrown away, the scum removed, the kraut re-covered with a clean cloth, the board and weight thoroughly washed and replaced; and, as perfect cleanliness is necessary for its preservation, this process should be frequently repeated during the winter.

It is ready for use in twenty or twenty-five days. It may be eaten raw, or boiled with or without pork or bacon.

## SLAW.

Slaw should be made from firm cabbage. Trim, pick, and wash the cabbage. Shred it very fine. The stalk should not be used. It may be served without any dressing or with vinegar, pepper, and salt. It may be eaten hot or cold.

## STEWED SALSIFY.

Scrape roots, dropping in cold water that they may not change color. Cut in one-inch pieces. Cover with hot water and stew until tender. Drain off two-thirds of the water. Stew ten minutes longer. Add pepper and salt.

## SPINACH.

Wash one-half peck in several waters, to free it from grit, etc. Pick over carefully and cut off the roots. Wash again and drain, shaking out all remaining water. Put it in a kettle and add a cup of water. Cover kettle, place over moderate fire, and allow spinach to steam twenty minutes. Drain in colander, turn into chopping bowl, and chop fine. It can not be too fine. Place it in a saucepan, with one tablespoonful of dripping or butter, salt and pepper to taste, stirring until very hot. Have heated dish ready and place spinach on small pieces of toast.

## EDIBLE MUSHROOMS.

Edible mushrooms are found in clear open sunny fields and elevated ground where the air is pure and fresh. They are most plentiful in August and September, and spring up after low-lying fogs, soaking dews, or heavy rains. They first appear very small and of a round form, on a little stalk; the upper part and stalk are then white; they grow very fast,

and, as the size increases, the under part gradually
opens and shows a fringy fur (called gills) of a delicate salmon color.  After the mushroom is a day
old this salmon color changes to a russet or dark
brown.  They have an agreeable odor, the flesh compact and brittle, and the skin is more easily peeled
from the edges than in the poisonous kinds.  The
seeds or spores are white and for the most part
roundish or oval.  An edible mushroom should not
have only one of the above characteristics, but
should combine them all.

## POISONOUS MUSHROOMS.

*Poisonous* mushrooms are found in woods, low,
damp ground, in shady places, and upon putrefying
substances.  Some species emit an agreeable, others
a fetid, odor.  The color of the gills in some is either
red, green, blue, yellow, or orange-red.  In others
the top, gills, and stalks are dead white.  In all
poisonous mushrooms there is the absence of the
delicate salmon color found in the edible species.
The flesh in some is soft and watery, in others it has
an acid or a bitter taste.  Some on being bruised
assume a bluish tint or exude an acrid milky juice.
The seeds or spores are generally angular.  The
above rules for determining the edible and the
poisonous mushrooms are a safe guide provided the
mushrooms are quite fresh; but if they have been
gathered for several hours they may have so changed
in color that it might be impossible to form a correct opinion of them.  Furthermore, if a person
does not know the difference between a yellow and
a salmon color, the result of his judgment might be
disastrous.  Finally, if a white peeled onion is cooked
with mushrooms and turns black, or if a silver spoon
used for stirring them while cooking turns black, it
is safest not to eat them.  Whenever there is the
least doubt of their quality, do not use them.

## BAKED MUSHROOMS.

Prepare the mushrooms as directed for stewing. Put them into a greased tin or earthen baking dish, gills uppermost. Put a piece of butter, beef dripping, or lard, preferably butter, around the stems, and season with pepper and salt.

Put the dish into the oven and bake in a uniform heat. Exercise care that they do not burn. Bake from twelve to fifteen minutes, basting frequently. Serve in the baking dish.

## FRIED MUSHROOMS.

Prepare the mushrooms as directed for stewing. Heat in a frying pan enough dripping or butter to thinly cover the bottom; put in the mushrooms and fry both sides a golden brown.

When cooked, put them into a hot dish and keep warm, and make a gravy as follows:

Heat in the frying pan about half a cupful of stock or gravy, then stir in one or two tablespoonfuls of blended browned flour; keep stirring until it comes to a boil; season with pepper, salt, and pour it over the mushrooms.

## STEWED MUSHROOMS.

Select mushrooms of uniform size. Wipe them clean with a soft cloth; peel, commencing at the edge and finishing at the top; cut off the lower part of the stem; put them into a tin or earthen vessel and half cover them with cold water, and stew gently for fifteen minutes, frequently stirring to prevent burning. Season with pepper and salt. When the stew is done stir into it one or more tablespoonfuls of dripping or butter, previously cut into small pieces, and rolled in flour; stir three or four minutes. Do not let it boil.

## SALAD DRESSING.

| 3 tablespoonfuls oil. | 1 teaspoonful mustard. |
|---|---|
| Yolk of 1 egg. | ½ to ¾ teaspoonful salt. |

1 tablespoonful vinegar.

Rub together the oil and egg; it is better to first beat the egg; then rub in the mustard, then the salt, and lastly the vinegar, gradually. A few grains of cayenne pepper may be added. A boiled Irish potato (mashed fine) may be substituted for the yolk of the egg.

If the oil and egg or potato do not mix well, a few drops of vinegar will facilitate the process.

Instead of oil, there may be used melted butter, cream, or the juice from boiled ham. When about to serve the salad, pour over the dressing.

This dressing may be used with every species of lettuce, chicory, endive, water cress, celery, cabbage, dandelion, onions, tomatoes, etc.; cold boiled cauliflower, beets, string and dried beans (boiled or baked), corn, potatoes, etc.; chicken, turkey, lobster, crab, boiled or baked salmon, shrimp, etc.

## BOILED DRIED BEANS, No. 1.

Pick over the beans: wash and soak them over night in cold water; soft water is preferable.

Drain and put the beans into a pot with enough fresh cold water to cover them plentifully.

To two quarts of beans add one teaspoonful of bicarbonate of soda; cover and boil for fifteen minutes. Remove the scum as it rises. Pour off the water; replace with boiling water. Cover, and boil steadily for two or three hours, or until tender.

Drain, and season with butter, pepper, and salt.

Boiled beans may be prepared as follows: After they are drained return them to the pot, pour over them about a half pint of hot stock, gravy, or the liquor from boiled beef or mutton; add two tablespoonfuls of butter and a seasoning of salt; put the pot over the fire, stir gently for five minutes, then add two teaspoonfuls of chopped parsley.

Or, add to the beans about six to eight ounces of dripping or butter; stir, and when the butter is melted, season with pepper, salt, two teaspoonfuls of chopped parsley, and one teaspoonful of vinegar, and stir gently to mix the seasoning.

### BOILED DRIED BEANS, No. 2.

#### With baked beef, mutton, or fresh pork.

Boil the beans until they are tender; drain them; and when the meat is about half baked put them in the pan with it and stir occasionally until the meat is done. Serve with the meat.

### FRIED BEANS.

Boil and drain the beans. Put into a frying pan enough butter or beef dripping so that when melted it will just cover the bottom of the pan. When this becomes hot put in the beans and fry brown; stir them occasionally so that they will brown uniformly.

### STEWED DRIED BEANS, No. 1.

#### With beef, mutton, or fresh pork.

2 quarts dried beans.     4 pounds beef, mutton, or fresh pork.
Pepper, salt, and such herbs and spices as may be desirable.

Prepare and boil the beans for fifteen or twenty minutes, as directed in recipe for Boiled Dried Beans, and drain. Cleanse and cut the meat into small pieces. Put beans and meat into a pot, and cover with cold water, put in the seasoning, cover, and simmer until all is thoroughly done, stirring occasionally. Serve beans and meat together.

There may be added to the stew two or three sliced carrots and four or five minced onions, raw or fried.

## STEWED DRIED BEANS, No. 2.

### With bacon or salt pork.

2 quarts dried beans.      About 1 pound bacon or salt pork.
Minced parsley; pepper and salt.

Boil the beans tender and drain them. Cleanse and cut the meat into half-inch pieces, put it in a dry pot over the fire, and fry brown; then add the beans, stir them together, and cook for twenty or twenty-five minutes either on the fire or in an oven, stirring occasionally. Season with the parsley; pepper and salt. Minced onion may be fried with the meat.

### BAKED DRIED PEAS.

3 pints dried peas.      7 quarts cold water.
3 pounds bacon or salt pork.

Pick over the peas; wash and soak them over night in cold water; drain and put them into a pot with the meat, the latter previously cleansed; cover and boil gently. Remove the scum as it rises. When the peas become soft, drain, mash, and put them into a baking dish, smooth the top, place the meat on top, put the dish into the oven, and bake brown.

The liquor from the peas may be strained, and thickened with Indian meal (about four or five tablespoonfuls to a pint), and boiled gently about an hour. When cold it may be sliced and fried.

### DRIED PEAS AND OATMEAL.

1 quart peas.      4 onions, sliced.
½ pound bacon or fat salt pork.   2 tablespoonfuls sugar.
6 quarts cold water.      Pepper and salt.
6 or 8 ounces, or enough oatmeal mush to thicken the mixture.

Cleanse and cut the meat into half-inch pieces; put it into a dry pot over the fire with the sliced onions and fry brown, stirring constantly. Exercise care that it does not burn; put in the pepper, salt, and sugar, then add the water and peas, the latter previously soaked and drained. Cover, and boil gently until the peas become quite soft, stirring frequently; then stir in gradually the oatmeal, simmer for twenty minutes, and serve hot.

## BOILED RICE.

Rice is generally spoiled in boiling, being reduced by the process to a gelatinous or a watery mass. The theory of its being cooked properly appears to be to use considerable water for boiling it partially done, then to drain off the water that may readily separate from it. The moisture that may then adhere to the rice is, in further cooking, either absorbed by the rice in swelling or evaporated.

One pound of rice contains about three and one-half times as much food as one pound of potatoes.

One pint of rice will swell to three pints when cooked and increase in weight from fourteen ounces to two pounds.

Time, thirty minutes. One pound of rice; four quarts of boiling water; four teaspoonfuls of salt. Pick the rice over carefully and wash it clean in one or two cold waters; drain and put it into the pot of boiling water, adding the salt. Cover, and boil steadily for fifteen minutes, then thoroughly drain off the water and cover the pot and put it into another vessel of boiling water and steam it for ten minutes. Uncover the rice, steam five minutes longer, and it is cooked. If the above is not practicable or convenient, proceed as follows: After the rice has been boiled for fifteen minutes and drained, wipe out the pot, and sprinkle a little salt over the bottom of it and rub it with a dry cloth. Empty out or throw away any remaining salt; put in the rice; cover and put it into a slow oven or set it near the fire for fifteen minutes to dry and swell. The rice should not be stirred while cooking and drying.

Rice cooked as above may be eaten with butter, salt, gravy, curry powder, or curry powder blended with gravy, or stock or tomato sauce, milk, sugar, or sirup, ground cinnamon, or grated nutmeg.

## ANOTHER METHOD OF BOILING RICE.

The rice should be thoroughly washed and then placed in a pot with plenty of water (latter at boiling point); boil without touching the rice twenty minutes; throw into a colander, covering same; let stand several minutes, this serving a double purpose—allowing rice to drain as well as steam.

The three cardinal points essential to a satisfactory result are repeated in order to accentuate: First, water boiling from start to finish; second, rice undisturbed while cooking, that grains may not be broken; third, thoroughly drained.

By following these directions every grain will be found separate and dry, like a first-class mealy potato.

In order to see whether or not the rice is done, take out one of the grains and press it between the fingers ; if well done it will mash easily and feel perfectly soft.

## STEWED RICE.

Two or three ounces of dripping or butter; one pound of rice; two ounces of onion, minced; one quart of stock, gravy, or the liquor from boiled beef; black pepper and salt; a pinch of cayenne pepper or its equivalent in *chile colorado* or curry powder.

Pick over and wash the rice carefully. Put the dripping or butter into a dry pot and when hot put in the minced onion and fry a light brown, constantly stirring it; then add the stock, rice, etc., with seasoning. Cover and stew gently for fifteen or twenty minutes, stirring frequently to prevent burning, and serve as soon as the rice is tender. If the stock, etc., is absorbed before the rice is done, add more (hot) to keep it moist.

Cheese may be added as follows: When the rice is done, stir in two or three ounces of grated cheese; let it remain on the fire for one or two minutes, constantly stirring without letting it boil; or, the grated cheese may be sprinkled on the rice after it is dished.

### RICE PANADA.

| | |
|---|---|
| 1 pound rice. | 2 tablespoonfuls salt. |
| ¼ pound suet (chopped). | 1 pound flour. |
| 2 tablespoonfuls sugar. | 2 quarts water. |
| 2 gills molasses or sirup. | |

Time, twenty minutes.

Pick over, wash, and drain the rice; put it into a pot of boiling water—enough to plentifully cover it, adding the suet, salt, and sugar. Cover, and boil for fifteen minutes. Mix gradually and thoroughly the flour, water, and molasses.

Stir this into the boiled rice and boil for about five minutes, stirring frequently.

### FRIED RICE.

Boil sufficient rice and let it stand until cold, then cut into slices of proper thickness and fry to a nice brown, turning it carefully so as not to break the slices. This is an excellent breakfast dish.

### BOILED HOMINY (COARSE).

Hominy sufficient to one-quarter or one-third fill the vessel in which it is to be boiled; cold water sufficient to fill up the vessel; a little salt.

Pick the hominy over carefully; wash it clean and free from husk; soak it all night or ten or twelve hours in cold water.

Put it, and the water it was soaked in, into a pot, adding the salt; cover and boil slowly all day and as far into the evening as the fire is kept going, and it may be left on the fire all night in order to complete its cooking.

The next morning it may be served for breakfast, and eaten with salt, or with butter or sirup; or, the cooking may continue until dinner time. In cold weather it may be packed in wooden or earthen vessels, and rewarmed as wanted.

Care must be taken while boiling the hominy that it does not burn; it is better to boil it on the back of the stove where the heat is not great; when necessary to replenish with water add boiling water carefully. When hominy has been boiled as directed above, it should, when cold, be an agglutinated, moist mass and free from water. An earthen vessel is the best for boiling hominy, as it answers for keeping the hominy in after it is cooked.

Cold boiled hominy may be fried in butter, beef dripping, or lard. When put into the frying pan season with pepper and salt, stir occasionally until it is heated throughout, then press it down lightly, and fry it until the under side is browned.

When done put a hot dish bottom up on the pan, turn over pan and dish and remove the pan, leaving the hominy in the dish, the brown crust uppermost.

### CRACKED WHEAT.

One heaping teaspoonful of salt to one quart of wheat. Cover the wheat with cold water and let it soak over night in a cool place.

In the morning put the wheat, with the water it was soaked in, into a pot. Cover closely and cook gently until soft, stirring it frequently to prevent scorching. It should cook in from one to one and one-half hours. If necessary to replenish the water, add boiling water carefully. When cooked it should be a moist mass.

Hot milk may be used instead of water, to be added as evaporation takes place. It is safest, in order to prevent scorching, to cook it in a double boiler.

## HOMINY GRITS.

Hominy grits may be prepared and cooked in the same manner as cracked wheat. It may be baked as follows: To a pint of boiled hominy grits, cold, add two eggs well beaten; a small piece of butter and sufficient boiled milk to make a moderately thin mass. Put into a baking dish, and bake thirty minutes.

## FRIED GRITS.

Wash one pint grits in cold water. Cover with two quarts tepid water and soak over night. In the morning put it in a boiler and boil one hour. Season with salt and pepper to taste. Pour into a square mold and put away to cool. When cold, cut into slices, dust each slice with flour, and fry in fresh dripping until a light brown.

## INDIAN-MEAL MUSH.

| 1 cup Indian meal. | 2 quarts boiling water. |
|---|---|
| 1 tablespoonful salt. | |

To prevent the meal from lumping, mix it with sufficient cold water to make a thin batter, then gradually pour in the batter so as not to reduce the water below the boiling point, stirring it in with a wooden spoon or round stick. Cover closely and let it cook gently from one to two hours, stirring frequently or continuously, to prevent scorching. The mush should be made thick. When finished, if too thick, add boiling water carefully.

Cold mush may be cut into slices from one-half to three-quarters of an inch thick, and fried brown on both sides in hot beef dripping, lard, or butter.

Before frying, each slice may be dipped into beaten egg (salted), then into bread or cracker crumbs.

The best way to make mush for frying is to put two quarts of water on the fire to boil. Stir into a quart of cold milk or water one pint of corn meal and two teaspoonfuls of salt. When the water boils pour in the mixture gradually, stirring it well in. Let it boil half an hour, stirring continuously to prevent scorching. Set aside to cool, and when cold cut into slices three-quarters of an inch thick and fry; or the slices may be dipped in egg and crumbs as above.

## OATMEAL MUSH.

Oatmeal mush is prepared as Indian-meal mush, with the exception that the meal must be sprinkled dry into the hot water.

## BOILED MACARONI.

Wipe the macaroni carefully, and break it into convenient lengths; put it into a pot of boiling salt water, say ten times as much water as macaroni. Boil fifteen to twenty minutes, or until tender. Take care that it does not burst or become a pulp from excessive boiling; drain at once and season with butter or dripping.

If a flavor of onion is desired, boil with it two onions for each pound of macaroni. The liquor drained from the macaroni may be used for broth or soup.

Or, as soon as the butter and flour bubbles, gradually pour in one quart of boiling water, stirring it until it becomes smooth; season with pepper and salt; put in the macaroni and let it remain over the fire for one minute. Have ready one or two onions, minced or shredded, fried brown. Dish the macaroni and pour the fried onions over it.

Boiled macaroni may be served with tomato sauce as follows: For one pound of macaroni put into a pot half a can of tomatoes, or twelve large fresh ones, one-half a pint of stock, gravy, or broth, a little thyme and parsley, six whole cloves, a sliced onion, cayenne pepper, and salt. Cover and simmer for one hour, stirring frequently; drain and press the mixture through a sieve; then stir well into it about two ounces of dripping or butter and one ounce of flour, previously mixed smooth over the fire; pour it over the macaroni.

### BAKED MACARONI AND CHEESE.

Boil and drain the macaroni and with it fill by layers a greased earthen dish, seasoning each layer with minced fat pork or butter, grated cheese, mustard, pepper, and salt; add bread crumbs for the top layer. Cover and bake with a moderate heat for half an hour. Remove the cover, and when the top is brown serve in the baking dish.

### STEWED CELERY.

Scrape and wash well the green stalks that are not fit to be used on the table. Cut in pieces one inch long and soak in cold water fifteen minutes. Place in saucepan of boiling water, with one teaspoonful of salt, and boil thirty minutes. When done, drain and throw into cold water while you make the sauce. Put one tablespoonful of dripping in frying pan, melt, and add one tablespoonful of flour. Mix smooth. Add three tablespoonfuls liquor in which celery was boiled; salt and pepper to taste. Add celery to sauce, stir until heated through, and serve.

### FRIED EGGPLANT.

Peel and slice thin and sprinkle each slice with pepper and salt; pile up evenly and put tin plate over and weight on top to press out juice. Let stand one hour.  Dip each slice in flour, sprinkle with salt and pepper, and fry in a frying pan in which have been thoroughly heated three tablespoonfuls of dripping.  Fry eggplant on both sides, and as fat is consumed add more, allowing it to heat thoroughly before putting in the plant.  These slices may be rolled in bread crumbs if preferred; or a mixture of flour and crumbs is good.  Drain slices on brown paper when done, and serve hot.

### STUFFED EGGPLANT.

Take large plants, cut in two lengthwise and remove inside, leaving one-half inch thickness of peeling.  Chop fine and mix well with an equal quantity of bread crumbs.  Salt and pepper to taste, and a little brown sugar.  Cook this mixture in dripping or butter in a frying pan, stirring constantly.  Cook ten minutes, fill shells with this, and bake in oven half an hour; serve in shells.

### FRENCH ARTICHOKES.

French artichokes have a large, scaly head like a pine cone.  Strip off coarse, outside leaves, cut the stalks off an inch from the bottom, wash well in cold water, throw in boiling water, with a teaspoonful of salt, and boil slowly until outside leaves are tender.  Take from the pot and place upside down on a platter to drain.  Arrange on a heated dish, tops up, and serve with sauce.

### JERUSALEM ARTICHOKES.

Wash and scrape, throw into cold water, and soak two hours.  Cover with boiling water and boil until tender.  Watch closely or they will harden.  Serve with sauce.

### STEWED ASPARAGUS.

Wash well in cold water.  Cut into pieces one inch long.  Cover with boiling water and boil thirty

minutes, in covered vessel. Drain in colander
and place in saucepan, with pepper, salt, and a little
water. Let it just come to a boil once, and serve.

## ASPARAGUS UPON TOAST.

Cut stalks of equal length, scraping white parts
and rejecting all woody pieces. Tie in bunch or
bunches and boil thirty minutes or until tender.
Have ready six or eight slices of toast. Dip in
asparagus liquor and lay on hot dish. Drain asparagus, lay upon toast, open the bunches, and salt and
pepper to taste.

## OATMEAL PORRIDGE FROM COOKED OATMEAL (ROLLED OATS, QUAKER OATS, ETC.).

| | |
|---|---|
| 1 measure oatmeal. | 3 measures fresh, cold, |
| Salt in proportion of 1 level | clear water. |
| teaspoonful to each quart | |
| of water. | |

Put the salt in the water, and bring the water to a
boil. Then pour in the oatmeal gradually with one
hand while stirring with the other, and keep stirring
till the mixture commences to thicken, when stop
stirring and place it at the back of the range, closely
covered, where it will keep hot, just simmering, for
twenty-five or thirty minutes. Serve it in a warmed,
covered dish.

The water should be fresh and clear, not taken
from the water back or from the teakettle, where
the life has been boiled out of it.

The stirring should cease after it has been placed
at the back of the range; too much stirring spoils
the porridge, making it pasty, unsightly, and unpalatable.

The utensil in which the porridge is made should
be scrupulously clean, and free from odor. Any
odor in the utensil or in the water will impair the
clean flavor that good porridge should have.

The three measures of water prescribed will usually be about the proper proportion. The shape of the utensil and the amount of evaporation allowed during the process of cooking are to be considered; the aim should be to have the porridge somewhat thin—it should certainly not be hard and thick. The flavor is better when moderately thin.

For oatmeal gruel use five measures of water.

## DRIED AND EVAPORATED FRUITS.

Dried fruits are an excellent food when properly prepared for the table, but unfortunately they are usually cooked imperfectly, and cook-books give scant information concerning them; in fact, the majority of cook-books do not mention them. The following recipes for cooking dried prunes, apples, peaches, and apricots contain directions which may be applied with slight variations for cooking all kinds of dried fruits.

### STEWED PRUNES.

Wash and pick over the prunes, rejecting imperfect ones; put them to soak over night in the water (cold) they are to be cooked in, using only enough water to cover them. Put the prunes on the fire where they can just simmer during three hours (prunes require longer cooking than other dried fruits because of their thick skin). Do not let them boil, nor use a vessel of iron. Keep them closely covered. If carefully cooked they present a plump appearance and are not broken or burst (this defect gives them a slovenly look, the reverse of appetizing). As the prune contains much sugar, more should not be added; the fruit taste is more prominent without additional sugar. If, however, increased sweetness is desired, the sugar should not be added till about five minutes before taking off the fire.

## STEWED DRIED AND EVAPORATED APPLES, APRICOTS, AND PEACHES.

Wash them thoroughly and soak them over night in the water (cold) they are to be cooked in, using only enough water to cover them. Put the fruit on the fire in a vessel not iron (an earthenware stone jar, well glazed, is very suitable) and simmer slowly (do not boil), closely covered, for two hours. Do not stir to break the fruit, and thus render it unsightly. When the fruit is cooked put in plenty of sugar; let it then cook five minutes. If sugar is added before the fruit is cooked it hardens it.

Dried peaches require more washing and rubbing than any other fruit in order to free the skin from fuzz, but the rubbing should not be so hard as to take off the skin, which contains the principal flavor of the peach.

The richest and best dried peaches are those dried with the skins on. The skins, however thick, entirely dissolve in cooking, and are imperceptible when the fruit is well stewed. Apricots require much sugar; it should be supplied liberally.

During hot weather fruit is liable to sour when put to soak over night; to avoid this put it in the refrigerator while soaking.

Flavoring should be used sparingly, and varied from day to day. Those especially recommended are allspice, cloves, cinnamon, mace, ginger, slices of lemon, or extract of lemon. If extract is used it should be added just before removing the fruit from the fire. Dried fruits are a convenient and wholesome vehicle for sugar as a food; any kind of sugar may be used, but on account of the peculiar flavor it gives many persons prefer a brown sugar, grade extra C.

All cooked fruits are better served cold. After they have been prepared, as here directed, they may also be used in many ways for pies, puddings, etc.

## STEWED CRANBERRIES.

Pick the berries carefully; then wash them in cold water; drain. Put them into fresh cold water and soak for five or ten minutes; drain, and then put the fruit into a well-covered vessel (not iron), with sufficient boiling water to cover it. Stew rather quickly, stirring occasionally until soft. They should cook in from twenty to thirty minutes. Five minutes before they are done stir in sugar to taste. Then pass them through a colander to remove the skins, if so desired.

Remove from fire, put into a cold dish, and set them away to cool. When cold they are ready for use; can be used as soon as cooked.

## STEWED RHUBARB.

Wash the rhubarb and cut it into pieces one inch long. Do not peel it. Allow one pound of sugar to each pound of rhubarb. Put rhubarb into saucepan, cover it with sugar, and put on back part of fire until sugar melts. Then bring it to boiling point without stirring. Turn it all out to cool and it is ready for use.

## EGGS.

Eggs are best twelve hours after they have been laid. They are good when translucent or will sink in water. They should be kept in a dry, dark, cool place. They may be kept for months by packing them (without touching one another) in salt, the small end down.

When eggs are cooked in a frying pan the pan must be particularly clean. When butter, beef dripping, or lard is put into the pan over the fire, it should be tossed about gently to melt it evenly, and to prevent it blackening. As soon as melted the eggs should be turned into it.

## BOILED EGGS.

Wipe the eggs clean with a wet cloth and put them into boiling water. If wanted soft, boil steadily for three or four minutes; if hard, from five to ten minutes.

Eggs may be put into cold water over a brisk fire, and when the water comes to a boil taken up and served. Time, about ten minutes.

## FRIED EGGS.

Heat in a frying pan over a good fire enough beef dripping or lard so that when melted it will cover the bottom of the pan one-quarter of an inch deep.

Break the eggs gently into a saucer or small plate, and slip them carefully, one at a time, into the hot fat until the bottom of the pan is covered, taking care not to allow the eggs to adhere together. Lose no time putting the eggs into the pan. The eggs are first emptied into a saucer to keep the yolks from breaking and to detect the bad ones. They are cooked when the whites become firm, and should be taken up before the yolks become hard. When cooked, take them up without delay and pour the grease remaining in the pan over them, or strain it and set it aside in a cool place for cooking purposes.

## PLAIN OMELET.

The fire must be brisk, as the quicker an omelet is made the better, and the less butter it requires.

If the frying pan needs cleansing, instead of washing, heat it and wipe it very clean with a coarse towel.

| | |
|---|---|
| 12 eggs. | ½ teaspoonful salt. |
| 1 cupful of milk or cream. | Pepper, butter. |

Separate the yolks and whites of the eggs; the whites beaten to a stiff froth. Beat the yolks; mix in the pepper and salt; add butter half the size of

an egg, and work them to a smooth thick batter;
stir in the milk; lastly, stir in lightly the beaten
whites.  Heat in a frying pan a piece of butter the
size of an egg; when it becomes hot pour the mixture gently into the pan.  As the omelet begins to
"set," loosen it with a thin-bladed knife from the
sides and bottom of the pan.  It should cook in ten
or twelve minutes.  Or, put the frying pan into a
hot oven when the middle of the omelet is set, and
bake to a delicate brown.

When cooked, to turn it out, proceed as follows:
Put a hot dish bottom-up on the pan, hold the
handle of the pan with the right hand, back of the
hand down, spread the left hand back uppermost
on top of the dish, turn both hands, emptying the
omelet into the dish, the browned side uppermost.
It should be eaten at once, as it falls rapidly.  It
may be eaten with pepper and salt or powdered
sugar or sirup.

Minced ham, tongue, and fish are sometimes mixed
with omelet batter and cooked as above.

To make jam omelet, as soon as one side becomes
brown, spread it over with jam, double, and serve.

### POACHED EGGS.

It is advisable not to poach more than three or
four eggs at a time; preferably one.

Nearly fill a frying pan with cold water, adding
two teaspoonfuls of salt and one tablespoonful of
vinegar to a quart of water.  When the water boils,
break a fresh egg into a saucer or small plate, slip
it carefully into the boiling water, and as near the
surface as possible.  Dip up some boiling water
with a spoon and pour it over the egg.  Boil gently
for three or four minutes.  When cooked take it
up with a perforated skimmer, giving the skimmer
a light shake over the pan to drain the water.  Lay
it on toasted bread and sprinkle with pepper and
salt.

## SCRAMBLED EGGS.

Break twelve eggs into a bowl or deep dish. Heat in a frying pan a piece of butter a little larger than an egg. When this is hot pour in the eggs, and at once stir them with a spoon from the bottom for fully three minutes, or until they become coagulated, seasoning with pepper and salt while cooking. When cooked turn them out into a hot dish or upon toasted bread.

Chopped parsley, sweet herbs minced, cooked ham or tongue, or chipped dried beef may be added to the seasoning.

## BREAD, ETC.

### Remarks on Breakfast Rolls.

The following rules are to be observed in making all rolls:

The dough must be prepared the night previous. It must be well kneaded, and be placed where the temperature is even, and never be allowed to chill.

In winter wrap the pan containing it in a blanket and set near the stove. In summer cover top of pan with a cloth.

After the morning kneading, the dough must be set to rise in a warm place about an hour before it is made into rolls for baking. The oven in which the rolls are baked must have a moderate and even heat maintained during the process of baking.

Baking pans must be clean, and well greased with dripping or lard.

### BREAKFAST ROLLS.

2 quarts sifted flour.      1 large teaspoonful salt.
1 large teaspoonful dripping or lard.    1 cup good yeast.
Tepid water (milk and water preferable) to make a soft dough.

Make sponge as follows: Rub the dripping or lard into the sifted flour, mix in the salt, then the yeast

and enough tepid water, or milk and water, to make
a soft dough. Knead thoroughly and set to rise
over night, the top sprinkled with flour.

In the morning again knead the dough and set to
rise again. When risen, knead again until the
dough feels light and puffy; then with floured hand
break or pinch off pieces about the size of an egg,
shape each piece into a ball, put into pan, and bake
in a moderate oven fifteen or twenty minutes to a
light brown.

### PARKER-HOUSE ROLLS.

2 quarts sifted flour.                       1 cupful fresh yeast.
1 large tablespoonful sweet lard.   1 teaspoonful salt.
Enough boiled milk (cold) to make a soft dough.

Mix as directed in breakfast rolls, and let it rise
all night. Knead well in the morning. Let it have
a second rising. Roll the dough to about one-half
inch thickness and cut into circular pieces. Fold
half the circle on itself; place a piece of butter in
the fold. Fold the other half to meet the first fold,
placing the butter beneath it. Bake to a light brown.

### BAKING-POWDER BISCUITS.*

2 quarts sifted flour.                   1 large teaspoonful salt.
4 large teaspoonfuls baking       1 tablespoonful dripping
powder.                                         or lard.
Cold water (sweet milk is preferable) enough to make a soft
dough.

Put flour into a deep dish; mix into this the baking powder and salt; then rub in the dripping or
lard. Put in enough cold water or milk to make a
soft dough. Handle as little as possible. Roll
quickly into a sheet three-quarters of an inch thick.
Cut into circular cakes, with a floured biscuit cut-
ter, or an empty can; roll the dough that is left into
a sheet, and recut.

---

* In using *baking powder* the directions printed on the packages should be strictly
followed, as one teaspoonful of some powders is as strong as two teaspoonfuls of
others.

Lay the biscuits thus cut into a well-greased baking pan close together and bake five or six minutes in a quick oven until they are browned.

## WHEAT MUFFINS.

| | |
|---|---|
| 3 cups sifted flour. | 2 cups milk. |
| 1 egg, well beaten. | 1 tablespoonful sugar. |
| ¼ teaspoonful salt. | 3 teaspoonfuls baking powder. |

Into the sifted flour mix the baking powder, salt, and sugar; add the egg and milk enough to make a thick batter.

Drop the mixture into greased muffin rings and bake.

## GRAHAM BREAD.

Make a sponge of one quart of Graham flour, three-quarters of a cup of yeast, one quart of warm water, and one cup of molasses. Set it in a moderately warm place to rise over night (or six or eight hours), then mix the sponge with white flour into a stiff dough, let it rise a second time, then make it into loaves to rise for baking.

## CORN-MEAL AND RYE BREAD.

| | |
|---|---|
| 2 quarts corn meal. | 2 quarts rye flour. |
| 1 teaspoonful salt. | ½ pint molasses. |
| ½ pint strong fresh yeast; tepid water. | |

Sift the corn meal and rye flour into a deep pan or bowl; mix them together, adding the salt; mix into the molasses one-half pint of warm but not hot water; then stir into it the yeast and pour it into a hole previously made in the middle of the meal; work into it with a spoon enough of the flour to make a thick batter; sprinkle the top with rye flour. Cover the pan with a thick cloth and set it in a warm place for three or four hours to rise. It is light enough when cracked all over the surface.

Then pour gradually into the middle of the batter about a pint of warm but not hot water; mix it thoroughly through the dough till it becomes a round mass. Sprinkle rye flour over it; flour the hands and knead it thoroughly, frequently turning it over, for half an hour, or until it ceases to adhere to the hands. Sprinkle it again with rye flour; cover, and set it in a warm place to rise. When perfectly light the dough will stand high and the surface will be cracked all over. Put it at once into a deep tin or iron pan, greased, and bake about two hours; as soon as baked wrap it in a clean coarse towel, wet with cold water, and stand it on end till cool. It is important that the oven should be ready and of the proper heat, so that the dough may be put in as soon as it has completely risen the second time. When dough has done rising it will fall if not put at once into the oven. If the dough has stood so long as to sour, dissolve a level teaspoonful of soda in sufficient warm water; sprinkle this over the dough and knead it well in and put it into the oven as soon as possible.

Excellent bread may be made as above of equal quantities of corn meal, wheat and rye flour; or, of one part of corn meal and three parts of wheat flour.

## CORN MEAL.

As corn meal contains very little gluten, wholesome and palatable bread can be made of it without the use of any material to lighten it, using only salt and water to mix it.

If corn meal is not fresh, a better bread can be made from it by scalding the meal.

## CORN BREAD.

Corn bread will often be found more desirable than wheat bread. It is much healthier for those engaged in muscular exercise, more easily digested, and more apt to be successfully prepared. An excellent recipe is the following: Corn meal, two quarts; salt, two teaspoonfuls; mix rapidly with boiling water, and stir till it drops lightly from the spoon. This may be baked in an ordinary Dutch oven, or, in thin cakes, in a frying pan. Eaten either warm or cold.

## CORN BREAD OR HOECAKE.

1 quart meal. 2 teaspoonfuls salt.
2 tablespoonfuls melted lard. Sufficient warm water (but not hot enough to scald meal) or warm milk to make a thick batter.

Put meal in a deep dish; mix in the salt; pour in sufficient warm water or milk to make a thick batter; last add the melted lard, beat thoroughly, and bake in a well-greased pan in a quick oven.

By the addition of more warm water or milk the batter can be thinned down and a griddle cake made from above recipe.

## WHEAT BREAD.

Should wheat bread be desirable it is better to use the patent self-raising flour; this only requires to be gradually mixed into a thin batter with cold water, and may be baked in a Dutch oven, or, into biscuits or hot cakes, in a frying pan. It makes most delicious bread and biscuits.

The addition for self-raising flour is baking powder and salt, in proper proportions, which makes it cost about 1½ to 2 cents more per pound than the straight flour.

Remember, always, that to bake in an oven (or Dutch oven) you must have the heat *on top* of as well as under the oven.

## POTATO BREAD.

| | |
|---|---|
| 1 quart boiling water. | 1 tablespoonful salt. |
| 3 large potatoes. | 3½ quarts flour. |

⅓ cup yeast, or ¼ cake compressed yeast.

Cover potatoes with boiling water and cook half an hour. Drain and mash. Pour boiling water on them and let stand until blood warm. Add the yeast and three quarts flour, beating with a spoon. Cover bowl with cloth and board or tin cover, and let it rise over night (nine or ten hours). In the morning beat in salt and half remaining flour, and use flour left for kneading bread on board. Knead twenty minutes to half an hour. Put dough back in bowl and cover. Let rise to double its size. Shape into loaves and let rise to double their size originally. Bake one hour in a moderate oven.

### RAISED BROWN BREAD.

| | |
|---|---|
| 1 pint yellow corn meal. | ¼ teaspoonful salt. |
| ½ cup yeast. | 1 salt spoonful soda. |
| ¼ cup molasses. | 1 pint rye meal. |

Put corn meal in a bowl and scald with boiling water just enough to wet it. Let stand ten minutes, and add cold water enough to make soft batter. When lukewarm add yeast, molasses, salt, soda, and rye flour. Beat well and let rise over night or until it cracks open. Stir it down, and put in a greased and floured tin to rise again. Sprinkle flour over top. Bake in a moderate oven two hours.

### POTATO YEAST.

| | |
|---|---|
| 3 large potatoes. | 1 quart boiling water. |

½ cup salt.

Peel and grate potatoes as rapidly as possible, so they will not turn dark. Pour on the boiling water and cook half an hour. Add sugar and salt shortly before it is done. When sufficiently cool, put in any good yeast to raise it. Stir well together. The next day it will be light as foam, and one teacupful will be enough to raise four or five loaves.

Keep in a cool place, and in summer renew every fortnight.

## HOP YEAST.

| | |
|---|---|
| 1 pint hot mashed potatoes. | ¼ pint flour. |
| ¼ pint salt. | ½ pint hops (light measure). |
| ¼ pint sugar. | 4½ quarts boiling water. |

½ pint yeast (or 1 cake compressed yeast).

Put hops in stew pan with one pint boiling water and boil twenty minutes. Mix potatoes, sugar, flour, and salt, and strain hop water on them. Beat this mixture well and add the four quarts boiling water. Let this stand until blood-warm, add yeast, and stir well. Cover the bowl and let stand twenty-four hours. Skim and stir the yeast several times, place in jugs, and cork tightly. Keep in cool place.

## BAKING POWDER.

8 ounces bicarbonate of soda.    4 ounces cream of tartar.
4 ounces cornstarch.

Roll smoothly and mix thoroughly. Keep in tight glass jar or bottle.

## REMARKS ON GRIDDLE AND PAN CAKES.

If the pan or griddle has been unused for some time cleanse thoroughly with soap and hot water, then wipe dry with a towel, and, lastly, rub thoroughly with dry salt to remove all moisture.

If the griddle is clean and smooth, only occasional greasing will be required; the best way is with a clean rag containing butter. The griddle must either be scraped or greased after each cake is cooked. Pancakes should be fried in a small pan. When the cake is cooked on one side, turn, and cook it on the other.

164        MANUAL FOR ARMY COOKS.

When yeast is an ingredient and the batter rises over night, the articles to be stirred in the morning should be added thirty minutes before the cakes are to be cooked.

The batter should be removed gently from the vessel to the griddle with the least possible disturbance to the batter.

Baking powder and sweet milk may be substituted for soda and sour milk.

### CORN-MEAL BATTER CAKES.

1 quart sour milk.   2 eggs, beaten.   2 teaspoonfuls salt.
1 teaspoonful soda in sufficient hot water to dissolve it.
Mix in enough sifted meal to make a thin batter.

Cook on a griddle, over a quick, clear fire. Each cake should be buttered as soon as cooked, and kept hot until served.

### FLANNEL CAKES, No. 1.

1 quart sour milk.   2 teaspoonfuls salt.   2 eggs, well beaten.
1 teaspoonful soda in sufficient hot water to dissolve it.
1 heaping tablespoonful melted lard or butter.
Mix in flour enough to make a moderately thin batter.

The melted lard should be put in last and thoroughly incorporated. Instead of sour milk and soda, sweet milk with an adequate amount of baking powder may be used. Cook and serve as directed for Corn-Meal Batter Cakes.

### FLANNEL CAKES, No. 2.

1 quart sweet milk.          1 teaspoonful salt.
3 tablespoonfuls yeast.      2 eggs, well beaten.
          1 tablespoonful butter, melted.

Put the milk (slightly warmed), yeast, and salt into a deep earthenware dish; into this then stir sufficient flour to make a tolerably thick batter, and set the dish in a warm place over night. Should there be danger of freezing, wrap the dish in a woolen cloth and set near the stove. If the batter becomes chilled or frozen it is useless. In the morning add the melted butter and eggs, and then cook. Should the batter, after the eggs and butter are added, be too thick, add warm milk to thin it. If too thin, add sifted flour. This rule is general for all raised cakes.

### FLANNEL CAKES, No. 3.

| | |
|---|---|
| 2 cups sifted wheat flour. | 1 cup sifted Indian meal. |
| 4 tablespoonfuls yeast. | 1 teaspoonful salt. |

Make into a batter. Set it to rise as directed in Flannel Cakes, No. 2.

In the morning stir into the batter one tablespoonful of melted lard, and cook.

### BATTER CAKES, No. 1.

| | |
|---|---|
| 1 quart sifted flour. | ¼ teaspoonful salt. |
| 2 heaping teaspoonfuls baking powder. | 1 teaspoonful brown sugar. |
| | 2 eggs, beaten light. |

Put flour into a deep dish, and mix with it the salt, baking powder, and brown sugar. Add warm milk sufficient to make a thick batter. Then add eggs. If eggs do not thin down the batter sufficiently, add more milk. Beat thoroughly and cook at once.

### BATTER CAKES, No. 2.

| | |
|---|---|
| 1 quart sifted flour. | ¼ teaspoonful salt. |
| 1 teaspoonful soda. | 1 pint sour milk. |
| 1 egg, beaten light. | |

Dissolve the soda in a small portion of warm water. Put flour into a deep dish. Mix in the salt; stir in gradually enough of the sour milk to make a thick batter, then the egg, and lastly the dissolved soda. Beat thoroughly and cook.

## BUCKWHEAT CAKES.

For all raised cakes a well-glazed earthen crock or stone jar should be used for the batter, and the general rules for the treatment of batter followed. Batter must be made the night previous.

One quart buckwheat flour (sifted); one-half pint Indian meal; four tablespoonfuls of yeast; one teaspoonful salt; two tablespoonfuls molasses (not sirup), or in lieu thereof one and a half tablespoonfuls brown sugar. Warm water (mixed milk and warm water is preferable) enough to make a moderately thick batter.

Mix the meal into the buckwheat flour; stir in gradually enough of the warm water, or milk and water, to make a moderately thick batter. Then stir in the yeast. Set to rise over night. In the morning add the salt, and lastly the molasses or brown sugar. Beat the mixture thoroughly; add milk and water if too thick, or buckwheat flour if too thin, before adding the salt and molasses, or brown sugar, and cook on a hot griddle.

During the winter batter may be made each night, for a period of a week or ten days, without additional yeast, by allowing a portion of the batter (say one or two teacupfuls) to remain in the jar, and adding thereto the ingredients.

Should the batter be the least sour in the morning, stir in a very small quantity of soda, dissolved in hot water, to correct acidity.

### RICE CAKES.

One quart of sifted flour; two cups of cold boiled rice; two teaspoonfuls salt; four eggs, beaten light; milk enough stirred into the flour to make a tolerably thick batter; then add the rice, salt, and last the eggs; beat thoroughly and cook at once.

## PANCAKES.

One quart of sifted flour; one level teaspoonful of salt; three heaping teaspoonfuls of baking powder; three teaspoonfuls of brown sugar; two or three eggs, the yolks beaten light, the whites to a stiff froth; one quart of water or milk (the latter is preferable), or enough of either to make a thin batter. Fry as directed in Remarks on this class of cooking.

Cakes should be served hot and eaten with sugar and butter, molasses, or sugar and ground cinnamon, mixed in the proportion of five parts of sugar to one of cinnamon.

## RHODE ISLAND PANCAKES.

To one pint of Indian meal add one pint of rye flour; two tablespoonfuls of molasses; one teaspoonful of saleratus; one teaspoonful of salt; three eggs, well beaten. Stir with these ingredients sufficient new milk to make a stiff batter, and fry it ten minutes in lard, as you would doughnuts.

Another rule is nearly as good when milk and eggs are scarce. Mix well one quart of Indian meal, one quart of rye flour, two large tablespoonfuls of melted shortening or butter, five tablespoonfuls of molasses, one tablespoonful of salt, one small teaspoonful of saleratus, and one quart of water. Fry it as above.

## PIE CRUST, No. 1.

Pie crust, or pie paste, should be made in a cool place, and handled as little as possible during the process. The heat from the hand makes the crust tough.

One quart of flour (sifted); one-fourth of a pound lard; one-fourth of a pound butter; one-half teaspoonful salt; enough ice water to make a stiff dough. Sift the flour into a deep wooden bowl or tin pan;

mix into it the salt; then the lard. With a keen
chopping knife cut up the lard into the flour until
it is thoroughly incorporated, with no lumps; wet
with ice water, stirring it in with a wooden spoon
until it becomes a stiff dough. Flour the hands,
and make dough into a lump with as little handling
as possible.

Remove lump to a well-floured kneading board,
and roll it out into a sheet one-quarter of an inch
thick, always rolling from you, and with as little
pressure upon the rolling-pin as may be necessary.

Into the rolled sheet stick small pieces of butter
at regular intervals. Dredge slightly with flour.
Roll up the sheet, commencing on the edge nearest
you. Roll out, again buttering and dredging, until
the butter is exhausted. If time will then permit,
lay the roll in a cold place or on the ice for twenty
minutes.

Place it again upon the floured kneading board,
roll out into a sheet as before directed. Butter the
pie plates; lay the paste lightly in them, fitting it
nicely.

Trim off the paste neatly around the edges of the
pie plates. Gather up the cuttings and roll them
into a separate sheet.

If the pies are to have a top crust, cover the tops
with the paste, cutting neatly round the edges, and
with a knife, spoon, or the fingers join securely the
edges of the top and sides to prevent escape of juices.
Then, with a sharp knife, make three or four incisions about an inch long to the center of the top crust.

If the top crust is lightly brushed with sweet
milk it will brown evenly.

Bake in a moderate oven to a light brown. Be
careful to have the heat as great at the bottom as
at the top of oven. If this is not looked to the
lower crust will be uncooked.

Should a richer crust be desired the proportions
of lard and butter can be increased.

## PIE CRUST, No. 2.

In preparing paste, the cook should place his hands under a tap for a few minutes, so that they may be quite cold before touching the ingredients.

Chop up the suet very fine, if to be used, and roll it; place sufficient salt, flour, and baking powder in a dish; well mix the whole; add some water, mix lightly until it forms a smooth paste; sprinkle some flour on the table, roll out the paste one-half inch thick, shake some flour over it; take one-third of the dripping or suet and distribute it over the paste, fold the paste over, sprinkle some more flour over the table, roll out the paste, fold and roll again, and repeat this once more; then add one-third of the dripping or suet as before, fold and roll three times; then add the remainder of the dripping or suet, fold and roll again three times; it will then have been rolled and folded nine times; it should then be left in a cool place for ten minutes, rolled out, and the pie covered.

## PIE CRUST, No. 3.

Chop up the suet very fine and roll it, place the flour, suet or dripping, baking powder, and salt in a dish; well mix the whole together and work it into a smooth paste with cold water; roll it out and it is ready for use.

When preparing this paste, the dripping must not be rubbed into the flour, but chopped first.

### REMARKS ON PUDDINGS.

Puddings are variously compounded, but are always either boiled or baked. When boiled a cloth or bag well floured inside should be used to envelop them.

It must be dipped into boiling water and then wrung out before the flour is applied.

The seams of the bag must be thoroughly secured or felled, and sufficient room allowed for the pudding to swell. The water must be boiling when the pudding is put in, kept constantly boiling during the cooking, and must cover the bag. Should it be necessary to add water as evaporation takes place, the added water must be boiling. The bag should be turned several times under water to prevent its resting against the bottom or sides of the vessel, to guard against scorching.

When the pudding is cooked take it from the pot and plunge it into cold water for an instant. Then turn it out from the bag or cloth on the dish in which it is to be served.

### PLAIN DUFF.

#### (Sufficient for 22 men.)

| | |
|---|---|
| 5 pounds flour. | 1 ounce salt. |
| 1¼ pounds suet or fat. | ¼ ounce pepper. |

Water.

Prepare the paste the same as for Bombshells. Have a clean pudding cloth ready, flour it, and place the paste in it, and tie it up lengthwise; it will take one and a half hours; if tied round as a ball, two hours. This quantity will do for 60 dumplings.

### PLUM DUFF.

To make Plum Duff omit the pepper and add two pounds of plums, raisins, or prunes.

### BAKED RICE PUDDING.

#### (Sufficient for 22 men.)

| | |
|---|---|
| 4 pounds rice. | ¼ ounce salt. |
| 1 pound sugar. | ½ ounce cinnamon. |

2 quarts milk.

Have two gallons of boiling water, in which place the rice, that has been previously washed; add the salt, and boil for twenty minutes; strain off any water that may remain.  Have a baking dish ready, well greased; mix the rice with two quarts milk, the sugar, and cinnamon, place it in the dish, and bake for thirty minutes.

### RICE AND POTATO PUDDING.
(Sufficient for 22 men.)

| | |
|---|---|
| 2 pounds rice. | 1 quart milk. |
| 6 pounds potatoes. | 2 pounds sugar. |
| 1 pound suet. | ½ ounce salt. |

Prepare the rice as in Baked Rice Pudding, then put it into a stewpan with the milk, sugar, and salt, and boil for one hour; if it is too dry, add water.  Boil the potatoes, peel and mash them, and add them to the rice; chop up the suet, and mix the whole; butter a baking dish, pour the mixture in, and bake in a *quick* oven for thirty minutes.

### INDIAN-MEAL DUMPLINGS.
(Sufficient for 22 men.)

| | |
|---|---|
| 3 pounds Indian meal. | 1 ounce salt. |
| 1 pound flour. | 1 pound suet or fat. |
| 1 pint molasses. | |

Soak the meal, skim it, boil it in three quarts of water for one hour, take it out, mix it with the flour, salt, molasses, and suet, cut small, flour some cloths, make the paste into balls about three inches in diameter, tie them up each in a cloth, and boil for one hour.

NOTE.—The above may be made plain with butter and milk, and carbonate of soda, or with a baking powder.

### CANNON BALLS.
(Sufficient for 22 men.)

| | |
|---|---|
| 6 pounds flour. | 3 pints molasses. |
| 1½ pounds suet. | 1 pint water. |

Chop up the suet, mix with the flour, mix the molasses with the water, put the flour into a bowl, and pour the molasses gradually upon it, mixing it with the flour; when the whole is well mixed, not too soft, form it into any size balls required, flour some cloths, tie up each ball separately in cloth, not too tight, and boil from one hour and upward, according to size.

NOTE.—These, with lime-juice sauce, are an excellent anti-scorbutic, and will keep good for twelve months, and longer. They could be made before going on any long voyage, and given out as rations.

In the tropics, where fruit is cheap, the fruit is mixed with the molasses, but less fat is used.

In Italy honey and verjuice, or vinegar, are used instead of treacle.

### RICE TOAD-IN-THE-HOLE.

(Sufficient for 22 men.)

| | |
|---|---|
| 4 pounds rice. | ¼ ounce salt. |
| 2 pounds sugar. | ¼ ounce cinnamon. |
| 2 quarts milk. | 22 apples. |

Treat the rice as in Baked Rice Pudding, and place it in the baking dish; have some apples peeled and sliced, lay them in the rice, sift sugar over them, and bake.

### ARTILLERY PIE.

(Sufficient for 22 men.)

| | |
|---|---|
| 8 pounds bread. | 4 dozen apples. |
| 1 pound suet. | 2 pounds sugar. |

Melt the suet in a frying pan, cut the bread into slices one-quarter of an inch in thickness, dip each piece into the melted fat, and place them in the oven to dry. In the meantime get the apples peeled, boiled, and mashed with the sugar. Cover the bottom of the baking dish with the bread, cover the bread with some of the apples, then some more bread over that, then the apples, and thus until all is used; place it in an oven and bake for twenty minutes. This may be made with any kind of fruit.

## BOILED YEAST DUMPLING.

Make a light dough, or procure from the bakery dough which is ready for the oven.

Flour the hands well and mold the dough into balls about the size of an egg. Drop them successively into boiling water. Boil fifteen minutes. Remove them from the pot with perforated skimmer, to allow the water to drain. Serve at once. Eat with hot sauce or sugar and butter.

## PLUM PUDDING, No. 1.

The ingredients of this pudding, with the exception of the eggs and milk, should be prepared the day before the pudding is to be made.

Two quarts sifted flour; two quarts bread crumbs; four pounds suet, freed from fiber and chopped moderately fine; four pounds raisins, picked, seeded, chopped, and dredged with flour; sixteen eggs, whites and yolks beaten separately; two quarts sweet milk (or equivalent of condensed milk); a fourth of a pound of citron, cut fine and dredged with flour; grated rind of one lemon; two nutmegs, grated; one tablespoonful ground ginger; one tablespoonful ground cinnamon; one teaspoonful ground cloves.

Into a deep pan or dish put the ingredients in the following order, incorporating them thoroughly: First, the beaten yolks of the eggs; then one-half the milk; then the flour, bread crumbs, suet, spices, and lemon rind; then the remainder of the milk, or as much of it as will make a thick batter; then the beaten whites of the eggs; and last the dredged fruit.

Beat the mixture for thirty minutes, put it into the prepared bag or bags, and boil seven hours. Serve hot with sauce.

The above recipe is enough for thirty men.

## PLUM PUDDING, No. 2.

Prepare the suet and raisins the day before this pudding is to be made.

Six quarts sifted flour; three pounds suet, freed from fiber and chopped moderately fine; three pounds raisins, picked, seeded, chopped, and dredged with flour; two pounds brown sugar, or, in lieu of sugar, three and one-half pints molasses; one tablespoonful salt; two quarts sour milk; if sour milk is not obtainable, put enough vinegar into either sweet or prepared condensed milk to sour it; two dessert-spoonfuls of soda or saleratus, dissolved in a little hot water; eight tablespoonfuls ground cinnamon; three teaspoonfuls ground cloves.

Mix ingredients in the following order: Having the flour in a deep dish or pan, stir into it the salt, suet, spices, and sugar or molasses.

Put the dissolved soda into the milk; then add the milk or so much of it as will make a thick batter; finally add the dredged fruit; beat the mixture for ten minutes; put it into prepared bag or bags and boil six hours. Serve hot with sauce.

The above is enough for thirty men.

## PLUM PUDDING, No. 3.

The quantities here given will serve for a mess of five or six.

One cup molasses; one cup beef suet, freed from fiber and chopped fine; one cup sweet milk; one cup raisins, picked, seeded, chopped, and dredged with flour; three cups sifted flour; one teaspoonful salt; one teaspoonful ground cinnamon; one teaspoonful ground cloves; one-half teaspoonful soda; one egg.

Put soda into molasses and stir very hard. Beat the egg well and stir it into molasses, then add the flour, salt, spices, suet, and fruits.

Put into prepared bag and boil three hours.

## PLUM PUDDING, No. 4.

The suet and raisins for this pudding should be prepared the day before.

Two quarts sifted flour; one tablespoonful salt; two tablespoonfuls baking powder; one pound suet, freed from fiber and chopped fine; one and one-half pounds raisins, picked, seeded, chopped, and dredged with flour; one and one-half pints molasses.

Put flour into a deep dish or pan. Into flour mix the baking powder, then salt, suet, molasses, and dredged fruit. To this mixture add gradually sufficient cold water to make a stiff, firm batter.

Put into prepared bag or bags and boil three hours. Serve hot, with a sweet sauce.

Ten men can be supplied from above recipe.

### BOILED OMAHA PUDDING.

| | |
|---|---|
| 2 quarts sifted flour. | 2 heaping teaspoonfuls salt. |
| 2 tablespoonfuls baking powder. | About 1 pint cold water (milk is preferable). |

In a deep dish mix the flour and baking powder, dissolve the salt in the water, add enough of the water to the flour to make a very thick batter. Mix quickly. Put into prepared bag or cloth and boil one hour.

Serve as soon as cooked and eat with sirup.

### BOILED ROLL PUDDING.

In this pudding stewed dried apples, peaches, prunes, canned fruit, jams, jellies, marmalades, or ripe uncooked currants, raspberries, strawberries, blackberries, or huckleberries may be used.

If dried fruits are used they must be prepared as directed for dried apples, etc., but if ripe, uncooked fruits are used they must be carefully picked, and when spread upon the paste must have sufficient sugar sprinkled upon them to make them palatable.

| | |
|---|---|
| 1 quart sifted flour. | Cold water. |
| ½ teaspoonful salt. | Fruit. |
| ¼ pound suet, freed from fiber, and chopped fine. | |

Put the flour into a deep dish, and mix into it the suet and salt. Then add cold water gradually, enough to make rather a firm paste. Mixing should be done with the hands and done quickly. Remove paste to a well-floured bread board. Dredge the paste liberally with sifted flour and roll it out into an oblong sheet about one-half inch thick.

Spread the paste thickly with the fruit to within an inch of its outer edge. Roll it up; close the free edges by pressure with the fingers to prevent escape of juices. Envelop it in a cotton cloth well floured on the inside. Tie the ends firmly and tack the edge of the cloth. Boil from one and one-half to two hours. Serve hot with sauce.

### BOILED APPLE PUDDING.

Pare, core, and slice the apples; make a paste as directed for Roll Pudding.

Roll the dough into a circular sheet about half an inch thick; place the prepared apples in the center of the sheet; sprinkle them lightly with sugar; leave enough of the dough so that it can be taken up and closed over the apples. Put into a bag or cloth and boil from two to two and a half hours.

Serve with a hot sauce, or rock butter. Peaches pared, sliced, and the stones extracted, can be substituted for apples.

### ROLY-POLY.

| | |
|---|---|
| ½ pound flour. | 5 ounces suet. |
| ¼ teaspoonful salt. | 1 pint jam or jelly. |

Free suet from fiber and skin and chop fine; add salt and flour. Mix well and add gradually enough cold water to make it stick together. Roll out one inch thick, on a well-floured board, spread jam or jelly thickly over paste, roll it up, tie in well-floured cloth, leaving room to swell. Place in a pot of boiling water and boil two hours, or steam two and one-half hours. Serve hot with sauce.

## BOILED BATTER PUDDING.

1 heaping quart sifted flour.      1 quart sweet milk.
7 eggs, yolks and whites beaten separately, whites to a stiff froth.
¼ teaspoonful (about) soda in sufficient hot water to dissolve it.
2 teaspoonfuls salt.

Flour in a deep dish or pan; put into it the milk, gradually working it into a smooth paste. Then mix in the yolks, salt, and dissolved soda. Stir hard. Finally, stir in quickly the whites.

Put into prepared bag or cloth, leaving ample room for pudding to swell, and boil two hours. Serve hot. Eat with sirup, butter, and sugar, or a hot sauce.

## BOILED CORNSTARCH PUDDING.

1 quart sweet milk.      3 tablespoonfuls cornstarch.
2 or 3 eggs, beaten light.      Light pinch salt.

Dissolve the cornstarch in a small portion of the milk; then add the eggs and salt. Heat the milk not used in mixing the cornstarch to nearly boiling, then add the cornstarch and milk. Boil four minutes, stirring constantly to prevent scorching.

Then turn it into a mold or bowl which has previously been dipped into cold water and set it away to cool. When cold turn out on a dish and serve.

To be eaten with cream and sugar.

## BOILED INDIAN-MEAL PUDDING.

1 quart Indian meal.      1 quart sweet milk.
3 heaping tablespoonfuls sugar.      1 teaspoonful salt.
¼ pound suet, freed from fiber and chopped very fine.
3 eggs, yolks and whites separated, whites to a stiff froth;
beat yolks and sugar together.

Heat milk to boiling and remove it from the stove. Then gradually stir in the meal, suet, and salt (these three ingredients having been previously mixed); when the milk, meal, etc., have become cold, stir into them the beaten yolks and sugar.   Then mix in the whites of the eggs and put the pudding into the bag.

For this pudding fill the bag only half full.

Follow directions for boiled pudding.   Cook five hours, serve hot, and eat with sauce or butter and sugar.

### REMARKS ON BAKED PUDDINGS.

When eggs are used the whites and yolks should be beaten separately, the whites to a stiff froth. Sugar should always be mixed with the beaten yolks.

The beaten whites should be the last ingredient to go into the compound unless the recipe calls for dredged fruits.

Baked puddings should go into the oven the moment the mixture is made; this is essential if eggs are depended upon to lighten the dish.   More time may be allowed if yeast is used.

The baking dish or pan must be well greased before the pudding is put in.   Lard is best for this purpose, although butter or sweet beef dripping will do.

Fruit, rice, cornstarch, and bread puddings require a steady, moderate oven whilst baking.   Custard and batter puddings require a hot, quick oven, and must cook rapidly.   To prevent the bottom of the pudding from burning, place the baking dish on an inverted pan or a gridiron in the bottom of the oven.

If the top of the pudding shows signs of burning, cover it with a sheet of writing paper or an inverted tin plate.

Remove the covering in time to allow the top to brown before serving.

Jarring the oven by opening its doors or walking about the kitchen floor should be avoided while the pudding is in the oven.

## BAKED BATTER PUDDING.

Make a batter as directed for Boiled Batter Pudding; pour it into a well-greased dish and bake fifty minutes; serve hot in the dish in which it was baked, and eat with butter and sugar.

## BROWN BETTY.

Cooking apples, pared, cored, and sliced; dry-bread crumbs, or well-toasted bread rolled into crumbs; sugar, butter, and ground cinnamon.

Grease well a deep baking dish. Into the bottom of this put a layer of prepared apples; sprinkle them lightly with sugar; scatter small pieces of butter over this, then dust with ground cinnamon; over this place a layer of bread crumbs from one-half to three-quarters of an inch thick; over this apples, butter, and cinnamon, and continue this process until the dish is full, or until sufficient material has been used. The top layer must be crumbs, and on this must be scattered small pieces of butter. If the top layer is moistened with a couple of tablespoonfuls of milk it will brown more evenly.

Bake in a moderate oven from one-half to three-quarters of an hour.

When a fork will easily penetrate the apples it is cooked. Alden dried apples may be substituted for the fresh fruit.

It can be eaten hot or cold with butter, sugar, or sauce.

## BAKED CORNSTARCH PUDDING.

| | |
|---|---|
| 1 quart sweet milk. | 4 tablespoonfuls sugar. |
| 3 tablespoonfuls cornstarch. | 1 teaspoonful ground cinnamon. |
| 2 or 3 eggs, beaten light. | Pinch of salt. |

Dissolve the cornstarch in a small portion of the milk. Into the remainder of the milk stir the sugar, salt, and cinnamon. Heat this to boiling point. Then add cornstarch and milk. Boil briskly four minutes, stirring constantly to prevent scorching. Set away to cool. When cold, stir in the beaten eggs, pour into a well-greased baking dish, and bake half an hour in a moderate oven.

### BAKED RICE PUDDING, WITH EGGS.

1 pint rice, picked and well washed.    2 tablespoonfuls melted butter.
1 gallon sweet milk.
1 lb. raisins, picked, seeded, cut in two, and dredged with flour.
12 eggs; beat whites and yolks separately, whites to a stiff froth.
1 pound sugar incorporated with the beaten yolks.
Flavor with nutmeg.

Cover the rice with a portion of the milk and soak it for an hour. Put rice and milk in which it was soaked on the stove and heat to boiling; boil five minutes; remove and set away to cool. When cool, stir in the beaten yolks and sugar, melted butter, nutmeg, and remainder of the milk, then the beaten whites of the eggs, and, last, the dredged fruit.

Put the mixture immediately into a well-greased baking dish and bake in a moderate oven to a rich brown. Time of baking, one to one and one-half hours.

Serve hot or cold. If cold, eat with cream and sugar; if hot, with sauce.

### BAKED RICE PUDDING, WITHOUT EGGS.

1 quart rice, picked and well washed.    2 teaspoonfuls salt.
6 quarts sweet milk.    1 pound sugar.
Enough nutmeg and cinnamon to flavor.

Cover the rice with a portion of the milk and soak it two hours; then add the remainder of the milk, and stir into this the sugar, salt, and spices.

Put into a well-greased baking dish and bake from two to two and one-half hours in a slow oven. Serve hot or cold.

## BAKED CRACKER PUDDING.

1 quart powdered cracker.
7 pints sweet milk.
¼ pound melted butter.

16 eggs, whites and yolks
separated, whites beaten
to a stiff froth.

Put powdered cracker into a deep dish. Heat the milk slightly and pour over the cracker and soak for ten or fifteen minutes; then stir in the beaten yolks and melted butter. Finally stir in quickly the beaten whites, and put the mixture at once into a well-greased baking dish, and bake in a moderate oven from three-quarters of an hour to one hour. Top should be nicely trimmed. Hard bread may be substituted for crackers.

## BAKED BREAD PUDDING.

1 quart bread crumbs, dry.
2 quarts sweet milk.
6 to 8 eggs, whites beaten to a stiff froth.
Grated nutmeg enough to flavor.

3 tablespoonfuls melted butter.
3 tablespoonfuls sugar.

Put crumbs into a deep dish. Heat milk to boiling and pour it over the crumbs. Soak until crumbs become soft. Add incorporated yolks and sugar, then the melted butter and nutmeg; finally stir in quickly the beaten whites.

Put mixture at once into a well-greased baking dish, and bake to a brown. Time of baking, one hour to one hour and a half. Eat hot or cold.

## BAKED BREAD-AND-FRUIT PUDDING.

1½ pints bread crumbs, dry.
3 tablespoonfuls melted butter.
6 to 8 eggs, whites beaten to a stiff froth.
1 lb. raisins, picked, seeded, chopped, and dredged with flour.

2 quarts sweet milk.
Flavor with nutmeg.

Mix ingredients as prescribed for Baked Bread Pudding, and put the dredged fruit in last.

A little longer time will be required to bake this than baked bread pudding, owing to the presence of the fruit.

## BAKED APPLE PUDDING.

Apples pared, cored, and sliced.       ½ teaspoonful salt.
Sugar, butter, and cinnamon.       1 quart sifted flour.
3 teaspoonfuls baking powder, incorporated with the dry flour.
2 tablespoonfuls lard (half butter is preferable).
1 pint milk (if milk is not available ice water will do).

Put flour into a deep dish or pan; mix into it the salt and lard; then add the milk, and work the mixture with the hands to a smooth light dough.

Roll the dough into a sheet about one-quarter of an inch thick. Have prepared a well-greased baking dish. Cover the bottom and sides of a well-greased baking dish with the rolled dough, press it lightly against the sides and bottom, and cut off the edges above the baking dish with a sharp knife.

Put into the bottom of the baking dish a thick layer of sliced apples, sprinkle it with sugar and ground cinnamon, then another layer of apples treated in like manner, and so on successively until the dish is full. The top layer of apples should have a dressing of sugar, cinnamon, and small pieces of butter. Wet the top layer with three or four teaspoonfuls of water, and then sprinkle it lightly with dry flour.

Take the remainder of the dough, roll it out thin, and cover the dish with it, pressing the paste down round the edges of the dish to join it with the paste that lines the sides. Make three or four incisions in the cover with a sharp knife.

Then bake in a moderate oven from one to one and one-half hours. When a fork easily penetrates the pudding, it is cooked. Eat hot with sauce. Alden dried apples, canned apples, canned peaches, or fresh peaches pared, quartered, and the stones extracted, may be used.

## BAKED APPLE DUMPLINGS.

The apples pared, cored, and quartered. Prepare paste as directed in Baked Apple Pudding.

When the paste is rolled, cut it into squares, and in the center of each square place the four parts of an apple; add to each apple a piece of butter the size of a chestnut and a sprinkle of sugar and cinnamon.

Envelop the apple in the paste, pressing the edges together. Place the dumplings thus prepared into a well-greased baking pan, edges down.

Bake one-half to three-quarters of an hour in a moderate oven. When a fork will easily penetrate the dumplings they are cooked. Alden dried apples may be used.

## BAKED PUMPKIN PUDDING.

| | |
|---|---|
| 1 quart molasses (not sirup). | 4 tablespoonfuls brown sugar. |
| 1 quart sweet milk. | 1 quart stewed pumpkin. |
| 4 tablespoonfuls ground ginger. | 6 eggs, yolks and whites beaten together. |

Mix the molasses and milk, adding sugar and ginger. Then stir in gradually the beaten eggs, and then by degrees the stewed pumpkin, or enough of the pumpkin to make a thick batter. Put into a deep dish and bake.

Stewed winter squash is an excellent substitute for stewed pumpkin.

## BAKED HOMINY PUDDING.

| | |
|---|---|
| 1 cup boiled hominy (cold). | 1 large teaspoonful butter, melted. |
| 2 cups sweet milk. | 1 teaspoonful white sugar. |
| 3 eggs, whites and yolks beaten separately, whites to a stiff froth. | |
| Pinch of salt. | |

Work the beaten yolks into the hominy alternately with the melted butter. When these ingredients are mixed, put in sugar and salt. Continue beating; soften the batter with the milk, added gradually; be careful to have the batter smooth. Lastly, stir in the beaten whites.

Put into a well-greased baking pan and bake until firm and lightly brown.

### DOUGHNUTS.

On baking day, take two pounds of very light bread dough that has been make in the usual manner.  Put it into a broad pan.  Rub into it half a pound of fresh butter and half a pound of powdered sugar, and a tablespoonful of mixed nutmeg and cinnamon.  Wet it with half a pint of milk, and mix in three well-beaten eggs.  Cover it and set by the fire to rise again.  When quite light, flour your bread board, and make the dough into oval balls; or, it may be cut into diamond shapes (handling it as little as possible).  Have ready, over the fire, a pot of boiling lard.  Drop the doughnuts into it and boil them; or, fry them brown in a frying pan. Take them out one by one in a perforated skimmer, draining back the lard into the pan.  Spread them on a large dish, and sift sugar over them.  Eat them fresh; when heavy and stale they are not fit. This is a German cake.

### COMMON CRULLERS.

The above mixture for doughnuts will make good crullers.  Flour your bread board, lay the dough upon it, roll it very thick, and cut it into strips with a' jagging iron.  Take off short pieces and twist them into various forms.  Throw them into a pot of boiling lard.  When done, drain the lard from them, spread them on a large dish, and dredge them with powdered white sugar.

The alpistera is a Spanish cruller, shaped like the five fingers united at the wrist.

## SAUCES.

### Apple Sauce.

Pare, core, and slice six tart apples, and put them in a kettle, with one-half cup of water. Cook and stir until soft (about ten minutes). Then mash them through a sieve. Add sugar and nutmeg to taste, mix well, and it is ready for use.

### Rock Butter.

Butter; powdered or granulated sugar, and nutmeg, lemon, or vanilla.

To the butter used, take twice the weight of sugar; beat together until the whole is brought to a smooth mass. This is called creaming. Flavor with nutmeg, lemon, or vanilla.

In cold weather soften the butter before beating, but do not melt it.

### Hot Sauce, No. 1.

Butter the size of an egg. Pinch of salt.
1 cup sugar. 1 pint boiling water.
2 tablespoonfuls of sifted flour or cornstarch, mixed in enough cold water to make a smooth, consistent paste.
Nutmeg and cinnamon to taste.

Put butter and sugar into a saucepan; pour in the boiling water; stir in the mixed flour or cornstarch, salt, nutmeg, and cinnamon; boil two minutes.

### Hot Sauce, No. 2.

¼ cup butter. 1 quart boiling water.
2 tablespoonfuls sifted flour or cornstarch, mixed in enough cold water to make a smooth paste.
2 cups sugar. Flavor with nutmeg or cinnamon.

Cream the butter and sugar in a bowl; pour in it the mixed flour or cornstarch; beat thoroughly; then pour in the boiling water.

## Hot Sauce, No. 3.

4 tablespoonfuls sugar.  2 eggs (the yolks only).
1 tablespoonful sifted flour or cornstarch, mixed in
  enough cold water to make a smooth paste.
1 pint sweet milk.  Flavor with lemon or vanilla extract.

Mix ingredients well together; put in saucepan, boil, stir constantly until it begins to thicken, when it is cooked.  Flavor with lemon or vanilla.

## Hot Sauce, No. 4.

A little less than a quart of boiling water; 1 cup of sugar; butter the size of a walnut; 1 tablespoonful sifted flour or cornstarch, mixed in enough cold water to make a smooth paste; flavor with grated rind of lemon, cinnamon, nutmeg, or extract of lemon or vanilla.

Stir into the boiling water the mixed flour or cornstarch and sugar.  If grated lemon rind or ground cinnamon is used, add it now.  Boil for two or three minutes.  Remove from the fire, then stir in butter.  If grated nutmeg or flavoring extracts are to be used add them after the butter.

## SPANISH STEW.

Cold cooked meat.  1 onion.
1 tablespoonful beef dripping.  1 chile pepper.
4 ripe tomatoes.

Heat dripping in a skillet.  Add meat cut fine. Fry for a few minutes, then add chopped onions, chile, and tomatoes.  Cover and simmer twenty minutes.  Just before removing from fire add a little thickening of flour or cornstarch.  Cook thoroughly two or three minutes, and serve hot.

## SPANISH STEAK.

| | |
|---|---|
| 2 pounds round steak. | 2 cloves. |
| 6 red chiles. | 1 tablespoonful flour. |

A little garlic, thyme, and dripping.

Seed the chiles and cover with boiling water. Soak until tender and then scrape the pulp into water. Cut steak into small pieces, fry brown in hot dripping or butter; add flour and brown it. Cover with the chile water; add garlic and thyme. Simmer until the meat is tender and the gravy of the right consistency.

## "ESTUFADO."

| | |
|---|---|
| 2 pounds beef (ribs) or mutton. | 1 tablespoonful dripping. |
| Onions and green peppers to taste. | 4 slices toast. |

A little black pepper, garlic, vinegar, thyme, raisins, olives, tomatoes.

Heat dripping in saucepan, put it into the ingredients (leave peppers whole and mince garlic). Cover closely and stew thoroughly. Serve on toast.

## DRIED BEEF, WITH PEPPERS.

| | |
|---|---|
| 2 lbs. "jerked" dried beef. | 2 ounces dripping. |
| 1 onion. | 4 red peppers. |

Browned flour.

Place beef in a pan in hot oven ten minutes, then shred, place in a frying pan with onion and dripping, and fry five minutes. Pour boiling water over peppers, pass them through a sieve, and mix with beef. Thicken with browned flour, season to taste, cook twenty minutes, and serve piping hot.

## "SALZA" (Sauce).

| | |
|---|---|
| 3 large ripe tomatoes. | 1 small onion. |
| 5 hot green peppers. | 2 tablespoonfuls vinegar. |

Salt.

Lay peppers on coals, turning them until blistered; throw them into cold water, and then remove seeds

and skins. Skin tomatoes and chop all together
until quite fine. Strain off juice and add salt and
vinegar.

To be served with soup or meat as a relish.

### "FRIJOLES."

| | |
|---|---|
| 1 cup Mexican beans. | 1 long red pepper. |
| ½ clove garlic. | 1 thin small slice bacon. |

Soak beans over night; boil slowly until soft—
from eight to ten hours. Add red pepper, garlic,
and bacon, and bake.

### "FRIJOLES CON QUESO."

(Beans with cheese.)

| | |
|---|---|
| 1 quart red beans. | 4 tablespoonfuls dripping. |
| ½ pound good cheese. | Salt. |

A little cayenne pepper.

Boil beans until soft, drain, and turn into a frying pan with dripping. Salt to taste. Add the
pepper and cheese, grated. Stir until cheese dis-
solves and thoroughly blends. Serve very hot.

### STUFFED CHILES (GREEN).

| | |
|---|---|
| 6 chiles (green). | 1 tablespoonful vinegar. |
| 2 pounds meat. | 1 tablespoonful sugar. |
| 2 onions. | Olives and raisins. |
| 1 large ripe tomato. | Salt and pepper. |
| 2 slices bread. | Dripping and flour. |

Remove stems and seeds from the chiles. Boil
meat until tender and chop fine. Add tomato,
onions, and bread, chopped fine. Add raisins,
olives, vinegar, and salt. Sugar and pepper to
taste. Fry all together in the dripping. Remove
from fire and stuff the chiles. Dip the chiles in
batter and fry in dripping.

## BRAINS (SPANISH STYLE).

Soak brains an hour. Vein and prepare thoroughly. Beat till fine and foaming like omelet. Add one egg; tablespoonful dried bread crumbs; salt and pepper and a trifle of grated onion. Spread eight slices of fresh bread with the prepared brains, place in a dripping pan, and bake in a hot oven about ten minutes. Remove from the oven and place the bread in a pan with hot dripping and fry carefully, so that the bread is a light brown on the underside. Serve immediately with Spanish rice.

## "TAMALES."

Take two quarts yellow, dried corn and boil in water mixed with one-half teacupful lime. Let it boil until well cooked. Wash thoroughly and grind on the "metate" three times, until it becomes very fine. Boil a piece of beef until tender, water being seasoned with salt. Remove and let cool; then cut in small pieces. Mix with corn (which has been rolled on the "metate") enough of the water in which the beef was boiled to make it soft, and add two cups of dripping. Season with a little salt and knead thoroughly. After this take three dozen red chiles, remove seeds, then roast in a moderate oven for a few seconds. Remove from oven and place in tepid water, then grind on the "metate" several times, together with almost a head of garlic. Strain carefully.

In a stewpan place some dripping, and when hot drop in one onion, cut fine, and a spoonful of flour. Let it cook a little while, and then drop in the chile. Let it come to a boil, then add the cut meat, a cup of raisins, a cup of olives, a teaspoonful of sugar, a little salt and pepper, and let it boil again. Then remove from the fire. Soak dry corn leaves in cold water; when well soaked shake them well and apply a thin layer of the corn dough on the half of each

leaf, then put a spoonful of the stew on the prepared leaf and cover with prepared leaves and tie
the ends with strings made of the same leaf.

When tamales are finished, place them in a large
pot with a little boiling water, and boil them one
hour. Any other meat can be used if desired. The
"metate" can be purchased at any Mexican store.

### "TORTILLAS."

| | |
|---|---|
| 1 quart flour. | 2 tablespoonfuls dripping. |
| 1 cup milk. | Salt. |

Make a dough and knead thoroughly. Take
pieces of the dough and pat between the hands
until it makes a large, round, thin cake. Bake on
a griddle until brown.

### "CHILE CON CARNE."

| | |
|---|---|
| Beefsteak (round). | 1 cup boiling water. |
| 1 tablespoonful hot dripping. | 2 large red peppers (dry). |
| 2 tablespoonfuls rice. | ¼ pint boiling water. |
| Salt, onions, flour. | |

Cut steak in small pieces. Put in a frying pan
with hot dripping, hot water, and rice. Cover
closely and cook slowly until tender. Remove
seeds and part of veins from peppers. Cover with
one-half pint boiling water and let them stand until
cool. Then squeeze them in the hand until the
water is thick and red. If not thick enough add
a little flour. Season with salt and a little onion, if
desired. Pour sauce on meat and serve very hot.

### SPANISH FRIED RICE.

| | |
|---|---|
| Rice. | Salt. |
| Dripping. | Black pepper. |
| Onions. | Hot water. |
| Garlic. | Tomatoes. |

Wash the rice and brown it in hot dripping. Then
add onions, tomatoes, and garlic. Cover the whole

with hot water. Season with salt and pepper. Let rice cook thoroughly, adding water as needed. but do not stir it.

## JAMBALAYA.

### (A Spanish Creole dish.)

| | |
|---|---|
| 1 lb. rice (wash and soak 1 hour). | 1 lb. sausage (cut up). |
| | 2 large tomatoes. |
| 1 lb. ham (cut up). | Small piece red pepper. |
| 2 onions. | A sprig of parsley. |

Fry these in a heaping spoonful of dripping or butter, then add about one pint of boiling water. Stir in the rice slowly, cover the pot and set it where it can cook slowly. Salt to taste and serve while hot. Jambalaya is nice made with oysters, shrimps, or chicken substituted for sausage.

## REMARKS ON COFFEE AND TEA.

*Rio coffee* is generally provided for the use of troops at eastern stations, while on the Pacific coast Central American is preferred, both being good strong coffees. Coffee should be regular in grain (so as to roast evenly) and uniform in color. All coffee improves in flavor by age.

The presence of wormholes in coffee should not occasion its rejection unless it is of inferior quality and strength, since they generally indicate age, weigh nothing, and disappear when the coffee is ground. All coffees should be well cleaned before being roasted.

*Mocha coffee* has a small irregular grain and is quite strong.

*Java coffee* is generally yellow or light brown in color and a large grain. It is the mildest coffee furnished by the Subsistence Department, and when strong coffee is wanted more than the usual quantity should be used, or it can be mixed with sufficient Mocha, Rio, or other strong coffee well ground together. To insure the best results both in strength and flavor coffee should be ground fine.

*Tea.*—The kinds of tea found to be most popular in the Army are Oolong and Souchong among the black teas, and of strictly green teas Hyson and Young Hyson are preferable to Gunpowder and Imperial, being generally cheaper for the same quality.

Souchong is commonly known as English Breakfast Tea, although Congou is frequently sold under the same name. The leaves are dark brown, almost black. Great care is needed in selecting it, as a poor "English Breakfast" is a very poor tea.

Oolong tea is coarse in the dried leaf, loosely wrapped, and of a dark brown color verging toward olive. The fragrance reminds one of new hay, but is stronger and spicier. It is generally the best tea, being stronger than "English Breakfast" and less stimulating than green tea.

Japan green tea is an excellent tea, and being generally of a natural color is less injurious than Hyson, Imperial, or Gunpowder, which are artificially colored.

### TO ROAST COFFEE.

Pick over the coffee carefully; wash it in clean, cold water; wash thoroughly and quickly; drain, and when dry put it into a coffee roaster or baking pan; roast quickly to a light brown, stirring frequently.

Coffee may be vastly improved before roasting by adding to every three pounds of coffee a piece of butter the size of a nut, and a dessert-spoonful of powdered sugar, and then roasting in the usual manner.

Coffee should be evenly roasted; a few burned berries will impart a disagreeable flavor to the coffee when made.

When the coffee has been roasted, turn it on a clean cloth; cover with a cloth and let it cool; when cold pick out the burned grains.

Then put the coffee into a vessel with a close-fitting top. Only sufficient to last four or five days should be roasted at a time. Coffee should not be ground until it is wanted for use. It is better to roast it daily.

### TO PREPARE COFFEE, No. 1.

Coffee is best when made from the freshly roasted berry. To one pound of coffee, roasted and ground, add ten quarts of boiling water in some convenient vessel, cover the vessel closely to prevent escape of aroma, and place it in a vessel of boiling water, being careful not to let it rest on the bottom of the outer vessel. Boil fifteen minutes.

The water in which the coffee is mixed does not boil but remains at a temperature a few degrees below the boiling point. It can be cleared by pouring it through a piece of flannel or a hair sieve. This will make a strong infusion.

### TO PREPARE COFFEE, No. 2.

The vessel should be clean and the water fresh and clear. Fill the vessel with the necessary quantity of water and put it over a brisk fire. When it comes to a boil stir in the coffee, previously moistened with warm (not hot) water. Cover closely; let it boil up for two minutes, stirring from the sides and top as it boils up. Exercise great care that the coffee does not boil over. To clear it remove it from the fire and dash over the surface a cup of cold fresh water; cover closely and set it on the back of the stove to keep warm but not to boil.

### A SIMPLE METHOD OF MAKING COFFEE, No. 1.

Allow one-half ounce or one tablespoonful of ground coffee to each person; to every ounce allow one-half pint of water.

Have a small iron ring made to fit the top of the coffeepot inside, and to this ring sew a small muslin bag (the muslin for the purpose must not be too thin). Fit the bag into the pot, pour the ground coffee into the bag; pour over as much boiling water as is required; close the lid, and, when all the water has filtered through, remove the bag, and send the coffee to the table. Making it in this manner prevents the necessity of pouring the coffee from one vessel to another, which cools and spoils it. The water should be poured on the coffee gradually, so that the infusion may be stronger; and the bag must be well made, that none of the grounds may escape through the seams, and so make the coffee thick and muddy.

### A SIMPLE METHOD OF MAKING COFFEE, No. 2.

Put the dry coffee in the pot; stir it while heating; then pour over it one *quart* of *boiling* water to each *ounce of coffee*, and set the pot where it will keep hot but not boil. After standing ten minutes it is ready to drink.

### TEA.

For mixed tea the usual proportion is four spoonfuls of black to one of green.

The water with which tea is to be made should be fresh from the well or cistern; it is better if from a spring or rapid stream; it should not be made from water that has stood on the stove or in the water back. The making should be accurately timed so that it may be served as soon as drawn.

Bring the water to a hard boil as quickly as possible; fill the teapot with boiling water and set it on the stove or before the fire for one minute in order to heat the pot. This is necessary, for if the pot is not heated it will chill the tea water. Having thoroughly heated the pot, pour off the water and put into the pot one teaspoonful of tea for every teacupful of tea that is to be drawn, and one for the pot; then pour on the *boiling* water and set the covered pot on the stove or near the fire to draw, but not to boil. It should draw long enough to liberate the essential oil, which constitutes its aroma, but not long enough to drive it off or to dissolve the tannin, which gives the tea an astringent and disagreeable taste. The time for drawing varies with the different teas, and may be stated generally as follows: Green tea, five minutes; Oolong tea, eight minutes; English breakfast, fifteen minutes. The faults commonly committed in making tea are as follows: The water is flat from having been long on the stove, or the tea not made from the water on its first boil; the water is only hot and *not boiling;* the teapot is not heated before putting in the tea; the tea is boiled instead of drawn (no tea should be boiled); the tea is made too long before it is to be drunk.

### CHOCOLATE.

*Chocolate* is produced chiefly from the seeds of the cocoa palm ground to a fine powder, mixed with sugar, and reduced by great pressure to thin cakes.

*Cocoa nibs* are the seeds roughly broken, and may be boiled, but they are not as soluble as the prepared chocolate.

Scrape fine an ounce of chocolate and add an ounce of sugar; throw these into a pint of perfectly *boiling* milk and water, of each one half, and immediately mill and stir them well for two or three minutes until the chocolate and sugar are quite dissolved. Some think that ten or twelve minutes' boiling improves it. Chocolate should never be made unless to be used immediately.

If suffered to become cold or boiled again the flavor is injured.

### COOKING CANNED GOODS.

Before using canned goods, see that the ends of each can are sunk in. If such is the case, the contents are good and wholesome, and there need be no hesitation in using them. If the ends of the can are springy or bulged outward, look upon it with suspicion. A swelled or bulged can usually means fermented contents and spoiled goods. The general rule as to bulged ends does not apply to condensed milk, which is frequently put up in cans that have a convex end.

After the can has been opened, pour contents immediately into a porcelain or glass dish; never leave them in the can, as this act is often the innocent cause of sickness, owing to the natural chemical action of the air upon the tin.

Always bear in mind that all canned goods have received a cooking, varying in length of time from five minutes to seven hours, according to the character of the goods, and that but little further cooking is necessary.

#### Fruits.

Canned fruits of all kinds should be emptied from the can several hours before being served, poured into an open porcelain or glass dish, and then chilled in a refrigerator. Served cold they are most delicious and refreshing, and taste totally different from what they did when first taken from the can.

#### Vegetables.

As a general rule peas, lima beans, and string beans prove unsatisfactory, owing to the fact that two-thirds of the housewives serve them in the brine that is in the can. They should be prepared as follows, and it will then be difficult to distinguish the difference between the canned and freshly picked:

Pour off the brine, throw it away, then place the vegetables in cold water, washing well, and let stand a few minutes to freshen. Cook but a few minutes and season to taste. Many use milk instead of water with these vegetables.

A small piece of pork added to string beans improves their flavor.

Corn should be only thoroughly heated, as it has been sufficiently cooked in the cans. Add butter, milk, salt, and pepper as desired.

To retain the natural flavor of tomatoes they should be cooked quickly over a hot fire; allowing tomatoes to simmer long tends to extract the bitter taste from the seed and gives dissatisfaction.

Pumpkins, as now packed, have been run through a fine sieve and are sufficiently cooked in the hot processing of the cans, and simply require spicing.

Asparagus is best cooked in the can before it is opened, by immersing the can in boiling water for from twenty to thirty minutes; then open the can and slide the contents carefully onto a dish, taking care not to break the delicate tips. Always lay asparagus cans on the side, never upright, as the latter is apt to break the tips.

Canned meat should be kept in a cool place. It will then, when turned out of can, slice evenly and present a better appearance on the table.

In order to prevent tearing out the contents of cans of meat or plum pudding, open them as follows:

Cut away the larger end of the can first, then puncture a hole in the smaller end to admit air, tap can lightly, and the contents will drop out whole.

Plum-pudding cans should be immersed in boiling water for from one-half to one hour, according to size; then open in the same manner as canned meat.

## Soups.

There are many grades of canned soups on the market. Buy only the best, which are skillfully and scientifically made. To serve, they simply need raising to the boiling point. Be careful not to scorch them.

Use a double boiler, if possible, or immerse the cans in boiling water for half an hour to thoroughly heat the contents, and then serve.

## Salmon.

The finest Columbia River salmon steaks are delicacies in cans. They are of a handsome high-pink color, flaky in texture, rich in oil, and the flesh is solid. A delicious salad can be made with salmon, lettuce, and mayonnaise dressing. If salmon is left over at meals pour oil or melted butter over it to exclude the air, and put in a cool place; when ready to serve, the oil or butter can readily be removed by skimming, or the butter, by heating and skimming.

## Lobsters and Shrimps.

Owing to the large quantity of sulphur in these crustaceans there is a great tendency to their turning black if their meat comes in contact with the tin when they are packed dry. To overcome this trouble they are generally packed in parchment or linen bags, or in wood-lined cans. A new process has just been discovered that overcomes all this trouble, i. e., the packing in gelatin, which completely envelopes the meat and prevents contact with the tin, and insures fine quality.

## ICING.

To every pound of white sugar allow the whites of four eggs and one ounce of fine starch.

Beat the whites to a strong froth and gradually sift in the sugar, which should be reduced to the finest possible powder, and gradually add the starch. Beat the mixture until smooth, then apply with a broad knife or spoon equally over the cakes.

## ICE CREAM.

| | |
|---|---|
| 1 pint milk. | 1 cupful sugar. |
| 1 scant cupful flour. | 2 eggs. |
| 1 quart cream. | 1 tablespoonful flavoring extract. |

Boil the milk; mix together the sugar, flour, and eggs and stir into the boiling milk. Cook twenty minutes, stirring often. When cool add another cupful of sugar, the flavoring, and cream. Freeze in ice and salt.

Fruit of all kinds, chocolate, coffee, etc., can be used as flavoring.

When cream is expensive and can not be procured, a good substitute is obtained by using cornstarch or condensed milk and following the recipes upon the packages.

## WINE JELLY.

| | |
|---|---|
| 1½ ounces gelatin. | 1 pint cold water. |
| 1 pint wine. | ½ pound sugar. |
| Juice and grate of 1 lemon. | 2 eggs. |
| A little nutmeg, cloves, and cinnamon. | |

Soak the gelatin in cold water for ten minutes, add the boiling water, and stir until dissolved, then add the wine, sugar, and flavoring. Beat well the *whites* of the eggs and stir briskly into the mixture; put on a slow fire and stir *very gently* till it boils, when it should be immediately taken off and allowed to stand one minute and then strained through a jelly bag, returning instantly to the bag what first comes through till it runs perfectly clear.

In warm weather it is well to use more gelatin or less liquids, or the mixture may not "jell."

### CURRANT JELLY.

Make the same as wine jelly, using a pint of currant juice instead of wine.

### WELSH RAREBIT.

| Slices of bread. | Butter. |
|---|---|
| Cheese. | Mustard and pepper. |

Cut the bread into slices about one-half inch in thickness; pare off the crust; toast it slightly without hardening or burning, and spread with butter; cut some slices of cheese not quite as large as the bread and lay them on the toast in a toaster; be careful that the cheese does not burn, and let it be equally melted; spread over the top a little made mustard and seasoning of pepper, and serve very hot.

### LEMONADE, No. 1.

Good lemonade is of high dietetic value. Few know how to make it properly, being too economical in the use of lemons and sugar, and too generous with the water. One who enjoys a reputation for making a superior lemonade always uses boiled water. The recipe is as follows:

"For a quart, take the juice of three lemons, using the rind of one of them. Peel the rind very thin, getting just the yellow outside; cut into pieces, and put with the juice and powdered sugar, of which use two ounces to the quart, in a jug or jar with a cover. When the water is just at the tea point pour it over the lemon and sugar, cover at once, and let it get cold."

## LEMONADE, No. 2.

| Rind of 2 lemons. | Juice of 3 large or 4 small lemons. |
| ½ pound loaf sugar. | 1 quart boiling water. |

Rub some of the lumps of sugar on the rinds of the lemons until all the oil is imbibed and put them with the rest of the sugar into a vessel, and pour in the lemon juice (but not seeds); then pour in the boiling water. When thoroughly dissolved strain; and when cool it is ready for use.

# PART II.

# CAMP COOKERY.

# CONTENTS OF PART II.

208                    CONTENTS.

RECIPES—Continued.                                    Page.

# MANUAL FOR ARMY COOKS.

## CAMP COOKERY.

Camp Cookery may be divided into three kinds: Permanent Camps, Temporary Camps, and on a continuous march.

The principles are the same in each kind, the differences being only as to the conveniences that are at hand in each case.

The appetite of men taken from quarters and placed in the field increases considerably for the first few days. Meats that would be indigestible from toughness, and simple dishes often neglected while living in barracks, are eaten with appetite.

## COOKING PLACES.

Each company should have its own kitchen on flank of, and in line with, its row of tents. The simplest kitchen consists of a trench dug in the direction parallel with the wind, of such width that the kettle, when placed on it, does not project beyond it more than an inch on each side; its depth should be 12 inches at the end from which the wind is blowing, and continue this depth for 4 feet, decreasing then gradually to 3 inches at the opposite end, where a space must be left equal to the breadth of the trench, to serve as a chimney. The fire is lit at the end where the trench is deep; it should not extend beyond 3 or 4 feet up the trench. The kettles are placed touching one another; dry sods should be used to stop up the chinks made by the roundness of the kettles, so that the space under them may form a flue. It is advisable to pile up sod, or, with stones and earth, to erect a chimney of at least one foot in height at the end farthest from the fire. All grass around the fireplaces should be cut to prevent accidents from fire.

If the command halts for more than one day, these kitchens are susceptible of great improvement; the chimney can be made of mud, or twigs and mud, and the draft may be increased by using short pieces of hoop iron as bars, stretched across the trench to support a filling in of clay around each kettle; or, in other words, to make a regular place for each kettle, into which it will fit exactly, so that its position may be changed. As the day following the wind may change to an exactly opposite direction, a similar trench must be dug in continuation of the former one, the same chimney being used. In this manner one chimney will serve for trenches cut to suit the wind blowing from all four quarters. The openings from these trenches into the chimney must all be closed with sod, except the one in use. In some places, where bricks or stones suitable to the purpose are to be had, it is better to construct these kitchens on the ground instead of below the surface.

In well-wooded countries, two logs side by side and parallel to the direction of the wind, the fire being kindled between them, make a good kitchen. In such places fuel is no object, so the construction of chimneys can be dispensed with, and the kettles hung from a stick resting at each end on a forked upright.

### HOW TO MAKE A COOKING FIRE FOR A SMALL CAMP.

Lay down two green poles (5 by 6 inches thick, and 2 feet long) 2 or 3 feet apart, with notches in the upper side about 10 to 12 inches apart. Let the ground be leveled meantime. Take two more green poles (6 by 8 inches thick, and 4 feet long) and lay them in the notches. Procure a good supply of dry wood, bark, brush, or chips, and start your fire on the ground between the poles. The air will circulate under and through your fire, and the poles are just the right distance apart to set your camp kettle, frying pan, or coffee pot on.

If you are going to cook several meals in this place, it will pay you to put up a *crane*. This is built as follows: Cut two green posts (2 inches thick and 3 feet long), which drive into the ground a foot from either end of your fire, and then split the top end of each with the ax (unless they be forked). Then cut another green pole, of same size, and long enough to reach from one of these posts to the other; flatten the ends and insert them in the splits. The posts should be of such height that when this pole is passed through the bail of the camp kettle, the latter will swing just clear of the fire. Other cooking utensils may be used as required.

## DISPOSAL OF REFUSE.

Particular attention is directed to the cleanly method of burning all kitchen refuse in the camp fire; it will not affect the cooking. Burn everything—coffee grounds, parings, bones, meats, even old tin cans, for if thrown out anywhere, even buried, they attract flies. Tin cans are flytraps—burned and cleaned out of fire daily they are harmless. Fires. should be cleaned of burnt refuse once a day, as refuse burned will not attract flies. Cleanliness is a good doctor. The burning of refuse, not burying it, is a splendid rule, especially in a large command or permanent camp.

## EXTEMPORIZED STOVES, OR COOKING PLACE.

### (With Plates.)

In the field the utensils furnished are of primitive character, consisting of camp kettles and mess pans, made of iron, etc.

To extemporize stoves and cooking places the usual and most simple mode is to dig a trench 18 inches wide, 12 inches deep, and from 4 to 6 feet long. At each end place a forked stick, of equal height, with a stout sapling, from which to suspend the kettles, extending from one to the other. (See plate 1.)

PLATE 1.

This, however, is neither the best nor most economical mode, as it consumes much fuel, wastes much of the heat, and causes great inconvenience to the cook. An improvement can be effected by casing the sides of the trench with brick, adding a little chimney at one end, and, in place of the forked sticks, using iron uprights and crossbar, to which half a dozen hooks for hanging kettles are attached. (See plate 2.)

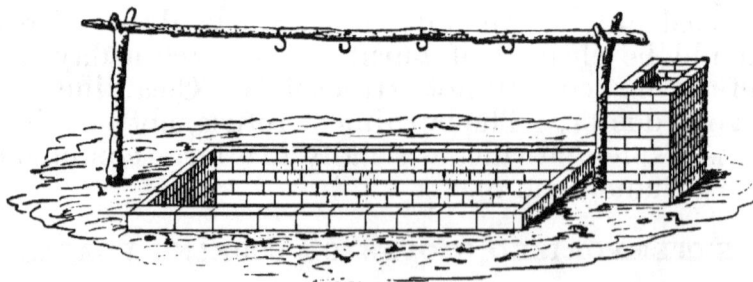

PLATE 2.

In a clayey soil, the following plan is perhaps the neatest, most economical, and most convenient that can be devised: Dig a hole about 3 feet square and

2 feet in depth, generally in the slope of a hill.  On one side run a shaft laterally, about 1 foot square and 6 feet in length, and 1 foot from the surface of the ground.  At the extreme end sink a shaft vertically, and form a chimney; and at equidistances pierce three holes of sufficient diameter to prevent the kettles from slipping through.  By this mode kettles can be placed over the fire to boil—or on either side, to simmer—with less difficulty than by any other means.  (See plate 3.)

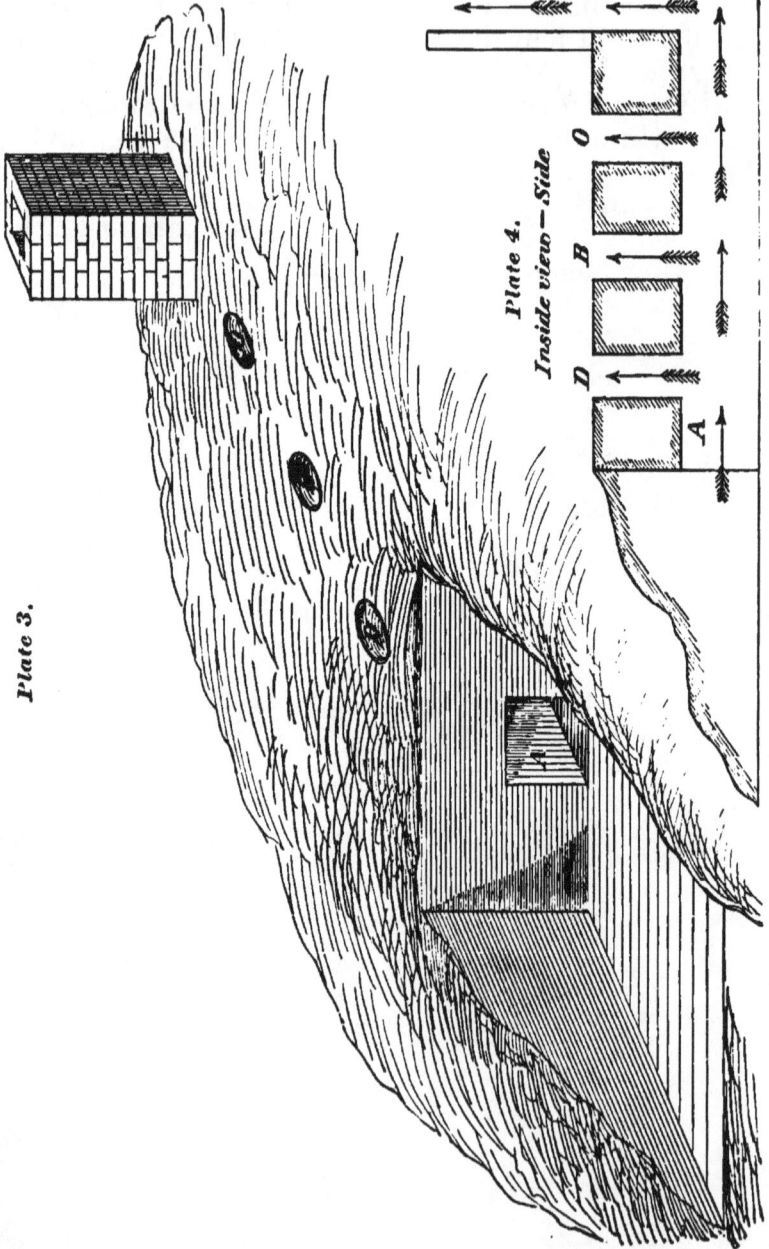

*Plate 3.*

*Plate 4.*

*Inside view — Side*

## SHIELD FOR CAMP FIRE.

Made of light boiler or heavy sheet iron. Composed of top and three sides, joined to top by hinges.

Fuel is inserted in front, which should be to the windward, and being open, any length of wood can be used. One joint of pipe is sufficient.

This is very portable, and in windy weather a comfort for the cooks and those who would gather around the camp fire. (See plates 5 and 6.)

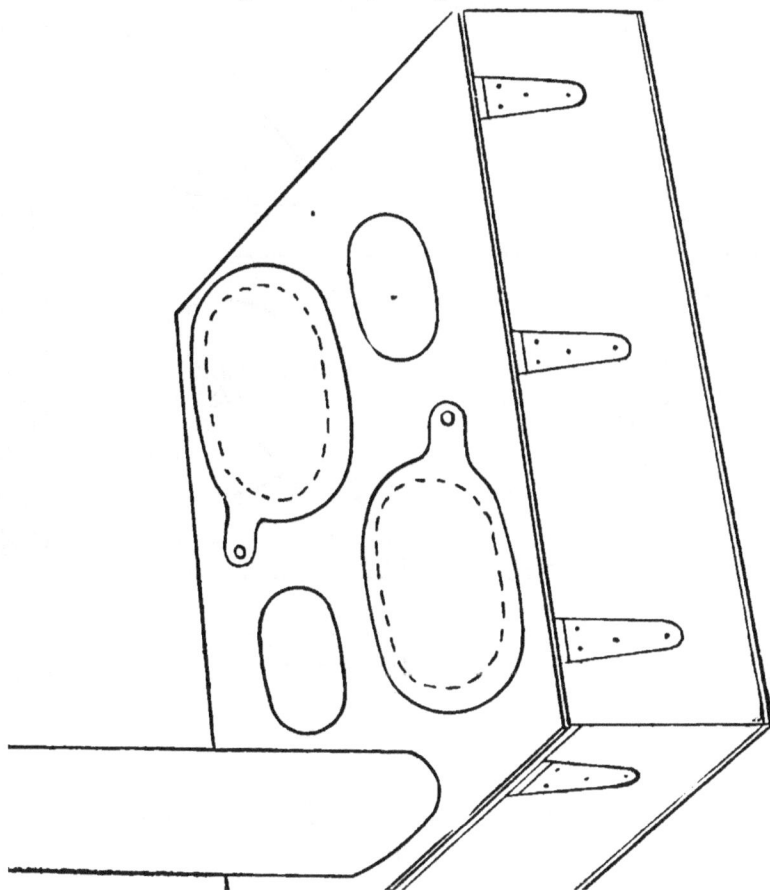

PLATE 5.—Dimensions Length, 30 inches; width, 26 inches; height, 12 inches.

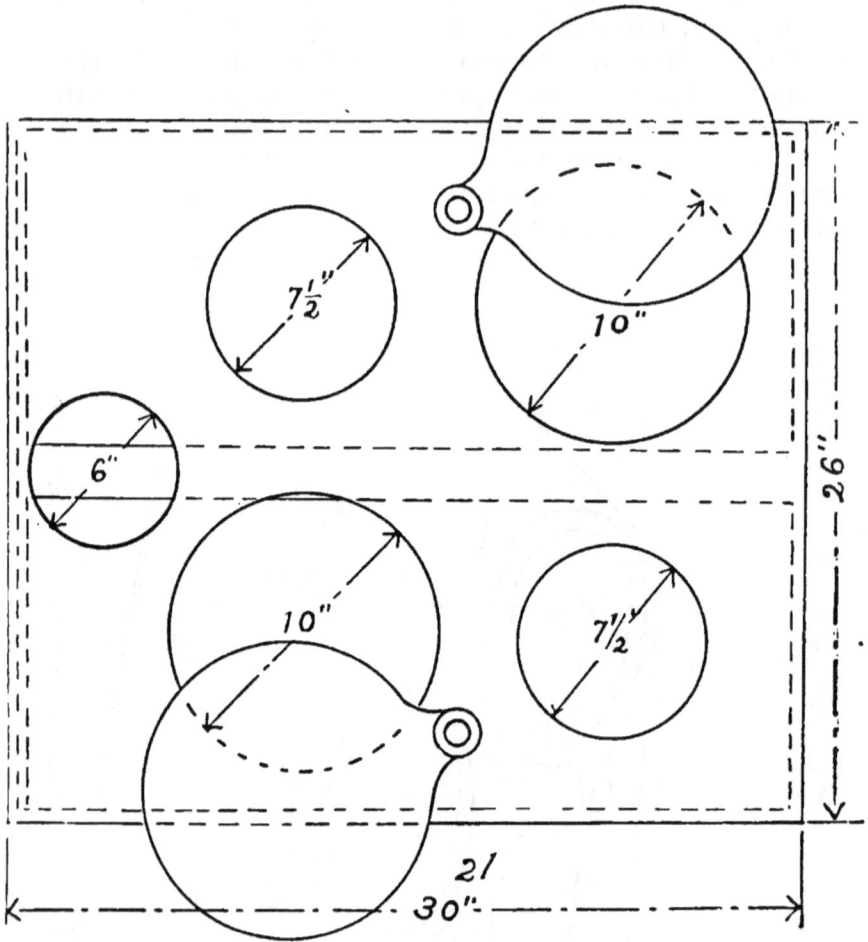

PLATE 6.

## BUZZACOTT OVEN.

Various portable stoves and ovens have been invented and placed upon the market for use in camp cookery.

The Buzzacott oven is now generally used in the Army; it is an adaptation from the Dutch oven. It consists of a large rectangular box; the bottom is made of sheet iron or steel, with a top of similar material.

It is compact and strong for transportation.

The outfit includes all the necessary utensils for *roasting*, *baking*, *frying*, *broiling*, and *stewing*, as well as many of the cooks' tools for the use of a full company of seventy-five men. It is issued by the Quartermaster's Department, upon requisition, to United States troops, for use in field and camp service.

PLATE 7.

Plate 7 represents the entire military outfit, as packed for transportation. Inside are the thirty to thirty-five utensils comprising the outfit. Size, 25 by 35 by 14 inches. Weight, 175 to 200 lbs., complete. In shipping, it forms its own crate, and when thus closed this skeleton stove forms an iron crate about the whole, fastens or binds it together and permits of any heavy objects being packed on top of it without danger of crushing.

PLATE 8.

Plate 8 represents the general appearance when set up for use. It can, however, be rearranged as circumstances require.

## WHAT THE OUTFIT COMPRISES.

One skeleton stove (grate stand).
One extension stand.
Two parts of oven.
One large cover for oven (used when boiling water, etc.).
Two large baking and roasting spiders. Rests.
Two small frying spiders. Rests.
Two lifting-hooks or irons.
Two large combination frying, roasting, or baking pans, with covers.
Three large boilers (a set), with covers to fit.
These articles are of special make, *handmade*, and of selected material, permitting of the rough and constant usage incident to field service.

## UTENSILS PACKED WITH THE OUTFIT.

One butcher cleaver, 8-inch blade.
One butcher knife, 8-inch blade.
One butcher steel, 10-inch.
One 10-quart (seamless) dish or mixing pan.
One large sieve or strainer.
One large 3-quart dipper, handle 12 inches long.
One medium cup-dipper or ladle, handle 12 inches long.
One large cook's spoon, solid handle, 12 inches long.
One large cook's flesh fork, 3-prong, handle 12 inches long.
Three large dredges (salt, pepper, flour).
One large pierced ladle or skimmer.
One graduated scoop or measure, $\frac{1}{2}$ pint to 2 quarts.
One large seamless colander.
One large turnover, solid handle, 12 inches long.

## CAPACITY OF UTENSILS.

The largest boiler, full measure, 12 gallons, 48 quarts.

The medium boiler, full measure, 10 gallons, 40 quarts.

The smallest boiler, full measure, 8 gallons, 32 quarts.

Combined capacity, full measure, 30 gallons, 120 quarts.

Largest pan, baking (1 time), 100 biscuits, 30 pounds bread.

Medium pan, baking (1 time), 75 biscuits, 25 pounds bread.

Largest pan, roasting (1 time), 75 to 100 pounds meat.

Largest pan, frying (1 time), 75 to 100 pounds meat, fish, etc.

Largest pan, baking and roasting together, 50 pounds potatoes and 50 pounds meats.

Largest pan, baking beans, pudding, etc., 35 to 40 pounds.

If oven is used as a boiler, 10 to 15 hams can be boiled together in it, or one barrel of liquid prepared. In an emergency only is this necessary.

### DIRECTIONS FOR USING BUZZACOTT OVEN.

If the wind is blowing heavily dig a hole for the oven and fire of sufficient depth to bring the top of the oven on a level with ground, piling the wood on the edges of the bank for additional protection. If weather is good there is no need of this.

When practicable use a tent fly as a shade for the cooks.

Use the best fuel for baking, and stack it so that it may dry. Splitting or chopping wood is not required, except to first kindle fire.

Build a fire of any convenient fuel, wood, buffalo chips, leaves (anything), and when well started, place over the fire your skeleton stove.

Adjust the "extension stand" always to *leeward* (from the wind), so as to catch or absorb the spare and draft heat, flame, etc.; use the "oven" on this stand, and shift the stand as circumstances require for your convenience.

When roasting or baking is desired in connection with boiling or frying, place the oven on the stand crosswise, as that allows room for the other utensils at the same time; or if preferable, place it on a bed of coals near the fire on the ground, or on a level fire.

Near the center of the inside of the oven place evenly apart the two large pan spiders (rests). These support the baking and roasting pans and contents and prevent an uneven circulation. Place these firmly and easily, and your foods will roast and bake splendidly.

Prepare the roast, bread, pudding, or whatever you wish in the pan, place it on the rests inside of the oven and cover with the upper part of the oven; heap some fresh burning coals on top and the roasting or baking commences instantly.

In using the oven keep a clean fire, free from sand and dirt. On top of oven build a little fire, if necessary, from chips, etc.; regulate your heat by the amount of fire—add to or remove when necessary.

Always build a fire or use live coals on top of the oven when either roasting or baking.

The two smaller pan spiders (rests) are intended to be used on top of the oven, over the fire that is built on top. On this do your boiling, stewing, broiling, and frying with the utensils (provided with the outfit) for the purpose.

Keep the oven covered as much as possible.

Basting is *never required*; to regulate the heat simply shift the fire, add to or remove as necessary; judge cooking by time and strength of fire; add water to the roasts for gravy, etc., and to assist its self-basting qualities.

When roasting or baking is completed, take off the oven, remove the cover and dump the ashes;

recover it, and you can carry the oven and its contents clean and warm, being careful to avoid spilling or capsizing the food.

When removing pans with lifters, be careful to steady contents and lift easily, lest they capsize and spill contents.

Use the oven for washing dishes, and the top for frying and stewing (in addition to regular frying pan if desired).

The washing of pots, kettles, etc., will be easy if they are washed immediately after use—before they cool—it will be done in one-half the time with one-quarter the work. Set them bottom up to drain and keep clean.

## THE BARNEY STEAM COOKER AND STERILIZER.

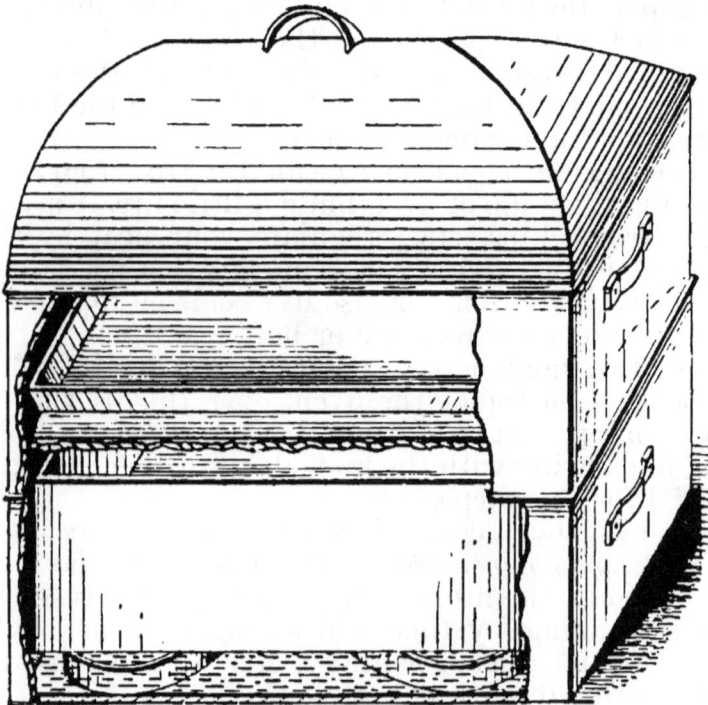

PLATE 9.

No. 1, Army; size, 18 by 24 inches; weight, 100 pounds.

The Barney Steam Cooker and Sterilizer operates under the principle of a complete circulation of steam. No water from condensation can come in contact with the food. It has been tested that onions, cabbage, fish, pudding, etc., can be cooked at the same time without taint or odor. As a sterilizer it is invaluable. No adulteration of food; no harmful germs. Requires no special attention. Can be used on gas, oil, coal, or wood stoves.

The 18 by 24 Barney Steam Cooker is composed of two sections—kettle rest and roasting pan; the sections are known as the bottom and top sections, and are made of the No. 24 galvanized sheet steel; the cover is made of the same material. The kettle is made of the best two-cross charcoal tin and has a capacity of 13 gallons of liquid substance, meaning 120 plates of soup or 160 cups of coffee, and will hold rations of vegetables for 100 men. The baking pan is made of No. 27 black iron, is $16\frac{1}{2}$ by $21\frac{1}{2}$ by $4\frac{1}{4}$ inches deep; this means a capacity of 75 pounds of roast beef. All food to be cooked in the Barney Steam Cooker is prepared the same as when cooked by the old method. The circular will give the desired information as to how the food is prepared and cooked in the steamer.

### INSTRUCTIONS FOR USING THE COOKER.

Fill the bottom with water to the top of rest on which the kettle sits; no more water will be required for 3 to 4 hours over a moderate fire; should the time necessitate, the cooker may be placed over a hot fire, only being careful to keep a supply of water in the bottom; other than this no watch or care is necessary. In making soup and liquid food there should be no more water used than is required to serve, as there is no boiling away of the water in the kettles. The reason of this is that, the heat being equal on all sides of the kettles, there is no evaporation; so it has been proved that 10 gallons of water, placed in the kettles and steamed over a hot fire for 10 hours, when again measured was found to be still 10 gallons. The water in the bottom of the steamer being directly in contact with the raw heat the gases will naturally be consumed, and so of course will have to be replenished after 3 or 4 hours.

For boiling rice, hominy, oatmeal, etc., just enough water is added to allow their kernels or substance to swell.

The stove is operated by first putting the legs or supports together and fastening them to the stove by placing them in the sockets prepared to receive them; if convenient there should be a small hole or ditch dug for the fire (although this is not necessary). The stove is then placed over the place thus prepared and a fire kindled, using wood broken or cut three feet or less in length, or any material that will make a good fire.

The cooking should be done in a sheltered place, if possible, although this is not entirely necessary, as the cooking can be done on the open plain in any weather. The advantage of a sheltered place is that it will prevent sand and dirt from getting into the food. In using the cooker, when the food is prepared and in the cooker place, close the same, and cook as in the kitchen. Any water, muddy or salt, can be used in the bottom for the purpose of making steam, only using fresh water for cooking the food. In cooking in summer, when the food is done the fire may be allowed to go out, and if the cooker is kept closed the food will keep warm for two hours, and by this means picket guards and scouting parties coming in late can always have warm food, and while left in the cooker the food will never get dry. In cold weather there should be a small fire kept under the stove. The steamer should never be opened until it is time for the food to be done, giving plenty of time.

## FIELD OVENS.

Field ovens for bread baking are of two classes: The first is constructed where the troops are located, by excavations in the earth, or from any material available, such as sod, wood, brush, etc.; these are immovable. The second class have a part or whole of the oven of a portable character, and can be worked with little or no delay or preparation after their arrival in camp.

*Dimensions.*—The maximum capacity of the hearth of a field oven should be such that at a single baking it does not exceed 150 or 200 rations, unless its arch be of brick or stone

The ration loaf of the United States Army, in pans, should occupy from 25 to 31 square inches. The greater the space the better the bread.

The following table gives the capacities of field ovens with the proportionate dimensions of their hearths:

| CAPACITY OF OVEN (NUMBER OF RATIONS SINGLE BAKING). | SQUARE INCHES OF SURFACE TO A RATION LOAF. | TOTAL DIMENSIONS OF THE HEARTH. | LENGTH OF HEARTH. | WIDTH OF HEARTH. |
|---|---|---|---|---|
| | | *Square feet.* | *Feet.* | *Feet.* |
| 100 — | 25 | 17.5 | 5 | 3.5 |
| 100 — | 30 | 20.28 | 5.41 + | 3.75 |
| 150 — | 25 | 26 | 6 | 4.33 + |
| 150 — | 30 | 31.25 | 6.58 + | 4.75 |
| 200 — | 25 | 34.58 | 6.91 + | 5 |
| 200 — | 30 | 41.25 | 7.5 | 5.5 |

Ovens made of earth, mud, sod, and frames of twigs would be more stable and durable if their capacity did not exceed 100 rations.

### AN OVEN IN A STEEP BANK (PLATE 10).

This is recommended as a very good and convenient oven. A bank from 4 to 6 feet high is the best for the purpose.   Two men with a spade and a long-handled shovel can build it, in light soil, in three-quarters of an hour.   If such tools are not available, it may be constructed with trowel bayonet, intrenching tools, or even with knives.   To build the oven, dig down the bank to a vertical face and excavate at the base a hole from 4 to 5 feet horizontally, care being taken to keep the entrance as small as possible; hollow out the sides of the excavation and arch the roof until the floor is about 2 feet 6 inches in its widest part and the roof 16 inches high in the center of the arch.   Then tap the back end for the flue. A hole from 4 to 6 inches in diameter will furnish a good draft.   A piece of tent stovepipe may be utilized for this purpose.   It will be advantageous, before using, to wet the whole interior surface of the oven and smooth it over neatly, drying it out and hardening it with a small fire.   The time required for drying out will depend upon the character of the soil; if ordinarily dry, a fire kept up for an hour will suffice.

Such an oven has a capacity of about 40 rations, and will bake good bread in about 50 minutes. With proper care it will last several weeks.   Bake-pans may be used in baking, if they can be obtained; if not, the bare floor, after the ashes are removed, may be used to bake on.   After the introduction of the dough, the flue and door should be closed, which may be done with logs of wood, pieces of hard-bread boxes plastered with mud, flat stones, a wet grain sack or piece of canvas.   After the oven has been heated, the degree of heat may be regulated by means of the door and flue—opening or closing them as may be necessary.

Plate 10.

An Oven in a steep bank

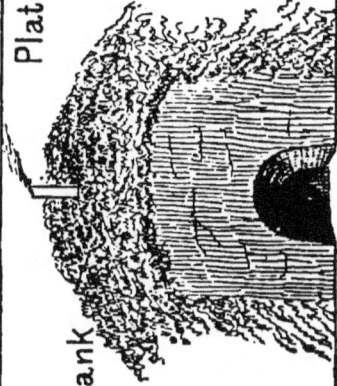

Nº 3

Nº 4.

No. 1.—Longitudinal section.
No. 2.—Plan.
No. 3.—Front view; not on the scale.
No. 4.—Transverse section of interior.

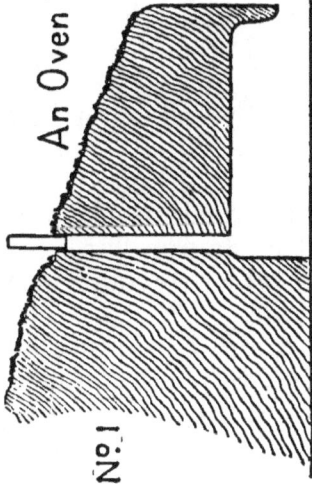

Nº 1

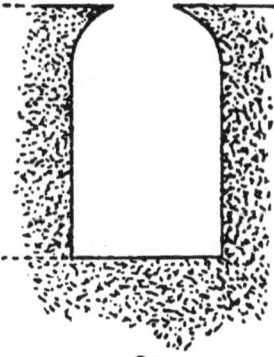

Nº 2

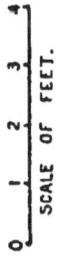

0   1   2   3   4

SCALE OF FEET.

## AN OVEN ON LEVEL GROUND (PLATE 11).

To build such an oven dig a hole about 4 feet long, 1 foot 6 inches deep, and 1 foot 6 inches wide. Without enlarging the top, hollow out the sides, from above downward, until the floor is about 2 feet 6 inches wide. The sides will thus form something of an arch, and be much better than vertical sides. At about one foot from the end dig a trench of convenient dimensions for one man to stand in, to attend to the oven. A suitable size would be 2 feet 6 inches in depth, 4 feet in length, and 2 feet 6 inches in width. Dig down the partition between the oven and the trench for the door. At the back end of the oven dig a small hole, slanting downward, for the flue. Lay green poles close together across the oven, and stop up the interstices with grass or weeds; then plaster over the covering with a thick layer of stiff mud, after which place more poles across and cover with another layer of mud. If pressed for time this last mud may be omitted, and grain sacks or brush may be spread over the second layer of poles and dry earth shoveled on. Dig a ditch around the oven and trench to keep out water in rainy weather.

Such an oven may be built by two men in one hour and a half. It is not durable, as the roof must soon burn out, but it has the advantage of being easily constructed and available for immediate use. Although much inferior to the clay or bank oven, it might sometimes be serviceable to troops on the march.

When there is no bank near, and it is expected to occupy camp for several days, the best plan, perhaps, is to make an artificial bank by digging a pit about 4 feet long, 3 feet wide, and 5 feet deep, and then to build a bank oven. The pit should be protected from rain.

Another method for level ground is to build, over a mound raised for the purpose, a semicylindrical-shaped oven of clay or earth. Any soil suitable for making adobes is good.  If lime is available, mortar should be used; if not to be obtained, chopped hay will add strength to the mud.

Plate II.

An Oven on level ground

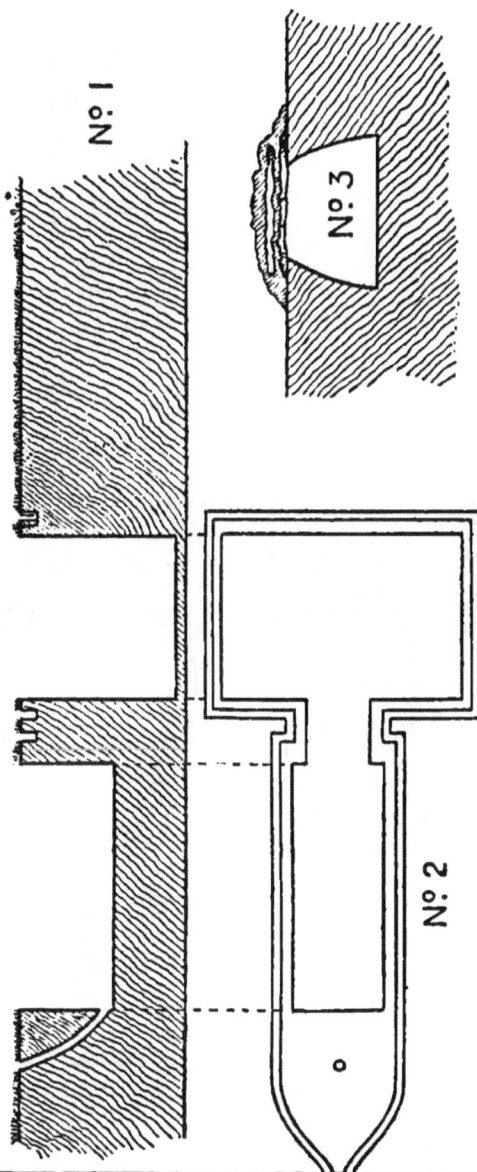

N° 1

N° 2

N° 3

No. 1.—Longitudinal section.
No. 2.—Plan, showing ditch.
No. 3.—Transverse section.

SCALE OF FEET.
0  1  2  3  4

Plate 12

An Oven above ground.

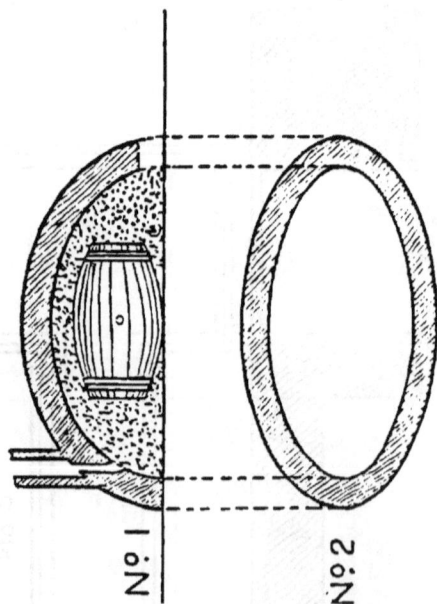

Nº I

Nº 2

Nº 3

No. 1.—Longitudinal section, showing method of construction.

No. 2.—Plan.

No. 3.—Transverse section at centre of dome.

SCALE OF FEET

1 2 3 4

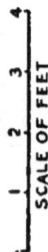

AN OVEN ABOVE GROUND (PLATE 12).

To build such an oven (plate 12) a rounded heap of dry earth or sand, about 5 feet long, 2 feet 6 inches wide, and 1 foot 9 inches high, should be

raised. This is the mold on which the oven is to
be formed. Sand is more suitable for the mold
than earth, it being more readily removed. Willow
twigs bent over and closely wattled together, or a
flour barrel laid flat and covered completely with
earth, will likewise suffice to give form to the
mold. Mix a stiff mud or mortar, and plaster the
mold over 5 or 6 inches thick, commencing at the
base. Allow one or two days for it to dry and
harden, plastering up all cracks which may appear.
When nearly dry, cut out the door at one end and
the flue at the top of the other end. A small mud
chimney raised over the flue will greatly improve
the draft. Carefully withdraw the loose earth
or sand from the interior. If a barrel has been used
for the mold it may be burned out without dam-
aging the oven. Keep a small fire in the oven for
at least half a day before attempting to bake. Dig
a pit in front of the oven for the convenience of the
baker.

Two men can build this oven in three hours, but
it will generally not be fit for use for two days. It
will last several weeks, and prove very satisfactory.

This oven may also be built dome-shaped, like the
household ovens used by the Mexicans. This kind
of an arch would be stronger than the semicylin-
drical form, but with the same quantity of material
used would not have as great a baking capacity.

The clay oven is peculiarly adapted for use when
camping on swampy ground. Under such circumstances it may be constructed upon a platform of
stones or logs covered with clay.

### DUTCH OVENS.

Considerable fuel is consumed in baking in Dutch
ovens where a company is to be supplied—the
capacity of each oven being small and several fires
being usually required. Fuel may be economized,
however, by building the fire in a trench of sufficient
length to receive all the ovens.

Care should be taken that the ovens and lids are quite hot before the dough is placed for baking. During the preparations for the baking the ovens and lids should be heated over the fire in the trench. When a good mass of coals has been obtained, the dough should be placed in the heated ovens and the lids put on. The ovens should then be embedded in the coals and the lids covered with coals and hot ashes. If there are not enough coals to cover the lids a small fire may be built over each.

Mess pans may be used in a similar manner for baking bread, but great care will be necessary to prevent burning, owing to the thinness of the metal.

### DOUGH.

Dough may be mixed in mess pans, on a piece of canvas, on a rubber blanket, or in the flour barrel or flour sack.

Dough should be set near the fire, and be allowed to rise well before baking. Very little fire is required at first.

If time and fuel are to be considered, biscuits will prove more suitable than large loaves.

### FIELD BAKE HOUSES.

During good weather a tent fly, awning, paulin, tent, or interior of a wagon will answer for a temporary shelter under which the labor of the baker can be performed, but in rainy or cold weather a board or more substantial building is essential.

To knead and raise bread successfully in the field with a temperature below 65° or 70° F. requires a long time, and is attended with difficulties and much uncertainty.

### UTENSILS NECESSARY FOR A FIELD OVEN.

One dough trough and cover made of pine plank 2 or 2.25 inches thick, about 2 feet 6 inches wide at top and 22 inches at the bottom, and about 18 inches in depth.   Length to correspond with capacity of oven.   For an oven with capacity of 100 rations, 5 feet long will be sufficient.

Two sets of boards for each trough to separate flour, sponge, and dough.

One board for dough about 4 feet long, 2 feet wide, and 2 inches thick.

One oven peel, wood; blade about 10 inches wide, pole 2 feet longer than the oven.

One short-handled brush.

Two large-sized common knives.

Two camp kettles.

One yeast tub (two better).

Two wooden pails, ordinary size, without paint.

A shelter in which to make and keep the bread warm.

## BAKING BREAD IN FIELD OVENS.

It not unfrequently occurs that the first baking in a field oven is of a bad quality; the bread is burnt at the top and not cooked enough at the bottom. This shows ordinarily that a hearth made on the natural soil is not as dry as the other parts of the oven, and if you have the time and means it should be paved.

In regard to French field ovens it is stated that the average temperature for baking is about 250° F., when the bread is placed in, and it is so managed that when it is baked the temperature has not fallen below 180° F.   (This would appear to be an error, or the loaves should be made very small and thin; even then a thorough soaking or crusting could not be satisfactorily done.)   If not baked in one hour's time it is permitted to remain in the oven about fifteen minutes longer, but after this delay it must be taken out, or it will lose more than gain by remaining.

The best temperature for baking in field ovens is from 380° to 450° F.   If higher, the fermentation, not always perfect in raising the dough in the open air, will be stopped too soon. If below this, it will require too long a time to properly bake.

### KNEADING TROUGHS.

An expeditious means of constructing a kneading trough in the field consists in digging two trenches of unequal size, parallel, *a* and *b*. The first should be lined with plank; the solid earth which separates the two trenches should, in the second trench, be sustained by boards also, or pickets at a proper slope. The bakers descend into the large trench *b* and knead the dough in the trench *a*, in the trough.

To make sure of the bread rising in the open air, make an excavation about 18 inches deep of convenient length and width. Heat it with pieces of wood in small sticks, and place the bread on brushwood, covering the excavation with branches, plank, hay, or grass.

Figs. *A* and *B* are two modes of making kneading troughs by excavation and plank. Vertical sections perpendicular to their length.

#### Fig. A.

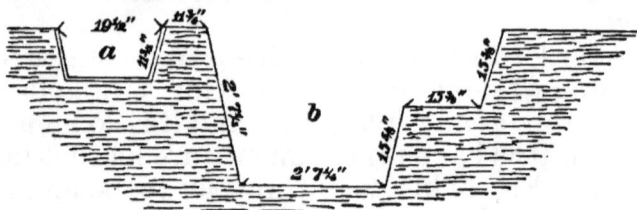

#### Fig. B.

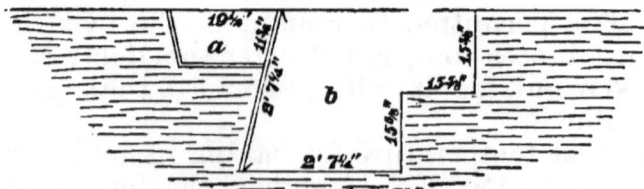

PLATE 13.

## PORTABLE OVENS.

This class of ovens is generally so constructed that they are ready for use at all times. Those on wheels form part of the train of an army. Many patented varieties were used during the late war, in the field, which gave satisfactory results. Constructed mainly of iron, it is claimed the quality of the bread baked in them is inferior to that made in brick or earthen ovens.

### SMALL PORTABLE FIELD OVEN (PLATE 14).

The body of each oven is made of two pieces of $\frac{1}{16}$-inch sheet iron. These sheets are 5 feet long by 2 feet 6 inches wide, and so curved that, when their upper edges are connected and the lower edges fixed in the ground, they form an arch, the span of which is 3 feet 9 inches and the rise 1 foot 4 inches. The lower edge of each sheet is bent outward into a flange, so as to secure a firm rest on the ground.

On the inside of each sheet are riveted 3 longitudinal bars, 1 inch wide and $\frac{3}{8}$ inch thick, and on the outside 5 transverse ribs, $1\frac{1}{4}$ inches wide by $\frac{3}{8}$ inch thick (fig. 2). The upper ends of the transverse ribs on one of the sheets are formed into hooks, and those of the other sheet into eyes, by means of which the sheets are securely attached to each other along the ridge of the oven when erected.

The front of the oven is closed by a two-handled iron door (fig. 1), which is kept in place by means of hooks and eyes.

When the soil is of clay, or of other favorable quality, the rear end of the oven may be closed by the natural earth; but if it is sandy or loose, a sheet-iron plate will be required to close it. No chimney is necessary.

When set up, the whole, excepting the door, is covered with a mass of earth 8 inches in thickness.

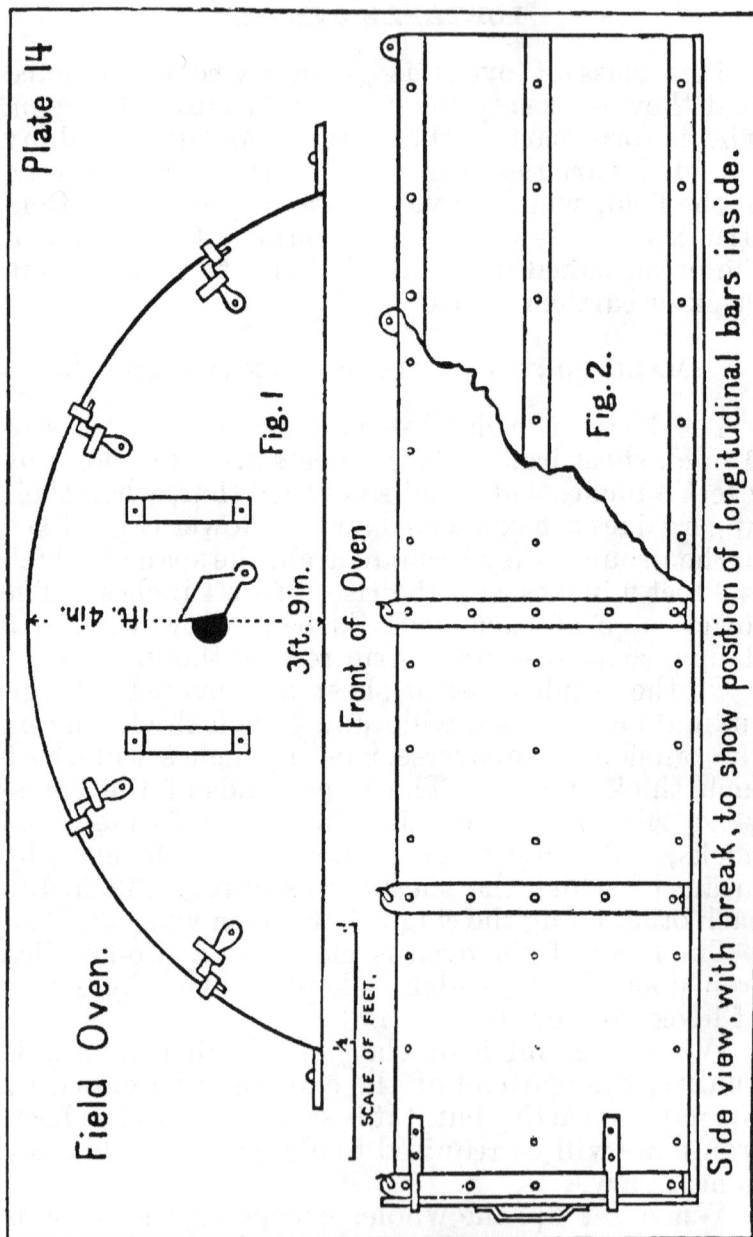

Plate 14

Field Oven.

Fig. 1.

1ft. 4in.

3ft. 9in.

Front of Oven

SCALE OF FEET.

Fig. 2.

Side view, with break, to show position of longitudinal bars inside.

This depth of earth is named for the reason that a larger quantity would be liable, from its weight, to bend the iron when heated, and a smaller quantity would allow too much heat to escape.

An excavation 3 or 4 feet in depth should be made a foot or two from the door, for the convenience of the baker.

Two hours are required for heating the oven at first starting, but for each heating immediately following one hour will be sufficient.

A small quantity of wood is placed in the oven at the extreme rear and ignited, the door being kept open to afford a draft and a vent for the smoke. Small quantities of wood should then be added as combustion progresses. In this way the fuel will burn more freely, and the oven be heated quicker, than if all the fuel necessary for the heating were put in at once.

As soon as the oven is at a white heat the ashes should be raked out, the floor swept clean, and the dough in pans introduced. The door should then be closed, and all interstices filled with moistened clay or earth. Bake pans may be dispensed with if the floor is made of bricks. If bread pans are used they should be of such size that four of them, or at most six, will cover the whole available space of the oven floor. The time required for each baking is about 45 minutes.

As each of the two principal pieces forming an oven weighs only about 85 pounds, the whole—consisting of the two sides, the door, and end plate— can be easily transported, and can even be carried on a pack animal if necessary.

To set up the oven no tools except a pickax and a shovel are required, the sides being merely placed on level ground, attached together, the rear end closed, and the whole covered with earth. It can be erected and prepared for use in 15 minutes, and if kept in constant operation for 24 hours can bake sufficient bread for 1,000 men. By the use of two of these ovens, therefore, a regiment of a thousand men, if it make a halt of 14 hours each day, can be supplied with fresh bread daily on the line of march.

The dough is kneaded in the field by hand, and the operation requires about 45 minutes. Ordinary kneading troughs for the purpose are made, which may be placed on trestles, or they may be fixed on the ground and trenches excavated near them for the kneaders to stand in.

### PORTABLE FIELD OVEN OF A LARGER SIZE (PLATE 15).

The body (top and sides) of this oven is made in two parts, each part being in shape nearly the quarter of a cylinder, and formed of three pieces of sheet iron 3 feet long by 2 feet 2 inches wide and $\frac{3}{16}$ inch thick, riveted together, and overlapping 2 inches (fig. 2).

Each side has three transverse bars of iron, $1\frac{1}{2}$ inches wide and $\frac{3}{8}$ inch thick, riveted on the outside. The upper ends of the bars on one of the sides are formed into hooks, and those of the other side into eyes, by means of which the two parts are connected and held firmly together along the ridge of the oven when erected.

The lower edge of each side for a width of 3 inches along its entire length is bent outward into a flange, the lower face of which coincides with the plane of the bed of the oven.

A longitudinal strip of light sheet iron, $2\frac{1}{2}$ inches wide, is riveted along the upper edge of the side on which the eyes are, and the edge of the other side slips under it in hooking (fig. 4).

To each side, on the under front end of the oven, are riveted two short iron bars, $5\frac{1}{2}$ inches long, $1\frac{1}{2}$ inches wide, and $\frac{3}{16}$ inch thick, each with a small hole in the outer end, and which are so bent as to

Plate 15

Field Oven

Fig. 3.

ft. Bin.

Front View

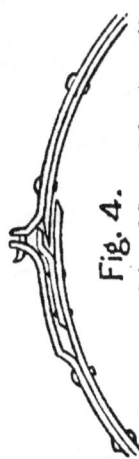

Fig. 4.
Manner of hooking sides together

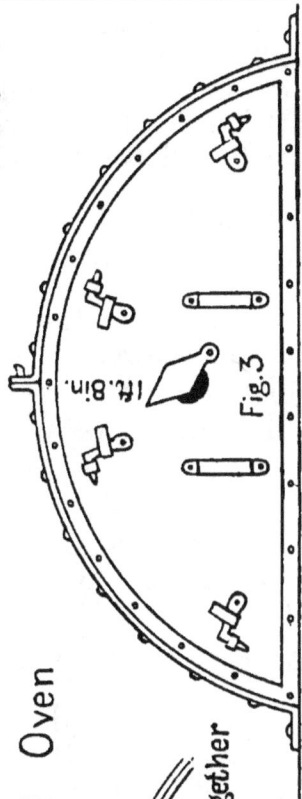

Fig. 2

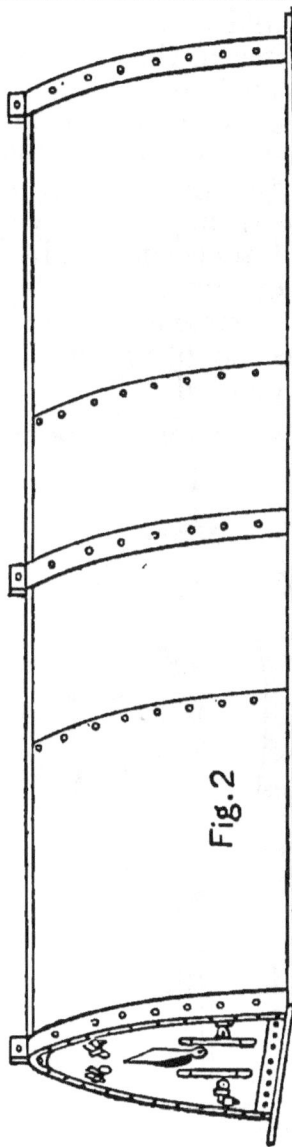

Side and End View

SCALE OF FEET

pass through slots in the face of the front of the oven, and are caught outside by corresponding hooks, as shown in the drawing (fig. 3).

Riveted to the door are two short iron handles, and cut in the face is a "draft hole," which may be opened and closed at pleasure by a lozenge-shaped door, turning on a rivet.

The front of the oven is strengthened with bar iron, 1 inch wide and ¾ inch thick, riveted around the edge on the outside.

The rear end of this oven is closed in the same way as that of the smaller oven, and the oven is set up and operated in the same manner as the smaller size.

COOKING AND MESS FURNITURE FOR FIELD SERVICE (PLATE 16).

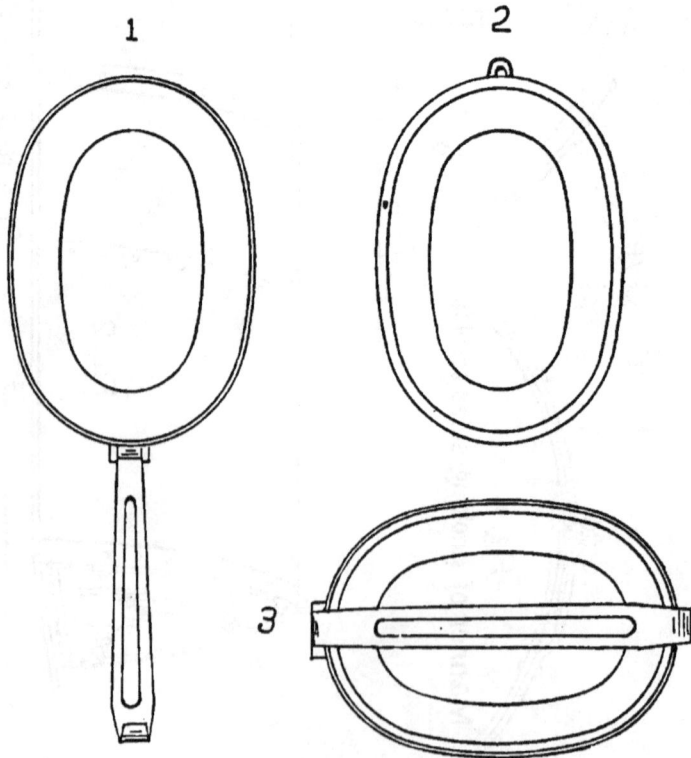

1 Soup plate    2 Plate...
    3 Meat Can, Closed.

The device for cooking, as now furnished by the Ordnance Department, is one meat can and plate combined, and consists of two oval dishes made of block tin, one deeper than the other, which fit together, forming a meat-ration can of the following dimensions:

Length, 8 inches; width, 6½ inches; depth of whole can, 1½ inches when closed; the lower dish to be 1 inch in depth; the plate ¾ inch in depth.

To the deeper dish or plate is attached a light iron handle, which folds over and holds the two together. The one with the handle may be used to eat soup out of; as a frying pan; or to warm up cold food, and many other purposes that will suggest themselves when it is used.

These articles are, on the march, placed in the haversack (the cup being attached to the strap), which also contains the rations required to be carried by the soldier and, with the canteen, which holds three pints, constitute the cooking and eating utensils that are deemed essential for use upon the most active service.

## HINTS REGARDING WATER AND WOOD.

Nothing is more certain to secure endurance and capability of long-continued effort than the avoidance of everything as a drink except cold water (and coffee at breakfast). Drink as little as possible of even cold water. Experience teaches old soldiers that the less they drink on a march the better, and that they suffer less in the end by controlling the desire to drink, however urgent.

After any sort of exhausting effort a cup of coffee or tea, hot or cold, is an admirable sustainer of the strength until nature begins to recover herself.

Officers in command of companies should impress upon their men the danger to which they expose

themselves in drinking bad water.  Poisonous matter of many descriptions may be taken into the
stomach in it.  (In Algeria, leeches have in this
manner been frequently taken into the body, causing dangerous internal bleeding.)  Dysentery and
diarrhea ensue and, in the opinion of the best
army surgeons, it is one of the chief causes of those
fearful diseases which have devastated armies in so
many wars.  It has lately been proved, that if bad
water does not produce cholera, its use predisposes
the body to take it when it is prevalent.

### TO PURIFY WATER THAT IS MUDDY, PUTRID, OR SALT.

With muddy water, the remedy is to filter; with
putrid, to boil, to mix with charcoal, or expose to
the sun and air; or, what is best, to use all three
methods at the same time.  With salt water nothing avails but distillation.

### TO FILTER MUDDY WATER.

When at the watering place there is nothing but
wet sand, take a good handful of grass and tie it
roughly together in the form of a cone, six or eight
inches long; then dipping the broad end into the pud-
dle and turning it up, a streamlet of partly-filtered
water will trickle down through the small end.  For
a copious supply the most perfect plan, if you have
means, is to bore a cask full of auger holes and
put another small one, that has had the bottom
knocked out, inside it; then fill up the space between
the two with grass, moss, etc.  Now, sinking the
whole in the midst of the pond, the water will filter
through the auger holes and moss and rise up clear
of, at least, weeds and sand in the inner cask, whence
it can be ladled.  With a single cask, the lower
part of the sides may be bored and alternate layers
of sand and grass thrown in till they reach above
the holes; through these layers the water will strain.

Or any coarse bag that is kept open with hoops, made on the spot, may be moored in the muddy pool by having a heavy stone put inside of it, and will act on the same principle, but less efficiently than the casks. Sand, charcoal, sponge, and wool are the substances most commonly used in filters; peat charcoal is excellent. A small piece of alum is very efficacious in purfiying water from organic matter, which is precipitated by the alum and a deposit left at the bottom of the vessel.

### PUTRID WATER

should always be boiled with charcoal or charred sticks before drinking, as low fevers and dysenteries too often are the consequence of its being used indiscreetly, but the charcoal entirely disinfects it; bitter herbs, if steeped in it, or even rubbed well about the cup, are said to render it less unwholesome. The Indians plunge a hot iron into putrid and muddy water.

When carrying water in buckets, put a wreath of grass, or something floating on the top of the water, to prevent splashing; and also make a hoop, inside which the porter walks, while his laden hands rest on the rim, the office of the hoop being to keep the buckets from knocking against his legs.

### TO CLARIFY MUDDY WATER.

Sprinkle a pinch of *pulverized alum* over the water in the bucket, and the impurities will soon settle at the bottom.

### TO KINDLE A SPARK INTO A FLAME,

the spark should be received into a kind of loose nest of the most inflammable substances at hand, which ought to be prepared before the tinder is lighted. When by careful blowing or fanning the

flame is once started, it should be fed with little
bits of sticks or bark, split with a knife or rubbed
between the fingers into fibers, until it has gained
enough strength to grapple with thicker ones.

### FUEL.

There is something of a knack in finding firewood.
It should be looked for under bushes.  The stump of
a tree, that is rooted nearly to the ground, has often
a magnificent root, fit to blaze throughout the
night.  Dry manure of cattle is an excellent fuel.
Dry fuel gives out far more heat than damp fuel.
Bones of animals also furnish an excellent substitute for firewood.

### FIREWOOD

should be cut into lengths of 1 foot and about 2
inches square.  When nothing but brushwood is to
be had, the trench should be deepened where the
fire is lit.  Damp or very sappy wood should be
avoided.  Bones can be used when other fuel is not
to be had.  During a march, it is well to pick up
and throw into the wagons all the dry wood that
may be found along the road.

### FILTERS.

Two barrels, one inside the other, having a space
of 4 or even 6 inches clear all around between them
filled with layers of sand, gravel, and charcoal, form
an excellent filter.  The inside one, without a bottom, rests on stones embedded in sand, the sand
reaching above the chine, and above this, between the
barrels, is a layer of charcoal and of coarse gravel.

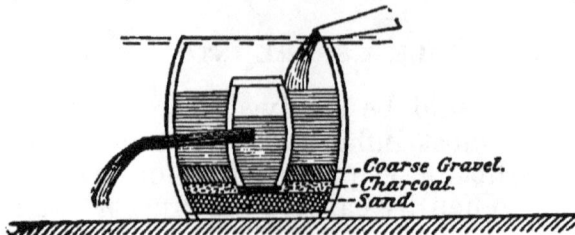

PLATE 17.

The water, flowing or being poured into the space between the two, and having thus to force its way through these substances into the inner barrel, becomes purified. The water is drawn off by means of a pipe running through ·the outer into the inner barrel.

## SUGGESTIONS RELATIVE TO COOKS AND THEIR DUTIES.

There should be required for each organization of 60 men one chief cook, one assistant cook, and one man detailed daily as cook's police. While the chief cook may be confronted by conditions entirely different from those to which he is accustomed in garrison, he will get willing assistance from other members of the company, and thus have more time for general supervision.

With the exception of the first sergeant there is no non-commissioned officer in the company so important to its well being as a competent, energetic chief cook.

His particular duties comprise (1) cooking, and baking bread, (2) care of rations, and (3) general superintendence of all work in the kitchen, and responsibility for all rations and cooking furniture. If there is a good baker in the company it might sometimes be found well to give him charge (under the chief cook) of all the bread baking.

The assistant cook assists the chief cook in his various duties, and is held responsible for the cleanliness of the cooking utensils.

The cook's police assists the cooks as directed— the cutting of wood and keeping up of fires usually being included in his duties.

In the cavalry it is usual to allow the cooks to ride with the wagons or pack train. When both wagons and packs are provided, the cooks ride with the latter, and should always have on the pack

mules sufficient rations and utensils with which to
prepare a meal upon arrival in camp.

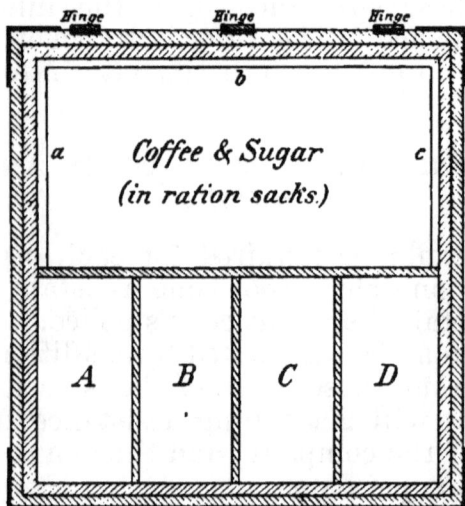

PLATE 18.

PLAN OF RATION BOX.
Scale ⅛.

*a, b, c,* cleats for supporting false lid, the upper edges of
which are on same level as tops of partitions.

*A, B, C, D,* compartments for beans, rice, candles, soap, salt,
and ground coffee, all in ration sacks. Yeast powder and pepper in cans and carefully packed. Coffee mill, etc.

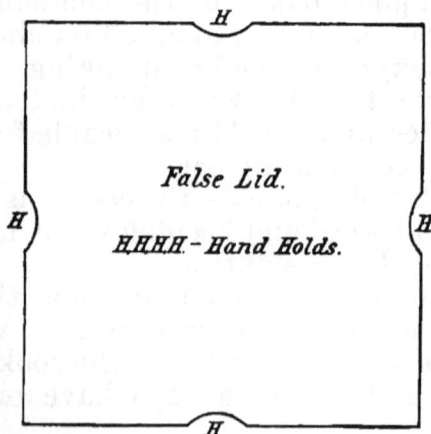

## SECURING AND TRANSPORTING RATIONS.

For use in garrison, as well as in the field, each company should be provided with facilities for carrying the ration. It will be found convenient to have a ration box of outside dimensions which will just admit of its being placed in the rear end of an army wagon, which is about 40 inches wide. The following is a description of a ration box which has been found by actual service to answer all requirements (see plate 18):

Its outside dimensions over all are 38½ by 38½ by 30 inches deep. It is made of white pine 1 inch thick and doubled or re-enforced for 3 inches at top and bottom; the edges should be dovetailed, the corners strengthened with angle iron and braces, and the sides provided with suitable handles. The interior, as shown in plan, is divided by vertical partitions, which extend to within 8 inches of the top. Exactly flush with the tops of these partitions, and extending around the interior of the larger compartment, are strips *a*, *b*, *c*, which support a square false lid of good 1-inch hard wood a little smaller than the inside dimensions of the box, and in the edges of which hand-holes are cut as shown in plan. This false lid may be used as a bread board, a chopping board, and for a variety of other purposes.

The real top or lid is secured by three strong hinges, and provided with suitable lock and key.

The space between the real and false lids is used for carrying fresh bread for the first camp, and smaller utensils, dishcloths, etc.

Such a box will weigh about 180 pounds, and will hold, in ration sacks to be described later, 1,000 rations each of sugar, coffee, salt, soap, and pepper; 200 rations of beans, a 10-pound can of lard, and 25 pounds of flour—the latter to be used in making gravies.

For field use, ration sacks of strong drilling or ticking with permanent ties, should also be provided.

Each ration sack should be marked in solid black indelible letters with the name of the article which it is to hold, and should ordinarily be large enough to contain 10 days' supply for the company of the component of the ration to be carried therein.

As soon as an original package is opened the contents should be transferred to its particular sack.

When *wagon transportation* is used, these sacks with their contents can be placed in their appropriate compartments in the ration box. When packs are used, an additional covering of gunny sack will be required.

When ordered for field service, and rations have been drawn, the first care must be to pack everything with the greatest possible care. Each side of bacon or piece of meat should be wrapped in several sacks. Coffee, sugar, salt, beans, rice, etc., except that which is carried in the ration box, should be double sacked.

Matches should be kept in closed tin boxes, or in wide-mouth bottles, and well corked, so that no dampness can reach them.

Candles should be wrapped up and placed in a candle box, or in a compartment of the mess box, to prevent their being broken.

Cases containing pepper and yeast powder should be opened and the contents carefully repacked with hay or straw, so as to prevent the cans from being shaken open and their contents spilled. Flour and vegetables should be double sacked and sacks securely sewed or tied. Boxes of hard bread require no special attention.

One full day's ration of soft bread and fresh meat should be drawn for the first day's march; also a proportion of one-fifth or more of hard bread, to meet the contingencies of wet weather or lack of fuel for baking purposes.

If the company be supplied with a Buzzacott oven, about all the utensils necessary for the mess will be found with the oven; otherwise, the following (all to be ascertained by inspection to be in serviceable condition) should be taken, if possible:

Four frying pans.

Six camp kettles (two sets or "nests").

Twenty mess pans (ten deep and ten shallow).

Three butcher knives.

One steel.

Two long-handled spoons.

Two long-handled forks.

Two dippers.

One skimmer.

One small coffee mill, and coffee roaster. (Plate No. 19.)

PLATE 19.

One iron kettle rod, twelve feet long and one inch in diameter, and supplied with six or more kettle hooks.

Two iron uprights, one inch in diameter and four feet long.

One spring balance (one which will weigh up to 200 pounds is to be preferred, as being useful when purchases of fresh beef, forage, etc., are made).

Two axes and one camp hatchet.

The smaller articles can be placed in a small wooden box fastened about with a strap, while the knives may be carried in leather sheaths attached to the cartridge belts of the cooks.

In packing the wagons the tents, bedding rolls, etc., should be put in first and a space left at the tail end of the wagon for the mess box and cooking outfit. If the wagon be crowded, the Buzzacott oven can be lashed to the rear of the wagon outside the tail gate, the side resting in the feed box.

The chief cook should know where everything is when wagons are packed, to save time in searching for articles should anything be wanted during a temporary halt. All articles necessary for the first meal should be so placed in the wagons that they can be taken out at once, and no delay occur in the preparation of the meal.

Before leaving a post the chief cook should roast a part of his coffee, so that if unexpectedly called upon to make coffee he will not find himself unprepared. Roasted coffee should always be kept on hand.

When *pack transportation* is provided each troop should have four mess boxes, ¾-inch lumber, dovetailed, 11 by 18 by 26 inches, and when packed in pack cover, without lids.

The rations should be carefully put up in 100-pound packs lashed solidly, and carried on the best pack mules; each pack is plainly marked with its contents and weighed.

Salt, sugar, coffee, and beans are double sacked and lashed in 100-pound packages. Bacon in 100-pound packages, is packed in from 5 to 8 pounds of clean straw or hay, double sacked, and lashed firmly.

Each cargo is in two side packs of about 100 to 125 pounds each, and should match in size, shape, and · weight, as nearly as practicable; each side pack having, as nearly as may be, the following proportions: width, one-half more than the thickness; length nearly one-half more than width—*e. g.*, 12 by 18 by 25 inches.

The salt, sugar, coffee, and beans should not all be placed in one cargo.

*When no transportation* is provided, which may occur in maneuver marches in the presence of the enemy, troops may be required to carry their rations on the person. It may safely be said, in general terms, that a soldier can carry three days' subsistence on his person—the infantryman in the haversack or pack, the cavalryman in his saddlebags. Under such conditions of course only bacon (one day's ration of which may be replaced by cooked beef), hard bread, coffee, sugar, salt, and pepper can be carried, the other components being replaced by such condensed forms of food as compressed soup, etc.

The regulation meat can, tin cup, knife, fork and spoon answer all requirements for cooking under such emergencies.

## CAMPING.

Upon arrival in camp as soon as ranks are broken in the infantry, or the horses provided for in the cavalry, the first sergeant commands: "All hands out for wood and water," when all available men prepare to gather fuel and carry water to the spot selected for the kitchen. If the transportation has arrived in camp, the cooks, while waiting the arrival of fuel and water, proceed to unload the articles necessary for a meal; the assistant cook and cook's police dig a shallow trench about 10 feet long, 18 inches deep, and 12 inches wide. The kettle rod is placed in position over this trench, the fire lighted, and the kettles with their contents hung on the hooks, as quickly as possible, and the meal prepared while tents are being put up. As a rule, a meal should be served about 30 minutes after the transportation reaches camp. This meal should, therefore, be of a simple character, such as bacon, bread, and coffee; the more elaborate meal to follow later in the day or evening. Immediately after the meal has been served, the chief cook proceeds to prepare the articles necessary for the next meal, and the assistant cook to cleaning and scouring the utensils. While they are thus employed, the police should dig another shallow trench at right angles to and connecting with the first trench. In this a small fire should be started to thoroughly dry the ground.

The fire for baking may then be easily gotten from the cook fire. The cook having made everything ready for the next meal, may then turn the care of them to the assistant and proceed to bake his bread for the next day.

The dough may be mixed on a rubber blanket or false cover of the ration box, according to the formula printed on the yeast-powder can, each particular brand of powder needing a different proportion; and may then be baked in the Buzzacott oven or mess pans. If mess pans are to be used, the dough is then placed in the deeper pans and covered with the shallow ones. An even bed of coals is then raked into the baking trench, the ovens or pans placed on this bed and live coals placed on top. Care should be taken not to use too many coals, as owing to the thinness of the pans, the contents are easily burned.

After the evening meal, which should usually be immediately after retreat, the necessary articles are prepared for breakfast, and everything that can possibly be spared is repacked into the wagons, so that there may be no delay in the morning, or confusion if obliged to start during the night. In making his calculation for breakfast, he should be careful not to overestimate, as he will find it difficult to carry the remnants from one camp to another, and consequently a loss may occur.

The cook fire is replenished during the night by members of the guard, care being taken to use as little fuel as possible.

The cooks are awakened usually about two hours before reveillé, so that breakfast may be served immediately after that formation.

If this be done there will be ample time between breakfast and the "general" for the cooks to have everything used at breakfast cleaned up and in readiness to be loaded into the wagon. If breakfast is delayed, pans and kettles can be thrown into the wagon dirty, and warm water will be readily available at the next camp to clean them.

A few close-fitting covers for the camp kettles will prove invaluable, as by their use many articles of food, such as soup stock, etc., may be carried from one camp to another, which would otherwise be thrown away. Beans in soak previous to baking may also be carried in this manner. If possible, all the dry sticks of wood should be placed on the wagon; a fire can then be started immediately upon arrival in camp, without waiting for the arrival of the camp supplies. In like manner, especially in traveling through a poorly-watered country, the water kegs should be filled before leaving camp.

Water kegs should *always* be filled before leaving camp, even if it is expected to find better water during the march; because, if obliged to camp before reaching water, there will be no lack of that necessary article. Upon reaching the watering place, the kegs can always be emptied and refilled.

### TEMPORARY CAMPS.

The internal economy of the company kitchen in temporary camp differs but little from that which obtains on the march, except in the following:

A brush wind-break six or eight feet high should be erected on the windward side of the fire.

This prevents in a great measure sand and dirt from being blown into the food, and the inclosure forms a capital kitchen.

Rations should be taken from the wagons, if to be in camp for two days or more, and thoroughly overhauled, piled up neatly and covered with a paulin or wagon sheet; everything being disposed of, however, in such a way that the wagons may be packed on short notice if the command is unexpectedly ordered to march.

There being more opportunity for the preparation of soups, stews, etc., than when on the march, they should be made more frequently.

In camp, whenever practicable, the bacon and any other components on which a saving can be made, should be exchanged for fresh meats and vegetables.

### RATIONS AND BILLS OF FARE FOR A TEN-DAYS' CAMP.—(100 Men.)

The following assumed issue of rations to one hundred men is carried out in detail, as a suggestion to officers as to what to provide and how to arrange the bills of fare, and give a reasonable variety at the soldiers' mess:

| ARTICLES. | RATIONS ISSUED. | RATIONS LEFT UNDRAWN FOR SAVINGS. |
|---|---|---|
| Pork | 60 | 40 |
| Bacon | 50 | 150 |
| Fresh Beef | 700 | |
| Mutton | | |
| Fresh Beef, canned | | |
| Corned Beef, canned | | |
| Fish | | |
| Flour | 1,000 | |
| Hard Bread | | |
| Corn Meal | | |
| Beans | 500 | 200 |
| Baked Beans, canned | | |
| Peas | | |
| Rice | 300 | |
| Hominy | | |
| Potatoes | 700 | |
| Onions | 100 | |
| Tomatoes, 2½ pounds | 200 | |
| Coffee | 650 | 200 |
| Tea | 150 | |
| Sugar | 820 | 180 |
| Vinegar | 300 | 700 |
| Adamantine Candles | 1,000 | |
| Soap | 500 | 500 |
| Salt | 1,000 | |
| Pepper | 500 | 500 |
| Baking Powder | 800 | |
| Matches, boxes | 10 | |

The value of the rations "left undrawn for savings" will be about as follows:

| | |
|---|---|
| 40 rations pork, 30 lbs., at 6¼ cents per lb _____ | $1.95 |
| 150 rations bacon, 112½ lbs., at 12 cents per lb __ | 13.50 |
| 200 rations beans, 30 lbs., at 3₁₅⁄₁₂ cents per lb __ | 1.02½ |
| 200 rations coffee, 20 lbs., at 21 cents per lb____ | 4.20 |
| 180 rations sugar, 27 lbs., at 4 cents per lb _____ | 1.08 |
| 700 rations vinegar, 7 gals., at 8 cents per gal__ | .56 |
| 500 rations soap, 20 lbs., at 5¼ cents per lb _____ | 1.02½ |
| 500 rations pepper, 1¼ lbs., at 16 cents per lb___ | .20 |
| | $23.54 |

The amount saved may be expended for any of
the articles kept for sale by the Subsistence
Department, or obtainable in the market; for
example, in order to obtain material for the
bills of fare, it is assumed that the saving is
used, thus:

| | |
|---|---|
| 45 lbs. apples (evaporated), at 7½ cents per lb__ | $3.36 |
| 30 lbs. crackers (soda), at 6 cents per lb _____ | 1.80 |
| 16 lbs. cheese, at 8½ cents per lb_____ | 1.36 |
| 30 lbs. codfish, at 6½ cents per lb _____ | 1.95 |
| 30 lbs. macaroni, at 6 cents per lb _____ | 1.80 |
| 18 lbs. peaches (evaporated), at 6 cents per lb__ | 1.08 |
| 25 lbs. prunes (evaporated), at 5½ cents per lb__ | 1.38 |
| 10 gals. pickles (plain), at 16 cents per gal____ | 1.60 |
| 4 gals. sirup, at 43¾ cents per gal_____ | 1.75 |
| Oatmeal and hominy _____ | 1.70 |
| | $17.78 |
| | $5.76 |

The balance is in the hands of the officer in charge
of mess for the purchase of small vegetables, ice,
milk, etc., or as a nucleus for a company fund.

The total quantity of provisions, etc., drawn and
purchased, with approximate prices, is shown in the
following table:

| ARTICLES. | No. of RATIONS DRAWN. | APPROXI- MATE PRICES PER UNIT. | QUANTITIES. |
|---|---|---|---|
| | | *Cents.* | |
| Pork | 60 | 6½ | 45 pounds. |
| Bacon | 50 | 12 | 37 pounds. |
| Fresh beef | 700 | 10 | 875 pounds. |
| Flour * | 1,000 | 1 $\frac{6}{10}$ | 1,125 pounds. |
| Beans | 500 | 3 $\frac{8}{12}$ | 75 pounds. |
| Rice | 300 | 5 | 30 pounds. |
| Potatoes | 700 | 0¾ | 700 pounds. |
| Onions | 100 | 1 | 100 pounds. |
| Tomatoes | 200 | 7 | 100 2½-pound cans. |
| Coffee | 650 | 21 | 65 pounds. |
| Tea | 150 | 63 | 3 pounds. |
| Sugar | 820 | 4 | 123 pounds. |
| Vinegar | 300 | 8 | 3 gallons. |
| Candles | 1,000 | 11 | 15 pounds. |
| Soap | 500 | 5 $^1_8$ | 20 pounds. |
| Salt | 1,000 | 1.15 | 40 pounds. |
| Pepper, black | 500 | 16 | 1 pound. |
| Baking Powder | 800 | 35 | 32 pounds. |
| Matches, boxes | 10 | 5 | |
| *Purchased from savings.* | | | |
| Apples, evaporated | | 9½ | 45 pounds. |
| Cheese | | 8½ | 16 pounds. |
| Codfish | | 6½ | 30 pounds. |
| Crackers, soda | | 6 | 30 pounds. |
| Macaroni | | 6 | 30 pounds. |
| Peaches, evaporated | | 6 | 18 pounds. |
| Pickles, plain (kegs) | | 16 | 10 gallons. |
| Prunes, dried | | 5½ | 25 pounds. |
| Sirup | | 43¾ | 4 gallons. |
| Oatmeal and hominy | | | 35 pounds. |

* Two days' supply of bread should if possible be baked at the post from whence the troops are detached.

These quantities make an average of 3½ to 3¾ pounds per man, per day.

The command is supposed to be furnished with the travel ration while en route to the camp.

By using articles drawn and purchased, the following bills of fare can be provided:

## BILLS OF FARE.

| | BREAKFAST. | DINNER. | SUPPER. |
|---|---|---|---|
| WEDNESDAY 1 | | Travel rations. | Fried bacon, baked potatoes, pickles, bread, coffee. |
| THURSDAY 2 | Irish stew, bread, coffee. | Roast beef with gravy, mashed potatoes, bread, rice pudding. | Cold roast beef, pickles, stewed apples, bread, coffee. |
| FRIDAY 3 | Beef hash, bread, coffee. | Tomato soup, stewed beef and dumplings, boiled potatoes, bread, coffee. | Stewed prunes, boiled rice, bread, tea. |
| SATURDAY 4 | Codfish balls, bread, coffee. | Boiled beef, baked beans, bread. | Macaroni and cheese, bread, coffee. |
| SUNDAY 5 | Fried pork and gravy, bread, coffee. | Tomato soup, roast beef, gravy, potatoes baked with beef, pudding, plain duff, bread, coffee. | Cold roast beef, pickles, fried potatoes, bread, tea. |
| MONDAY 6 | Beef hash, bread, coffee. | Boiled beef, stewed onions, boiled potatoes, bread. | Cold beef, pickles, stewed prunes, bread, coffee. |
| TUESDAY 7 | Oatmeal mush, sirup, bread, coffee. | Bean soup, roast beef and gravy, stewed tomatoes, bread, coffee. | Cold meat, stewed apples, bread, tea. |
| WEDNESDAY 8 | Beef hash, bread, coffee. | Steak and onions, fried potatoes, bread, rice pudding. | Baked beans, pickles, stewed peaches, bread, coffee. |
| THURSDAY 9 | Boiled hominy, sirup, bread, coffee. | Tomato soup, stewed beef and dumplings, boiled potatoes, bread, coffee. | Boiled rice, sirup, bread, tea. |
| FRIDAY 10 | Hashed codfish, bread, coffee. | Roast beef and onion gravy, baked potatoes, bread. | Cold beef, pickles, stewed apples, bread, tea. |
| SATURDAY 11 | Beef hash, bread, coffee. | Tomato soup, roast beef, boiled potatoes, bread, coffee. | Travel rations. |

Simple recipes for cooking the above dishes may be found herein.

# RECIPES

FOR

## CAMP COOKERY.

(259)

# RECIPES FOR CAMP COOKERY.

## MISCELLANEOUS HINTS.

Bread and soup are the great items of a soldier's diet in every situation; to make them well is an essential part of his instruction. Those great scourges of camp—scurvy and diarrhea—more frequently result from want of skill in cooking than from any other cause whatever. Officers in command, and, more immediately regimental officers, should therefore give strict attention to this vital branch of interior economy.

Men should never eat heartily just before a great undertaking, because the nervous power is irresistibly drawn to the stomach to manage the food eaten, thus draining off that supply which the brain and muscles so much need.

It is always best to prepare hot meals when possible. If preserved or cooked rations have been served out, and there is time, they should be warmed or made into soup or *bouilli* before being eaten.

Fresh meat ought not to be cooked before it has had time to bleed and cool; and meats should generally be boiled, with a view to soup; though sometimes roasted or baked, for variety.

Fresh meat issued to the soldiers in advance, in hot weather, may be preserved by half boiling it; or, if there be not time for that operation, the meat may be kept some twenty-four hours, by previously exposing it for a few minutes to a very thick smoke.

Salted meats should soak eight or ten hours, or the water they are boiled in should be changed several times.

Vinegar added to water that tough meats are boiled in, tends to make them tender.

Meats to be eaten cold should be placed in boiling water. This sets the juices; while meat put first in cold water and then gradually heated and boiled, has its juices extracted; best done this way in soups, stews, etc.

Vegetables, especially fresh ones, should be immersed in boiling water; dried vegetables in cold water.

Meats that are to be used cold, ham especially, should be allowed to cool in the liquid in which they were boiled, as they will then be especially sweet, juicy and tender.

## SOUP.

Hang the camp kettle on the crane, and use a cover to keep out ashes, sand, or dust. If any fresh lean meat is available, put in a small piece, after cutting off every particle of fat. After breakfast build a fire of logs under the camp kettle, and let the meat boil in an abundance of water for two hours or longer, or until the meat is almost ready to drop to pieces; then add Irish potatoes and onions, all cut up, and simmer until the vegetables are done.

While boiling, frequently skim from the top every particle of grease that rises. When done, season with pepper and salt to taste, and eat hot. If it is not thick enough, mix enough flour and water in a tin cup to the consistency of molasses, and pour slowly into the soup, stirring with a spoon as poured. Good soup may be made with bones, cracked with a hatchet and boiled for a long time, or with vegetables alone, thickened and seasoned. Canned tomatoes make a nice soup.

## PEA SOUP, WITH SALT PORK OR BEEF.
### (Sufficient for 22 men.)

Meat.                   Flour or broken biscuits.
Mixed vegetables.       Pepper.
Split peas.             Water.

Peel, clean, and cut up the vegetables; place the fresh cold water in the camp kettle; add the vegetables and peas, and boil gently until the peas are soft. Then put into the soup about two pounds of meat, which should have been previously well washed in cold water, and simmer gently till it is cooked; then take it out and cover it up to keep warm.

Mix some flour into a smooth batter with cold water, and add it to the soup, keeping it well stirred to prevent it burning; boil for thirty minutes and serve. If flour is not to be had, use instead powdered biscuits, previously soaked in cold water.

The remainder of the meat should be soaked and well washed in cold water, then put into the camp kettle, with sufficient water to cover it, and allowed to boil for thirty minutes; the water in which it was boiled should now be thrown away, the camp kettle refilled with fresh cold water, and the meat boiled till done.

### BOILED SOUP DUMPLING.

Make a light dough, or procure from the bakery, dough which is ready for the oven.

Flour the hands well and mold the dough into balls about the size of an egg. Drop them successively into boiling water. Boil in the soup about fifteen minutes.

### STEWS OF BEEF OR MUTTON.

Joint or cut up your meat in small pieces, and place in the stewpan; add a couple of slices of bacon, cut thin; a few raw onions, peeled and cut up; pepper and salt to taste.

Pour in hot water until you have covered the meat with about two inches of water on top; put the lid on and simmer slowly until the water has boiled down, say one-half, or until it becomes thick or milky from the juices extracted from the meats. If it is too thin to be palatable, thicken with grated hard bread, or a paste of water and flour, mixed in a tin cup and poured into the stew.

## IRISH STEW, WITH SALT BEEF.

| Meat. | Potatoes. |
| Onions. | Pepper. |

Wash and clean the meat in cold water; separate it from the bone, and cut it into small pieces of about two ounces each, and wash it well again in cold water; peel and clean the potatoes, peel and slice the onions; place the meat, potatoes, and onions in the camp kettle, add a little pepper and sufficient cold water to cover the whole; put the lid on the kettle and cook gently over a slow fire, frequently skimming the fat off the top.

### A GOOD STEW.

Use meats, game especially, of any or various kinds—prairie chicken, quail, duck, rabbit, turkey —or if you have no fresh meats or game, use fried bacon or pork.

Into a kettle put a layer of bacon, meats, etc., and season; dredge with flour, then add a layer of potatoes, onions, etc.; repeating this until the kettle is nearly full, as desired. Over all pour sufficient broth or water (the former preferable) to cover, and stew slowly from one to three hours, according to size. During the last hour stir in a quart of batter to thicken; season to taste and serve hot.

### HOT MEAT STEW, WITH GARNISH.

Take cold meats, game especially, cut up into pieces of small and equal size; put them into the largest pan with broth or cold water, a few quarts of onions, can of tomatoes, etc., and stir slowly for one to two hours, seasoning to taste; then to the quart of flour add six tablespoonfuls of mustard or curry powder, stir in; boil ten minutes more and serve. Use as a garnish either rice, boiled or mashed potatoes, corn, etc.

This is a good hot winter dish.

## STEW, WITH CANNED MEATS.

| Meat. | Onions. | Salt. |
| Potatoes. | Pepper. | Water. |

Peel and slice the potatoes and onions; put them in the camp kettle, season with pepper and salt, pour in sufficient water to cover them, and stew gently, keeping the lid of the kettle closely shut until the potatoes are nearly cooked; then open the tins of meat and cut up the contents and put them in the kettle with the potatoes; let the whole simmer for ten minutes, then serve.

## BROWN STEW, WITH CANNED MEATS.

| Meat. | Flour. | Salt. |
| Onions. | Pepper. | Water. |

Peel and slice the onions, melt the fat of the meat in the camp kettle, add the onions and fry them until brown, mix the flour into a smooth batter with cold water, season with pepper and salt, and pour it into the camp kettle; stir the whole well together; cut the meat into slices, put it into the kettle, and, when warmed through, serve.

## TO ROAST MEATS IN A DUTCH OVEN.

Put about one inch of water in oven, and season with salt and pepper, so as to have a gravy for basting the meat while cooking, thus preventing its becoming too dry. Make a mop by tying a clean rag to the end of a stick; remove the lid frequently, and baste the roast with the gravy. When done remove the meat to a dish; put into the gravy a pinch of flour to thicken, and pour over the roast. If your roast is thick or tough, parboil in camp kettle from thirty minutes to an hour before placing in the oven; then roast to a nice brown.

## BROILING STEAKS OR CHOPS.

Build a good log fire, and let it burn down to a bed of coals, so that there will be no smoke. Cut your steak or chops almost one inch thick and season with pepper and salt. Put your meat between the bars of your broiler, and place on the red-hot coals. Broil quickly until rare, or well done, as you desire, frequently turning the broiler from one side to the other, so that the meat will not have time to char.

If a little charred, scrape with a knife; place on hot dish, season with salt and pepper, and serve while hot.

### BAKED BEEF HEAD.

#### (Without cooking utensils.)

Dig in the ground a hole of sufficient size and build a fire in it. After the fuel has burned to coals put in the head, neck downward. Cover it with green grass, coals, and earth. Build a good fire over the buried head and keep it burning for about six hours.

Unearth the head and remove the skin. A head treated in this way at night will be found cooked in the morning. The head of any animal may be cooked in this way.

### SALT BEEF AND DUMPLINGS.

Meat.     Flour.     Suet.

Soak and well wash the meat in cold water, and place it in the camp kettle, with plenty of water, and boil gently for one hour; then throw away the water in which it was boiled, and replace it with fresh cold water, and boil till the meat is cooked. Chop the suet up fine, mix it with the flour, and pour in some cold water and well mix the whole, and form it into dumplings about two inches in diameter; place the dumplings in a kettle with the beef about thirty minutes before the latter is cooked, and let both boil together until done.

## SALT PORK AND HARD BREAD.

| Meat. | Hard bread. |
| Onions. | Parsley. |
| Pepper. | Water. |

(a) Soak the hard bread in cold water for one hour; wash, clean, and boil the pork; drain the water off the hard bread, and cut up the pork into thin slices; peel and slice the onions, wash and chop up the parsley; pour a little water into the camp kettle; place a layer of the slices of pork at the bottom of the kettle, with some onions, parsley, and pepper, then a layer of the soaked hard bread on top, then another layer of pork, and so on alternately, until the kettle is nearly full. Cover the whole with water, and cook gently over a slow fire for one hour and fifteen minutes, and serve.

(b) Treat the pork, onions, parsley, as in (a); soak the hard bread for two hours, then squeeze it dry; mince up the pork and mix it with the hard bread, onions, parsley, and pepper; then roll it into balls, and place them in a camp kettle with sufficient water to cover, and cook gently over a slow fire for one hour, and serve.

These recipes can also be prepared in the camp kettle lids, by placing the layers of pork and hard bread or balls in one camp kettle lid, and covering it with another, and placing a few live embers underneath and on the top of the lids.

## TO COOK FISH WITHOUT COOKING UTENSILS.

Dig a hole in the ground about eighteen inches deep, and of sufficient size to contain the fish; build a fire in it and let it burn to coals. Remove the coals, leaving the hot ashes at the bottom, upon which place a thick layer of green grass; place the fish on top and cover with another layer of grass; then rake back the live coals and loose earth and build a small fire on top. At the end of about three-quarters of an hour the fish will be found cooked with the juice retained; the skin will peel off and leave the flesh clean and free from ashes and dirt.

## BAKED FISH

Should be dressed and cooked whole. Make a stuffing of bread crumbs, pork, onions, etc.; fill the body with same and close with a skewer. Put a little water in the pan; dredge the fish well, season; put a few slices of bacon fat on top and bake from forty-five minutes to an hour. Fish from six to eight pounds are best for baking, or a number of them together.

## PLANKED SHAD.

This is the very best way of cooking shad: The plank should be three inches thick, two feet long, one and a half feet wide and of well seasoned hickory or oak. Take a fine shad just from the water, scale, split it down the back, clean it, wash it well and immediately wipe dry. Dredge it with salt and pepper. Place the plank before a clear fire to get *very hot*. Then spread the shad open and nail it, skin side next to the hot plank, with four large-headed tacks. Put it before the fire, with large end down. In a few minutes turn the board so the other end will be down, and do this every few minutes until the fish is done. To tell when it is done pierce with a fork; if the flesh be flaky it is done. Spread with dripping and serve on the plank, or draw the tacks out carefully and slide the shad onto a hot dish. The whitefish caught in the lakes are excellent when cooked in this manner.

## TO BOIL POTATOES WITH THEIR JACKETS ON.

After washing, place in camp kettle and pour on boiling water. Boil slowly until a fork will pierce them with ease. Serve thus, or peel while hot; mash into a paste, season with pepper and salt, and eat hot.

## STEWED POTATOES.

Peel and cut into thick slices, stew in stewpan, with enough water to cover them, and add two thin slices of bacon; put on the lid and cook until potatoes are soft and nearly dry, but stir frequently to prevent burning or sticking to the bottom of pan. Add salt and pepper. A raw onion or two cut into the stewing potatoes gives a flavor that a hungry soldier always enjoys.

## BAKED BEANS, No. 1.

Soak the beans over night, if possible, and boil with a piece of pork or bacon about two hours, or until a bean will mash easily between the fingers; then strain them into a pan (pots are the best) and cover them with the liquid boiled in; season well, adding a cupful of molasses or sugar. If pork is salty, more salt will not be required. Draw a knife blade crosswise through the rind of three or four pieces of bacon or pork; bury them in the beans and bake slowly two to three hours or more. Brown the top before serving, but do not let the bottom get dry. Add more liquid as it becomes dry, and do not have too great a heat on bottom; stir from bottom if necessary. Some add vinegar, molasses, and mustard; a small quantity mixed with the beans increases the flavor. If water is hard, a small quantity of saleratus when the beans are boiling will soften it.

## BAKED BEANS, No. 2.

Boil the beans for a long time over a brisk fire, until they are perfectly soft, and settle at the bottom of the stewpan. Pour off the water, and let them dry in the stewpan by placing it on hot ashes or coals for a few minutes. When perfectly dry, mash into a fine paste; season with pepper and salt, and place in a conical or round shape on a tin plate. Lay two thin slices of bacon on top; place in a Dutch oven (tin plate and all) with lid on; heap live coals of fire on top of lid, and bake until the bacon is done, or to a light crust of brown.

### TO BAKE PORK AND BEANS WITHOUT OVEN.

Have a trench 18 inches wide, 18 inches deep, and from 4 to 6 feet long; keep a fire in this for several hours; let fire die down so that there shall be a bed of coals and hot ashes; it is then ready for use. Prepare beans as usual for baking and place in mess kettles; pour in three quarts of hot water; cover with tin plate or mess pan; scrape out the embers until kettle will be near bottom of trench; cover first with ashes, then with coals, and leave undisturbed for six to eight hours.

It is a good plan for cooks to soak beans over night and carry them to the next camp. This will permit the furnishing of baked beans at supper while marching.

### RICE.

Remember that rice swells very much in boiling, and that a teacupful makes a large dish when cooked. Place in camp kettle, and cover the rice with about two inches of water; boil slowly, or rather simmer, until it is tender, then by gradually slowing the heat let the water evaporate, thus leaving the grains swollen and dry. Rice thus prepared can be used as a vegetable or a pudding by adding salt and pepper in the former and sugar in the latter case.

### HOW TO BOIL RICE.

Pick your rice clean and wash it in two cold waters, drawing off the last water just as you are ready to put the rice in the saucepan for boiling.

Prepare a saucepan with water sufficient to more than cover the rice by two inches, and in which a little salt has been shaken. The water should be brought to a boil and kept there until it is drained off. When the water is boiling sprinkle in the rice gradually so as not to stop the boiling. Boil for about twenty minutes, keeping the pan covered. Then throw into a colander, covering same; let stand several minutes, this serving a double purpose, allowing rice to drain as well as steam.

Every grain should be found separate and dry.

Remember, boil rapidly from the time you cover the pot until you take it off; this allows each grain to swell to three times its normal size, and the motion prevents the grains from sticking together. Don't stir it, as this will cause it to fall to the bottom and burn.

In order to see if the rice is done, take out one of the grains and crush it between the fingers; if well done it will mash easily and feel perfectly soft.

## BAKING-POWDER BISCUITS AND BREAD.

To six quarts of flour add eight tablespoonfuls of baking powder, two spoonfuls salt, and stir thoroughly together; then add about eight tablespoonfuls of clear cold bacon fat; stir again, and add sufficient cold water (never warm water) quickly, and stir to a smooth but not stiff batter. Mix or stir it as little as possible—never knead it—or you will lose the strength (gases) of the powder. Roll or break into equal-sized biscuits; or, best, drop from a large spoon into well-greased pans. Put into a good hot oven, especially hot on top, and bake until done—usually from 15 to 20 minutes, if oven is good.

Never knead the dough, as kneading kills the leavening properties of baking-powder bread. Yeast, or baker's bread, on the other hand, requires much kneading and a good stiff dough.

If in a hurry, or inexperienced, biscuits are the most easily made; the great fault in preparing either is not so much inexperience as lack of careful attention to the above details.

## BREAD.

In making baking-powder bread observe the same rules as mentioned above; mix into a fairly stiff batter, using a large spoon, not the hands; have your greased pan and hot oven ready; drop or pour the batter into it until about half full, and set into the oven. Get a good even heat below and plenty on top (so as to fill the oven with hot air). When done the loaves will rise to the top of the pan. Bake from 30 to 45 minutes, or until a sliver will pass through the bread and on withdrawal be found dry; if sticky dough adheres to the sliver the bread is not yet done. Regular heat and quick mixing insure most excellent bread in large quantities in an easy way.

### FIELD BREAD.

Take five quarts of flour and one and two-thirds tablespoonfuls of yeast powder; mix thoroughly while dry, adding a little salt to suit the taste; then mix in well one tablespoonful of dripping or lard; then add water, and in small quantities at a time, until a biscuit dough is made; knead slightly. Take a Government mess pan and cut off about one inch and a half of the rim, leaving a rough edge. Into this mess pan put dough enough to fill it two-thirds full; cover with another mess pan. A hole should previously have been dug in the ground eighteen or twenty inches in diameter and depth, and a fire burned in it five or six hours. Then take out all the cinders except a bed two or three inches deep; upon this place the mess pans and surround and cover them with hot cinders; over all spread a covering of earth, and leave for five or six hours.

ಠ

The bread will not burn, as in rising it will not reach the bottom of the upper mess pan. The rough-cut edges of the lower mess pan afford egress to any gases that may be disengaged.

## FIELD BREAD, BAKED IN FRYING PAN.

Prepare the dough as above described; grease the frying pan and set it over hot embers until the grease begins to melt; put the dough, rolled to a thickness of half an inch, in the pan and set it on the fire; shake the pan every few moments to prevent the dough from adhering; after the crust has formed on the bottom take the bread out of the pan and set it up on edge, close to the fire, turning it occasionally to insure its being baked through.

## PIE CRUST.

To four quarts of flour sift three spoonfuls of baking powder, and a spoonful of salt; add one to two quarts of good bacon fat; cold water enough to make a good stiff dough without kneading. Roll with a bottle to a thin even sheet; line inside of pan— leave sufficient for a covering; cut hole in center of upper crust and bake in hot oven one hour. As a good filling for meat pies, observe the general rules seen in meat stewed, etc., using game and cooked meats if possible.

## SUET, OR FIELD PUDDING.

Cut up fine about two quarts of bacon, or salt fat pork, or suet in small dice-shaped pieces. To six quarts of flour add six spoonfuls of baking powder, two quarts of molasses, or one and one-half quarts of sugar, two quarts of currants, raisins, or chopped fruits, one quarter pint of mixed spices. Mix into a good stiff batter with a spoon, and it is ready for the bag and pot. Prepare from a flour bag (inside one) a bag; dip into boiling water and flour well inside, this prevents the pudding from sticking to the bag and absorbing water. Into this bag pour your pudding batter, allowing room for the pudding to swell (be sure of this), and tie up tightly, taking care that no water can get inside of bag. Have boiling two or three boilers of water and drop in your pudding while the water boils; boil two or three hours, according to the size of your pudding.

NOTE.—If the water stops boiling your pudding is spoiled.

To remove the pudding from the bag when done, dip it into a bucket or pan of cold water. It will then slide out easily when the string of the bag is cut. Before putting in the pudding to boil, drop a tin pan or plate into the boiler; this will prevent it from sticking to the bottom of the pot and burning.

## PLAIN SAUCE FOR FIELD PUDDING.

To a quart of sugar add a sufficient quantity of hot water and boil, adding a little spice; boil ten minutes, then thicken with flour, stirring continually. Toward the last add a little vinegar until taste is satisfactory. Use more spice or sugar if necessary. Boil until it thickens, and serve separately from pudding. If possible use condensed milk.

## STEWED DRIED APPLES.

Pick over the apples carefully; then wash them in cold water and drain. Soak them over night in sufficient cold water to cover them. Put them, with the water in which they have been soaked, into a pot (iron should not be used; an earthenware well-glazed crock or stone jar is preferable); cover closely to simmer until they are tender.

## STEWED DRIED PEACHES.

Rules as to cooking, flavoring, etc., for dried apples are applicable to dried peaches.

## STEWED DRIED PRUNES.

Pick carefully, wash thoroughly, drain, cover the fruit with cold water and soak thirty minutes.

Proceed then as directed for dried apples. Cook thirty to forty-five minutes only. Longer cooking will break the fruit; this is to be avoided.

They are flavored, served, and can be used as prescribed for dried apples.

## CANNED AND DRIED SOUPS.

Many reliable varieties of canned soups are on the market and easily obtainable. The cans contain the directions for preparation.

There are also preparations for dried soups, put up in packages on which are printed directions for preparing.

In preparing articles of the foregoing class the directions, as printed by the manufacturers, should always be followed.

## MEAT PIE.

(Sufficient for 22 men.)

| | |
|---|---|
| 16½ pounds meat. | 1 pound onions. |
| 5 pounds flour. | 2 ounces salt. |
| 1½ pounds suet. | ¼ ounce pepper. |

Make the paste; cut up and stew the onions with jelly from the meat added; cut the meat into dice and place it in a baking dish; add the cooked onions; season with pepper and salt; cover with a light crust, and bake in a quick oven for twenty minutes.

## STEW.

(Sufficient for 22 men.)

| | |
|---|---|
| 16½ pounds meat. | 1 pound onions. |
| 2 pounds carrots, or other vegetables. | 2 ounces salt. |
| | ¼ ounce pepper. |

Cut up the vegetables and onions, which place in the boiler with sufficient water to cover them; add some jelly from the meat; well season with pepper and salt, and stew gently, keeping the lid of the boiler closely shut until the vegetables are tender, then add the meat; let the whole simmer for ten minutes and serve.

## SEA PIE.

### (Sufficient for 22 men.)

Ingredients the same as for stew, with five pounds of flour and one and one-half pounds of suet or dripping added.

Make the paste; prepare and cook the vegetables and onions as for stew; when the vegetables are tender add the meat; cover the whole over with a light paste, and boil or steam for twenty minutes.

## CANNED LIMA BEANS.

Open can one hour before using and empty into bowl. Drain liquor off and cook in boiling water twenty-five minutes. Drain, and add pepper and salt to taste.

## CANNED STRING BEANS.

Cook one-half an hour in their own liquor, first cutting in good lengths to look well in dish. When almost done, add salt and pepper. Simmer ten minutes longer and drain off liquor. If can has not enough liquor to cover beans, add water in cooking.

## CANNED CORN.

Open can one hour before cooking. Put in kettle and cover with boiling water; let stand ten minutes; drain, and cover corn with hot water, a little salted. Set in vessel of hot water and cook one-half hour. Add pepper and salt, and serve.

## CANNED CORN AND TOMATOES, STEWED.

To two cans of tomatoes add one can corn. Stew one-half hour with a little chopped onion; pepper and salt to taste.

## SALMON IN CAMP COOKERY.

One pound of salmon, one-pound can of tomatoes; arrange in alternate layers; season with salt, pepper, and two ounces of salt pork cut into dice; add the liquid from both cans and cover the top with powdered hard bread; put a little dripping on top, and bake a light brown.

## A CAMP MORSEL.

Take a can of mackerel, salmon, or lobster; chop with raw onion and pickles, and pour vinegar over.

## CANNED SALMON, BOILED.

The simplest way of preparing salmon for the table is to open the can, place it in a pan or pot partly full of water, and when quite hot it is ready for the table. No water should be allowed to enter the can as it depreciates the flavor. After the salmon is put on the dish, remove the skin and arrange it as neatly as possible. The liquid in the can should be used for the basis of the sauce with the addition of a little seasoning, and if liked, a little flour for thickening.

## CANNED SALMON, DEVILED.

Fry one quarter of an onion until brown; add a gill of water, a teaspoonful each of flour and English mustard, salt and pepper. Simmer and add the liquor from the can of salmon; do not let it burn. Place a pound of salmon (hot) upon a dish, spread the thick sauce over it, and set it in a hot oven a moment to singe the surface.

## CANNED SALMON, DANISH MODE.

Peel a dozen medium-sized potatoes; put them in a pan with a little dripping and bake them. When done, arrange a pound of salmon (previously warmed in the tin) in the center of the dish with the potatoes round it; thicken the drippings with a little flour, season it with salt, pepper and a clove of garlic; pour it over the fish and serve.

## CANNED CLAM FRITTERS.

| | |
|---|---|
| 1 teacupful flour. | 1 teaspoonful baking powder. |
| ½ teaspoonful pepper. | ¼ teaspoonful salt. |

(1 dozen clams chopped; add their liquor.)

Drop from a spoon in hot meat dripping.

## CANNED CRAB, DEVILED.

Cut crab meat into small pieces. To six ounces of crab meat mix two ounces of bread crumbs, juice of half a lemon, cayenne pepper and salt. Mix all with milk (condensed), sprinkle fine bread crumbs on top, and color brown in a quick oven.

## CANNED LOBSTER, DEVILED.

Prepare the same way as crab, adding a little grated nutmeg to seasoning.

## CANNED LOBSTER, STEWED.

Cut the meat up fine and let it boil up once in its own liquor. Add a little pepper and salt, and serve plain or on toast.

## CANNED OYSTERS AND MACARONI.

Boil four ounces macaroni in plenty of water, twenty minutes. Cut in pieces one inch long. Put layer of this in bottom of baking dish, a layer of oysters, salt and pepper sprinkled over. Then another layer of macaroni and so on until all is used, having top layer macaroni. Sprinkle grated cheese lightly over top and bake in moderate oven twenty minutes. Serve in same dish.

## CANNED OYSTER SAUTÉ.

Drain oysters dry, sprinkle with pepper and roll in flour. Cut one-fourth pound bacon into thin slices, put in frying pan and try out all the fat. Remove bacon and cover bottom of pan with oysters. When brown and crisp on one side, do other side the same. Serve on squares of toast.

## TO ROAST (PARCH) COFFEE.

Coffee requires great care and constant attention in roasting—don't leave it to do something else.

Half fill the pan with coffee beans, about fifteen pounds, place it in the oven or on the fire (an even and slow heat is best) and when it gets heated through stir thoroughly from the bottom. Try to stir it so the under berries will come to the top, and vice versa. If fire is quick keep stirring constantly. Use the turnover in stirring, not a spoon. When about half done add half pint of fat or water and stir thoroughly until of a rich brown color, then set off to cool. Some prefer to use the oven and by having heat on top can observe the progress of parching more easily and thoroughly, acting accordingly. Time, about one hour or more to the half-pan full. Great care should be exercised, as good coffee is the backbone of many a meal.

## TO MAKE COFFEE.

Into a small coffee boiler, the smallest one, put sufficient cold water for the command, allowing a good quart per man or more; add to it the coffee, ground fine (two quarts ground coffee to fifty men at least), and when the whole boils remove it from the fire, ten minutes before service, to settle.

*Another way:* First boil the water, then add the coffee: boil ten minutes and remove; boil slowly or it will boil over—a cupful of cold water will prevent it from boiling over when it is boiling too fast,

but it must be removed quickly—it will also settle
the grounds.   Don't ever boil coffee too long as it
loses strength and flavor, and don't be too liberal
with the water.

*Another way:* Allow one heaping tablespoonful
of coffee to each pint of water.   If five quarts are
required put in six or seven quarts of water, thus
allowing for evaporation and boiling down.   First
boil the water, then set the pot near the fire, put in
your coffee, let it simmer and boil for thirty minutes
on hot ashes and coals, and then set aside close to the
fire to keep hot until your meal is ready.   A third
cup of cold water poured in will clarify it.

## TEA.

Scald the pot after each meal.   Place the pot
close to the fire, but not on it.   Allow one heaping
teaspoonful of tea for each person.   Place it in the
pot, and pour in boiling water in sufficient quantity;
cover the top securely to retain the heat and aroma,
and let it draw for twenty or thirty minutes.   It is
good either hot or cold.

After tea has been drank at the meal, the old tea
leaves may be resteeped, and the tea thus formed
can be carried in the canteens.   It will be ordinarily
better than the water that may be found along the
march.

# INDEX.

(281)

www.ingramcontent.com/pod-product-compliance
Lightning Source LLC
Chambersburg PA
CBHW020500270326
41926CB00008B/678